AGNES MACPHAIL

and the Politics of Equality

TERRY CROWLEY

James Lorimer & Company, Publishers
Toronto, 1990

Cover Photo: Agnes Macphail portrait by Karsh

Photo credits:
Page 1, photos courtesy of Jean Huston, London Ontario
Page 2, Jean Huston, London Ontario
　　　　View of farm life, *Farmers Magazine*, April 1920
Page 3, the National Archives of Canada
Page 4, sketch, the National Archives of Canada
　　　　photo, Glenbow Alberta Institute
Page 5, the National Archives of Canada
Page 6, CCF photo, the National Archives of Canada
　　　　post election photo, Jean Huston, London Ontario
Page 7, caricature, the National Archives of Canada
　　　　portrait, Archives of Ontario
Page 8, Archives of Ontario

Canadian Cataloguing in Publication Data

Crowley, T.A. (Terence Alan), 1946
Agnes Macphail and the Politics of Equality
Includes bibliographical references. ISBN 1-55028-328-6 (bound) ISBN 1-55028-326-X (pbk.)

1. Macphail, Agnes Campbell, 1890-1954. 2. Canada. Parliament. House of Commons Biography. 3. Ontario. Legislative Assembly Biography 4. Women Legislators Canada Biography. 5. Politicians Canada Biography. 6. Feminists Canada Biography. I. Title

FC541.M26C76 1990 328.71'092 C90-095149-4
F1034.M26C76 1990

James Lorimer & Company, Publishers
Egerton Ryerson Memorial Building
35 Britain Street
Toronto, Ontario M5A 1R7

Printed and bound in Canada

Contents

Preface

PART ONE: YOUTH

1 Born in the Scotch, 1890–1910   3

2 Young Country Woman:
Teaching and the Farm Movement, 1910–1920   14

3 History Is Made in Southeast Grey:
The 1921 Election   32

PART TWO: PRIME

4 Violating the Gentlemen's Club:
The First Term in Parliament   55

5 Equality Rights:
The Campaign for Women's Rights, 1926–1930   78

6 The Great Divide:
The Depression and the Creation of the CCF   104

7 Prison Reform:
"The Boss Wants to Get Aggie"   128

8 A Rare Vintage:
The Drift towards War and Defeat, 1936–40   147

PART THREE: GREY POWER

9 Return to the Fold:
CCF Member of the Ontario Legislature   175

10 Feminism and Pay Equity:
The Last Campaign and the Later Years   192

Notes   209

Select Bibliography   232

Index   236

Preface

The first woman elected to the House of Commons — and later the first to be seated in the Ontario Legislature — Agnes Macphail served in Ottawa and Toronto as the sole representative of her gender for seventeen years. With electoral successes that sustained her at the federal and provincial levels longer than any other woman, Macphail constantly smashed barriers that corralled her sex. In 1929, along with British Columbian politician Mary Ellen Smith, who was appointed to International Labour Organization, Macphail was one of the first women to represent Canada internationally. Named as a delegate to the League of Nations assembly, she was not content to be side-tracked into some inconsequential female ghetto. At Geneva she secured a place as the first woman on the League's disarmament committee and won kudos for her able conduct from more experienced diplomats.

The importance of Agnes Macphail to history lies less in the trails she blazed than in the courage, commitment, and industry that marked her three decades in political life. Elected eight times and defeated in four elections, she never wavered in her determination to transform Canadian political institutions through the power of the ballot box. A radical democratic populist sprung from the farmers' revolt following World War One, Agnes Macphail helped to forge a new alliance aimed at transcending the limitations of the two-party system and making parliamentary democracy more responsive to the electorate. After a decade of active political life she emerged as Ontario's leading politician during the creation of the Cooperative Commonwealth Federation (the forerunner of the New Democratic Party). Elected to the Ontario Legislature for the CCF in 1943 and 1948, she continued to fight for policies aimed at advancing women and assisting others unable to reap the full benefits of Canadian life..

An outspoken feminist committed to equality and human rights, Agnes Macphail served as an essential bridge between first-wave feminism at the beginning of the twentieth century and its contemporary counterpart. Keenly aware that woman's reproductive function separated her from man, Agnes Macphail sought to revolutionize gender relations well before they became a central focus of debate. While her key importance lay in helping to change Canadian government into an instrument serving more people, she was no less significant in prompting women to assume their rightful place in all walks of life. Macphail worked for new initiatives in both private and public sectors to assist the disadvantaged in a competitive world where people are created neither equal nor alike.

As a woman who swam against the main currents of her time, Macphail's commitment to feminism, equality, and social justice dictated that she remain an opposition politician throughout her career, despite her determined efforts to see her policies prevail. While it is ironic that a populist frequently found herself expressing views that the electorate as a whole rejected at the polls, Macphail perceived structural barriers that prohibited fuller democratic expression in Canadian government. Early on she advocated the reform of electoral representation, the disclosure of business influence over the media, and the control of parliamentary lobbying as ways to further governance by the people. When such reforms proved impossible to implement in the face of Liberal and Conservative intransigence, Macphail turned to the CCF as the party most closely approximating her own vision of a freer and more just society. This transition from leadership in an agrarian social movement to political partisanship occurred haltingly. Politics were too important to the lives of all Canadians, she felt, to be abandoned to the control of men intricately bound by the alliance between business and the old-line parties.

My interest in Agnes Macphail evolved out of the changing nature of historical scholarship as well as from my teaching at the University of Guelph. Broader intellectual horizons in the discipline of history opened to me during graduate study developed at Guelph into research exploring new areas in rural history and women's studies. Students prompted my interest in the latter. A decade and a half ago when they asked that the history of women form part of the curriculum, I joined with my colleague in the Department of History, Mary Rogers, in creating the first women's studies course. A study of Agnes

Macphail seemed a natural way to consummate a marriage of two areas that frequently diverge.

Researching this book revealed an exceptional individual brimming with vitality and humour, but also, one who masked her inner doubts and insecurities. An expansive and expressive personality, sometimes idiosyncratic and not infrequently explosive in reaction to prejudice, Agnes Macphail grew intellectually and politically throughout her life. Never defeated by ill health or other setbacks, she remained firm in her convictions and refused to be enticed by the prospect of a cabinet position. Temperamentally unsuited to other than populist politics, her adherence to her beliefs mitigated against aspirations towards the leadership role the press saw for her at the height of her personal popularity.

This study attempts to balance the requirements of biography with those of contemporary scholarship. Like most politicans, Agnes Macphail tried to conceal her private life from public view. Because her family background and personal struggles are essential to understanding her character and achievements, they form a continuous element in the pages that follow. Her role and that of the United Farmers of Ontario in the breakup of the two-party system in Canada following World War One lead to a revision of traditional interpretations of events that are generally viewed from a Western Canadian perspective. Since her commitment to populist politics, first as a radical democrat and then as a social democrat, explains the circuitous political route Macphail followed, it has been highlighted. Previous studies have also played down Macphail's dedication to feminism, which this life makes central. A devotion to making women equal partners with men in all walks of life concerned her from the beginning of her political career. But whatever her other attributes, Agnes Macphail was first and foremost a politician who thought that equality could be most fully realized through the victory of the democratic left. These interwoven themes of democratic reform and feminism ensure her continuing relevance.

Achivists, librarians, and others have been unfailingly helpful during the preparation for this book, especially Gloria Troyer at the University of Guelph library and Wendy Chmielewski of the Swarthmore College Peace Collection. Marilyn Armstrong Reynolds of Canadian Parks Service, Environment

Canada, volunteered her research skills at a critical moment. Frances Icovetta of the University of Toronto kindly lent me materials on Cairine Wilson. Kathy Sutherland-Huard and Christina Nyers served as able research assistants, and Cynthia Comacchio of Wilfrid Laurier University and Wendy Mitchinson of the University of Waterloo read parts of the manuscript in draft. Joanna Boehnert of the University of Guelph's Department of Psychology provided me with a Bible belonging to Agnes Macphail early in her life, and the Old Testament passages at the beginning of chapters are among those Macphail found particularly significiant. A sabbatical leave from the University of Guelph afforded the time required to complete this project. The financial support of the Ontario Arts Council and the Social Sciences and Humanities Research Council of Canada towards research costs is gratefully acknowledged. I alone am responsible for errors or omissions.

Terry Crowley

PART I

YOUTH

1

Born in the Scotch, 1890–1910

The good hand of the Lord is on everyone who looks to him, but his great anger is against all who forsake him.

Ezra 8:22

Agnes Campbell Macphail* was a rebel from birth. A wilful child who defied the authority of her parents, she loved to read and to lead others along the path she charted. She naturally questioned the conventions by which most people conducted their lives and was angered by restrictions placed on her because she was female. Her rebelliousness was bred of both ancestry and character. Her family had left mid-nineteenth century Scotland to escape the petty tyranny of aristocratic landlords and intolerant Presbyterians in order to establish economic independence by working their own farms in southwestern Ontario. One of her forebears was reputed to have been the first commoner to win a case against a noble in a Scottish court. From this Scots-Canadian background Macphail derived the qualities that helped her become the first woman elected to Canada's Parliament and to remain a prominent politician for three decades.

The mean log house in which Agnes Macphail was born on 24 March 1890 reflected her family's poverty rather than its ambitions. Her mother, in particular, dreamed of escaping from the inconvenient three-room dwelling, with its leanto

---

* Agnes Macphail changed the spelling of her family name from MacPhail to Macphail in 1925.

summer kitchen and adjacent log barn. Etta and Dougald Mac-
Phail shared the circumstances of many other farmers who
worked small parcels of poor land south of Georgian Bay in
Grey County. Still, they knew that they were better off than
their ancestors had been when they arrived in Canada West.
With the opportunity to own land rather than to farm as
tenants, succeeding generations could work to improve their
lot. The strict moral ethic that governed their lives combined
with a gospel of hard work to instil a belief that lives conducted by immutable standards brought a variety of rewards.
"A good man isn't afraid of hard work" was a common
aphorism that made their real existence into a philosophy of
life complete with gender distinctions.[1] Women worked as
hard as men, perhaps harder because their heavy labours were
constant throughout the year. Mornings frequently entailed
marathons of "floor scrubbing, cucumber hoeing, potato dig-
ging, bean and tomato picking, canning, pickling, washing,
starching, sprinkling, ironing, waxing, baking." Even when at
supposed repose on the verandah in the afternoon, as writer
Alice Munro records, they "were not idle there; their laps were
full of work — cherries to be stoned, peas to be shelled, apples
to be cored."[2]

Life was governed by the seasons and marked by numerous
social occasions. Apart from days in winter when storms
forced all to remain at home or in spring when muddy roads
became impassable, friends and neighbours gathered regularly. Sunday was the universal visiting day. Conversation
sweetened with some food was the usual entertainment, but
when a fiddler or some other musician was around, singing
and dancing added to the merriment. At family gatherings,
lore about the hardships faced by past generations, of bigotry
confronted and intolerance exposed, was passed on to young
people, and the constant repetition of the family history left an
indelible impression on Agnes Macphail.[3]

Her grandfather, Alexander MacPhail, had been sixteen
when his parents settled in the Huron Tract between Guelph
and Goderich. Several years later he followed a common pat-
tern for footloose young men. Heading north to find land on
which to support himself, he carried his meagre possessions
tied to a pole. When he could not hitch a ride, he walked.
Eventually he made his way past the village of Mount Forest,

and then, 18 kilometres west of the hamlet of Dundalk, he squatted on the land on the twelfth concession of Proton Township to which he later acquired title. His wife's family, the Jacks, arrived from Scotland at Hamilton and then walked some 160 kilometres with their belongings in tow until they reached the same vicinity.

Jean Jack married Alexander MacPhail when she was twenty-one. The couple began their family in a one-room shanty and produced twelve children. The house that was built eventually burned in one of those conflagrations that commonly afflicted primitive wooden constructions. In habits they remained Scottish, eating oatmeal in a concoction called "brose," and in the early years they were so poor that in winter their offspring could not walk to school because their clothing was inadequate for the cold temperatures.[4] Eventually the couple became relatively prosperous. They were the first family in the area to own a team of horses, and later, Alexander MacPhail was elected as second reeve of his township. A public-spirited man, he devoted himself to municipal and community work to such extent that his family suffered. He built a Sunday School for the Presbyterian Church before he got around to enlarging his own house. Attentive to the greater needs of widows and their children in the immediate area, Alexander hardly had time for his own wife and children.

Life had been no easier for the distaff side. Grandfather John Campbell had contended with his brother for the affections of Jean Black, a pretty and amicable dairymaid. When he won, the couple married and emigrated to Canada in 1852. The Atlantic crossing took ten weeks and dysentery claimed their infant son.[5] Without money, the couple took what jobs they could get: seaman and stewardess on board ship; brickmaker, sawmill operator, and fencer or laundress and cook on land. Slowly they acquired enough capital to purchase property and build a one-storey fieldstone house on the fourteenth concession in Proton Township near the MacPhails. Two brothers joined them shortly.

Proton Township was located in the southern part of Grey County. Much of the land was low-lying and unsuitable for agriculture. Grandmother Campbell frequently wondered why her family had walked such a great distance only to stop at such wretched land in the virgin forest where they were the

only settlers at the time, as far as she knew. Not far away clean
rivers abounded in the elevated terrain serving as the source
for six rivers — the Humber, Credit, Grand, Saugeen, Beaver,
and the Nottawasaga. To the east of the Campbell and Mac-
Phail farms the majestic Beaver Valley unfolded, and further
to the north lay the Blue Mountains.

Even in families more economically advantaged than the
Campbells or MacPhails, children began work early on farms,
sometimes as soon as they were past the toddler stage. Children's jobs were more repetitive than arduous, but all family
members were expected to contribute productive labour to the
home. Work gradually became more gender specific in
nineteenth-century Ontario, especially among those in the
rural community concerned with their social standing. Girls
helped with the housework, the three "C's" — cleaning, cook-
ing, and child-rearing — but together with the women they
also shared responsibilities for the vegetable garden, raising
poultry, and dairying. Boys were assigned to field work and
assisted their fathers with other chores such as ditching and
chopping wood.

As a young man, Agnes Macphail's father had resented the
additional burdens placed on him by his own father, who was
so concerned about community responsibilities that the farm
work fell to his children. Born in 1864, Dougald MacPhail set
out to acquire money for himself at the age of seventeen by
hiring out as a custom thresher. He grew into a tall man who
sported a bushy, handlebar moustache later in life. With his
high white forehead and sun-scorched skin drawn tight over
high cheek bones, Dougald MacPhail was the image of a
farmer. Since he had younger brothers and sisters to think
about, he did not marry until he was twenty-five. By 1889 he
had amassed eight hundred dollars and was ready to settle
down permanently.

Henrietta Campbell, his bride, was a small, pretty woman
close to him in years and with a fair complexion. Although the
Campbells were opposed to orthodox religion, the couple's
wedding took place in the Esplen Presbyterian manse. With a
team of oxen, a few sticks of furniture, and some second-hand
implements, the two began their life together on a farm that
contained too much swamp and drafty log buildings.[6] Etta
MacPhail complained incessantly about the house. During the

winter months, a kettle left boiling at night was frozen solid by the morning. Eventually the log barn, not the house, was replaced by a new building. Their first child, Agnes, realized early that while a farm was a joint enterprise, it was a partnership in which rewards were distributed unequally. Some maintained, she said, "that in farming women break fifty-fifty with the men, but if this is true it is fifty dollars to the men and fifty cents to the women, and I doubt if that is overstating the case."[7]

Two more girls, Gertha and Lilly, soon joined Agnes. The three loved to play in the big kitchen that their mother denounced so regularly. Still, no matter how humble their abode, Etta MacPhail was determined that it would be ready to receive guests whenever they called. Holidays never interfered with her routine. Monday was wash day, and if Christmas — less important as a Scottish celebration than New Year's — fell on a Monday, the laundry was still done. So maniacal were Etta MacPhail's obsessions with propriety that hired help later referred to her as "killing clean." Gertha and Lilly eventually assimilated her values, but to Agnes housework remained pure drudgery. Laundry was the worst.

The MacPhail home had a reputation for being a social centre where neighbours young and old gathered. Around them lived a host of other British descendants with names like Muir, Oliver, and MacLeod. Mother and daughters dutifully baked pies each Saturday in the expectation of visitors the next day. If no one arrived, the pastries were carefully stored in the larder.[8] On the following weekend someone was sure to come around, and they could be restored in the warm oven. Otherwise, the family went off on its own visiting. Agnes loved these occasions. Her mother told people that this child had talked before she even learned to walk. One Christmas when she was very small she received a red wagon as her present. When her grandfather tired of wheeling her around the kitchen, he tried to get her to talk to the adults in the room. As he stopped pulling, Agnes protested that she could ride while talking. The insistent baby developed into a headstrong child. Ordered by her mother to lie down because she was ill, she objected impudently that she was too sick to be in bed.[9] Life later became a juggling act for a woman so determined that she always wanted to do more than one thing at a time.

At the age of five, the mercurial child trundled off to S.S. No. 4 Proton, the local one-room school. Adept at games, she early showed promise of leadership and quickly gained a reputation as the champion of less fortunates picked on by others. She always knew that she wanted to be a teacher some day. When snowdrifts kept the children at home for weeks on end, Agnes gathered up her immediate companions and conducted a school of her own.[10] Intensely moody, she was prone to complete elation one moment and absolute despair the next. Constant quarrels with her mother led her to resent injustice vehemently. Etta MacPhail hated shows of emotion; she was a rigid disciplinarian who believed that children must be taught to control their feelings as she had learned to repress her own. Seldom did she sympathize with her children's hurts or their troubles once they were grown. Agnes early turned against many of the things her mother held most dear. Apart from housework, she despised frugality and hated to be surrounded by junk hoarded in the event of a rainy day. In their own ways, mother and daughter were each as hard on themselves as they were on each other.

Contrasting Personality

Temper tantrums were something Etta MacPhail knew all too well. She had been attracted to her husband because his expressive personality contrasted vividly with her own. Dougald MacPhail's colourful manner carried with it a quick temper that flared in an instant but subsided just as rapidly. He possessed a sharp tongue, which he wielded as a weapon, a characteristic that his eldest daughter inherited. He cared little for his wife's domestic fastidiousness, but she relieved him of such cares. After 1897, Dougald MacPhail put his lively sense of humour and ready wit to good use by branching out into the auction business and later into cattle-dealing. Farmers' lives were keenly attuned to the annual and seasonal vagaries of prices paid for their produce. They knew value when they saw it or when Dougald MacPhail convinced them. "But that calf has only three teats, Dougald," someone piped up at a country sale one day. "Your mother only had two," the auctioneer flashed back with a twinkle in his eye, "and look what a fine calf she raised."[11] People soon began to say that this

Scotch devil could sell haggis to the English on St. George's Day.

Auctioneering brought material rewards but no change in lifestyle. Money earned was money to be saved. Farms required large capital investments relative to their scarce and variable cash flow. When he acquired horses to replace the oxen, Dougald was able to make the long journey to the market town of Guelph and tap the higher prices offered for produce. He needed better land to support his expanding family and more equipment with which to work it. There was furniture to be bought, and the occasional new hat showed the neighbours the fruits of hard work and right living. Otherwise, work overalls could be bought two sizes too big, to allow for future expansion, and dresses creatively made over.

More than their heritage made the MacPhails hard-working and self-reliant. Life provided few cushions apart from the support of relatives, and they were only to be called upon in the most dire emergency. The dispersion of settlement in rural areas hid discrepancies between wealth and poverty so apparent in cities.[12] Members of poor families engaged in wage labour, and young women in search of employment frequently drifted off to the cities, while their male counterparts packed up more commonly for the West. The destitute found themselves inmates of the house of refuge, the county poorhouse.

The MacPhails were determined not just to avoid such a fate, but also to better their condition in life. Finally, they made the first step. Etta MacPhail inherited several thousand dollars, and when Agnes was twelve, the family was able to abandon their substandard farm. This time they bought a hundred and fifty acres close to Six Corners in Artemesia Township, not far from the village of Flesherton and its railway station in the hamlet of Ceylon.[13] At last Etta MacPhail had a respectable Ontario cottage with an additional half-storey for proper bedrooms perched beneath the rafters of its hipped roof. The purchasers of their previous farm demolished their house and built a new one.

As she grew older Agnes soon learned that society observed a double standard with regard to women and men in all spheres of life. Even in the conduct of the grandmother she adored Agnes learned about gender inequities. Each year Jean Campbell made enough butter and cheese to last through the seasons. She saved the money from what she sold to buy presents for her children, but her daughters were none too pleased when she purchased expensive items like a gold watch for a favourite son while they had helped to churn the butter and produce the cheese. Agnes did not have to vie with brothers for the affections of her parents, but what she was permitted to do was still circumscribed. She wanted to work in the fields, but that was not a respectable activity for a girl. Still, as the oldest, she was allowed to fetch the cows for milking and catch the horses in the pasture before harnessing them.

The young girl frequently turned to her father when she was upset. A close bond developed between them, but Dougald was unwilling to depart substantially from his wife's decrees. At times when conflicts flared and her life seemed ruined forever, Agnes turned to her grandmothers. Both were willing to listen to the anguish of a wounded teenager and assuage her feelings with stories of past trials. To the adolescent struggling to find herself, her grandmothers possessed indomitable spirits that had enabled them to surmount life's real difficulties, and their tales of hardships fired her imagination.

Grandmother Jean MacPhail had been forced into early adulthood at the age of twelve when her mother died. Not only placed in charge of the household, she also had to care for an infant brother. The first product she had to sell for a little money was maple sugar. She strapped it on her back and walked to Mount Forest, the product weeping in the hot sun. Butter had not initially been easy to make since cows in the bush ate wild leeks that tainted their milk. Nor were there earthen milk houses in which to keep dairy products cool. When the butter was good, Grandmother MacPhail had carried it in two ten-kilo pails to Mount Forest as well. The old woman never tired of quoting Robert Burns. "I'm sure it was Burns who made a rebel out of me," Agnes reflected later in life.[14]

Grandmother Campbell had been even more deprived economically, but her warm personality won the young girl's heart fully. Jean Campbell's coal miner father had died when his five children were still very young. Without formal education, she had learned to read by following her uncle's finger on the page of the weekly newspaper while he read aloud to the family. Through all life's vicissitudes, Jean Campbell

forged on, acquiring new skills and never giving in to cyni-
cism. Once in Canada, she found herself doing most things a
man was supposed to do and doing them just as well. With
other women, she had burned the bush while men felled the
trees and then hurried home to have dinner ready on the table
when the others returned. Several times she drove off bears
threatening the family's livestock and never shed a tear when
bandits stole their provisions, turned her family out of their
houses, and burned them to the ground. She couldn't cry, she
said, because she had been so angry. Later in life Jean Campbell tackled the last remaining vestige of her underprivileged
background and learned to write. She believed all people were
one, and she would not tolerate any form of racial discrimination. Agnes idolized her because she continued to learn
throughout her life, but most of all because of her abiding faith
in humanity. She "loved people with a great love," her granddaughter recalled, "people who were bad, people who were
good, and people who were in between."[15]

Agnes excelled at school and loved the world it opened to
her. She early developed a sense of her own self-worth and
fantasized about the things she would achieve in the distant
future when the agony of dependence had ended. "I'm going
to Europe some day," she announced to an astonished family
when she was about thirteen years old. "You are a crazy
child," her mother replied. "You would never have that much
money." "Yes, I will," responded the defiant youngster,
charting a future course that was blocked when her parents
decided that she did not need to continue beyond primary
school.[16] High schools existed only in the towns, required tui-
tion, and severely weeded out those desiring to attend by a
stringent examination known as "The Entrance." Agnes would
have to board in Owen Sound with money that the family,
paying for its new farm, considered it could ill afford. Her
parents needed her to work at home. The teenager brooded
incessantly over the cruel fate she suffered by being born
female, feelings she shared with other girls of her generation
like Thérèse Casgrain, the Quebec suffragist with whom she
became friends much later.[17]

Even as a youth Agnes was resentful that women's life
cycles were governed by childbirth. Was it not possible, she
wondered, for women to live their own individual lives as

complete persons in addition to bearing children or in place of their maternal role? In search of answers, she looked for concrete examples but could find no immediate role models, so she turned to books. The local school library contained a copy of Sarah K. Bolton's *Lives of Famous Men and Women*, which she read repeatedly. She decided that she could emulate many of the things done by the eminent males described in its pages but that the women all seemed to be philanthropists, singers, or artists. This placed her in an even greater quandry since she possessed neither wealth nor artistic or musical talent. [18] The forced two-year hiatus in her life intensified her identity crisis, but ultimately it strengthened her resolve to find satisfaction in work just as men did. Eventually she succeeded in winning over her mother and grandmother, and she was allowed to return to school. The "Entrance" posed no particular hurdle. Elated by her double achievement, she went over to her neighbours shouting, "I'm going, I'm going."[19]

When Agnes stepped on the train for Owen Sound, she embarked on the first of her life's big adventures. "At last I was a real person starting out on my own," she later recounted idealistically.[20] To the sixteen-year-old, the boarding house seemed like a barracks, but she soon adjusted. Until this point in her life, she had only viewed town life from the outside; living within it came as a revelation that was excruciating for a temperamental teenager. Owen Sound Collegiate was riddled with cliques; Macphail's plain country dresses were mocked and she felt ostracized. "I had ground into me," she recalled, "the difference in the recognized social standing of urban and rural people."[21] Nevertheless, these experiences reinforced her own sense of self, as did the behaviour of some of her teachers.

The principal of the collegiate was a man named Murray. He belonged to the brusque and bullying sort of sexist teachers who believed in the school of hard knocks. Intimidation toughened, especially demure young women. Pupils must learn to work under pressure. He did not frighten Agnes, but he terrified others. In class one day, he asked a girl to step up to the blackboard to solve a problem in geometry. As he prodded and harrassed his victim, she became ever more muddled. "I knew this before I came up here," she bleated apologetically. Not prepared to stand back, Agnes impudently called out that "Nobody could know a straight line from a crooked one with you after her."[22]

A tall and wiry young woman, Agnes grew proficient at athletics and attracted the admiration of those teachers who disagreed with their principal's teaching methods. She became captain of the girl's basketball team and was accepted among her peers for her outstanding abilities. She prided herself on knowing everything that was going on in school and joined the literary society. After she completed her junior matriculation in two years rather than the normal four, no one questioned her determination to prepare herself for a career. In 1908 her parents made arrangements with an aunt and uncle in Stratford, Daniel and Margaret McGregor, for her to board with them while she studied for senior matriculation and attended the town's new teacher's college opened that year.

The McGregors were members of the Reorganized Church of Jesus Christ of the Latter Day Saints where Daniel served as a lay reader. In order to foster the religious self-education of her niece, Margaret McGregor presented her with a Bible early in 1909. Agnes read sections carefully over the ensuing years, and since she also found the Latter Day Saints to have a greater social conscience than other denominations she had encountered, she joined them, though the affiliation was not to last. She regretted that the church frowned on dancing, a prohibition she could not respect, but her beliefs in human dignity were strengthened.

The power of the state was impressed on her in these years too. Passing the county jail one day, she saw a black flag flying. Agnes Macphail reacted instinctively against cold-blooded murder in the name of justice. Society needed protection from criminals, she reasoned, but not in the form of capital punishment.[23] The event left a deep imprint on her memory that was to surface years later in her concern for prison reform. Meanwhile, she looked forward to the happiest but also the most difficult period in her early life. She was soon to be free, engaged to be married, and earning money through a profession that satisfied her need for service to others.

2

Young Country Woman: Teaching and the Farm Movement, 1910–1920

"Write down the revelation and make it plain on tablets so that a herald may run with it."

Habakkuk 2:2

In the decade between 1910 and 1920, while she earned her living as a rural schoolteacher, Agnes Macphail awakened to national political issues and found her constituency among the farm people she sprang from. Before leaving Stratford in 1910, she applied for five teaching positions and got them all. She chose Gowanlock's school, six kilometres east of Port Elgin on Lake Huron, the first of several locations in which she would live during the next ten momentous years. Boarding with the family of Wattie Gowanlock was a great joy because there were three other young people her own age who were equally free-wheeling. As a youth, Agnes had been gawky, but she matured into an vivacious young woman whom men found appealing, although she was certainly neither beautiful nor pretty. She loved the company of the opposite sex, and they liked her. Her large, radiant smile, intense eyes, and sharp wit were her most compelling features. Slightly knock-kneed and bespectacled, she had thick hair, a high forehead and cheek bones, a pronounced nose, and a small mouth, which she closed for photographs to hide her teeth. Agnes herself made the definitive pronouncement on her physical appearance in declaring on the platform that "I belong to the plain people, you can see that."[1]

Forthright about what could not be hidden, the young woman was considerably more circumspect about her internal emotions. Pre-Freudian in sensibility, she never wrote about her sexual life and expected others not to inquire. How she came to terms with her sexuality remains a mystery, but Agnes attempted to pursue her love life free of adult comment. How many times did she not wish that her family's gray mare were black so that its hair would not show on her coat and alert a neighbour, who liked to tease her, that she had just returned from a date? On occasion she flaunted her popularity, dangling two young men on a string at once following her grandmother's practice. Her father found it difficult when he was forced to greet two medical students she was dating who arrived at the farm in over-rapid succession. "I do wish you would make up your mind which of these young men you want," he told her before asking what he was to say to the second one driving into the yard. "Ask him to come in," Agnes replied with the confidence that showed she would be able to handle the delicate situation adroitly.[2]

As much as she liked her job at Gowanlock's, Agnes was eager to return home to see her family at Thanksgiving. Before she left, the school board paid the first instalment of her five-hundred-dollar salary. That initial ninety dollars seemed like a million. It was the first substantial sum truly her own, and she used the layover between trains in Walkerton to go on her first shopping spree. She bought herself a fashionable hat with curled feathers, and for her family, she purchased an assortment of presents designed to impress them with her new status. When she distributed the gifts, her parents' response was unexpected. They reprimanded her for extravagance, and her mother reminded her that she had promised to pay back the money spent on teacher's college. Her father objected that ninety dollars would quickly evaporate at the rate she was spending it. Deflated, Agnes harnessed the gray mare and escaped with a boyfriend.

Back at Gowanlock's Agnes threw herself into her school work. She soon found that the real world differed substantially from the theoretical one in teacher-training. In her one-room school she had children of various ages and levels demanding attention at the same time. But she found her first year of teaching exhilarating. She organized a school concert in which all could participate, and she joined in local social activities. She enjoyed merry sleigh rides along the country lanes and sang popular songs like "McNamara's Band" beneath the winter skies. All the parents with larger homes were expected to hold dances for the young people. "A couple of sleigh loads of young people, two fiddlers and a caller, and the fun was on and lasted until the wee sma' hours," Agnes later wrote. Gertha visited for a couple of days to meet the people whom Agnes had talked about so much. She met a young man named W. Meredith Reany, who lived one farm over from the Gowanlocks, and later fell in love with him. When Macphail narrowed her interest to one of her medical students, Robert Tucker, the sisters shared the joys of young love and the adventures of emerging womanhood together.

Despite her delight with her position and the positive impression she had made in the community, Agnes followed the advice of an instructor in Stratford who had informed his charges that proper conduct required the submission of their resignation at the end of their first year so that the school board might assess their performance. Without asking anyone, Agnes naively followed his advice. The board chose not to reappoint her. They were happy with her performance, but thought her resignation signified that she was dissatisfied and advertised for a new teacher. Agnes was forced to move on. She readily found another job at Kinloss, another hamlet in Bruce County, and it was there that her political passions were to be aroused over agrarian issues.

Ontario Farm Movements and Reciprocity 1911

Wedged between Lake Huron and Georgian Bay, where the soil was frequently poor, Bruce County had been one of the last areas of southwestern Ontario settled for farming. Bruce and neighbouring Grey County had proved fertile for the Grange, or Patrons of Husbandry, the first farm movement to sweep through the province. Established in the 1870s to promote self-help through cooperatives and education of farm men and women, the Grange expanded too rapidly and contracted quickly. Two decades later, a second brush fire of farm discontent swept through the country when the Patrons of Industry focused agrarian interest on politics and set out to challenge two-party dominance in Canada. Advocates argued that since farmers were the well-spring of the nation, they needed their own organization to match groups formed by manufacturers and labour. The name they chose indicated that they thought of themselves not simply as agriculturalists but, within the physiocratic tradition stemming from the eighteenth century, as the country's primary wealth producers. Reacting against John A. Macdonald's National Policy with its high tariffs that favoured industrialists over farmers and urban over rural constituents, the Patrons subscribed to a labour theory of value. They attempted to develop a populist movement from a reform coalition of tillers and toilers.[3] In the Ontario provincial election of 1894, seventeen Patrons succeeded at the polls, including four who captured the seats representing Grey and Bruce. But their failure in the 1896 federal election sounded their deathknell as Laurier and his Liberals came to power in Ottawa. The newspaper that the Patrons had spawned, the *Canada Farmers' Sun*, continued to publish but under the more orthodox liberal policies of Toronto historian Goldwin Smith.

Tariffs and trade were vigorously debated in rural Ontario. Despite momentary disruption caused by the Patrons, most farmers were dedicated Liberals or Conservatives. Partisanship brought more than access to patronage in the time-honoured Canadian manner. Party identification involved psychological commitment to differing visions of the country's future, and emotions ran high on the trade issue. The Conservatives shrewdly wrapped their protective policies in the flag of the British Empire and appealed to Ontario's latent anti-Americanism. The branch plant industries created behind the tariff barriers contributed to the growth of cities which provided farmers with new urban markets. The Liberals had initially stumbled in attempting to formulate a response to the National Policy, but finally they had settled on a program of unrestricted reciprocity with the United States. This continentalist orientation was also intended to appeal to the pocketbooks of small producers by allowing greater sales south of the border and cheaper prices for imported machinery if the Americans could be persuaded to change their own high tariff policies.

At home, Agnes had frequently heard her father call for lower tariffs, and she had listened as one of her uncles made verbal sport of Tory-bashing. Boarding with Sam Braden and his wife in Kinloss broadened her awareness and marked the beginning of her adult interest in public affairs. The Bradens' business was a typical country general store where farmers gathered to do a little shopping and a lot of talking and to play some cards or a game of crockinole. Political debates reached a new crescendo late in 1910 when farmers from across the country laid siege to Ottawa and secured a hearing on the floor of the House of Commons; they demanded a new national policy of reciprocity and reduced tariffs. The Laurier government was currently involved in trade negotiations with the United States in the hopes of securing just such a deal. A month later a reciprocal trade agreement that would cover natural products and specified manufactured commodities was announced.

Sam Braden was a committed Liberal, and so was Agnes Macphail. With the reciprocity agreement in the offing, they thought their hour of triumph had finally arrived. Braden enjoyed talking with the friendly schoolteacher and caught in a difficult argument with Tory cronies, he would holler up the stairs for Agnes to "Come on down and help me, these tories may win this argument if you don't." Delighted, Agnes joined the debate while she perched on the store's counter with her young legs swinging. Mrs. Braden was scandalized. "Miss Macphail could be a lady," she told one of Agnes' friends, "if she would only take the trouble." Agnes Macphail never learned to observe such proprieties. In fact, she grew increasingly intolerant of artifical behaviour or undue attention to any sort of nonessential in dress or decorum as she grew older. What she did love was debate and that meant being among men. Also of Scots background, Sam Braden believed that there were two sides to every question, although his party was always right. He encouraged Agnes to read the Liberal viewpoint conveyed in the *Globe* and to contrast it with the position taken by its Conservative rival, the *Mail and Empire*. Other topics, including women's suffrage, emerged in the discussions within the general store's cracker barrel debating society. Agnes reacted against the violent activities of the militant suffragettes in Britain, but she knew she wanted to vote if given the chance.

The 1911 election was the most rancorous in two decades. Emotions flared as each side avidly defended its position in the great trade debate. Robert Borden's Conservatives whipped up a frenzy of impassioned patriotism. The country, the flag, and the empire were all said to be threatened by the blasphemy that flew in the face of British tradition. Big business in central Canada was adamantly opposed to the deal because industries had been built on tariff protection. Eighteen prominent Toronto businessmen bolted Liberal party ranks in sensational grandstanding. Such actions only confirmed the views of farmers throughout the country that economic protectionism had favoured trusts and combinations over the pressing needs of smaller producers like themselves. For her part, Agnes thought human nature had reached a new low. Reactionaries like the Conservatives seemed beneath contempt.

Once the arguments had been aired and election day arrived, Braden's store provided the only connection with the outside world. Since there was no telephone or radio in that part of Ontario, everyone gathered at Braden's to receive the results on the telegraph. By nine o'clock the outcome was clear. The Liberals had lost, and Braden was dejected. He went upstairs to tell Agnes, but he steadfastly refused to convey the election's outcome to his Tory opponents until forced to the wall. The crowd went wild with excitement when they finally heard the news and paraded out into the street with brooms soaked in coal oil as torches. Agnes came down to watch. As the tiny throng swung past the store for the last time, they taunted her to join them. "No, thanks," she retorted truculently, "I'll freeze to death first."[4]

Expanding Horizons

While she experienced her initiation into the joys and anguish of politics, Agnes matured in her teaching. She abandoned much that she had been taught about rigid discipline and rote-learning of lessons in order to arouse her students' interest in the world around and outside of themselves. She brought newspapers into the classroom, played games, and had heart-to-heart talks with the children about what they wanted to do with their lives. There were fifty-two in her class, some of the boys much bigger than herself, but disciplinary problems did not arise. Not quitting work at the end of class, Macphail met with parents to discuss their children's progress, and soon they were seeking her advice about problems in their own lives. In her spare time, she continued her active social life and frequently found herself returning home at three in the morning and sleeping late on weekends as she had as a teenager.

The Bradens were convinced that Agnes played and worked too hard. They were right. During her second year at Kinloss, her health began to deteriorate as great waves of weariness suddenly overwhelmed her. She tripped over objects and burst into tears without provocation. Finally, several doctors diagnosed her malady as inward goitre, an affliction caused by a lack of iodine in the diet and then common in southern Ontario. She wanted surgery to correct the thyroid hormonal imbalance that had changed her behaviour so dramatically, but her doctor demurred because he had recently lost two patients during such operations. Rest was prescribed, and she was told that she would never be able to work again if the advice were not followed. Forced to leave Kinloss, Macphail was showered with flowers at a picnic the children and parents threw in her honour. The tributes were so poignant that she found it difficult to hold back the tears.

Macphail returned to the farm for an unsettling year of forced recuperation. Her condition remained unaltered, but this second involuntary confinement allowed her an opportunity to think further about her life. Despite her success at teaching, she was unhappy. Believing fully in her own abilities, she tried to think of ways to achieve a larger impact. In a Bible class in Kinloss studying the Book of Job, the minister had made a remark that left a deep impression. He informed her that she was very bright and should go to university. Such positive reinforcement had made her intensely proud. As she read and studied one of the great treatises on injustice and human suffering, she determined that she would seek ways to right some of the social wrongs that disturbed her.[5] Finally, her medical condition improved following a medical visit to Toronto. Agnes then headed for Alberta where she taught ten pupils in a school some eighteen kilometres from Oyen. Through the United Farmers of Alberta, she came into contact with an organized farmers' movement for the first time. Although she was enchanted by the vast prairie landscape, a close call with death in a winter storm led her to cut short her stay. Clearly shaken from battling the elements to reach a shanty after hurriedly dismissing her class, Macphail answered tartly when one of her hosts asked if Ontario did not have storms. "Oh yes," she replied, "but then we have houses too."

Teaching next at Boothville and at another rural school near the village of Sharon in East Gwillembury Township, Agnes Macphail made lasting friends wherever she went. She became ever more unorthodox in her teaching methods as she detested the school system's emphasis on exam preparation. She got her board to subscribe to a magazine and daily newspaper for her classes to study. Each day they focused on some element in the news, but she found that if she did not choose the topic, the children concentrated on any horror stories. She also brought the books of Grey County native Nellie McClung into the classroom so that the older children could share her reformist and feminist ideas. In order to assist the board with refurbishing the building, Macphail and her students created projects to raise money. One of the school board members obliged her in return by teaching her to drive a car.

During her time at Sharon World War One broke out, and at its end her plans for her personal life were completely altered. Robert Tucker had left Grey County to attend medical school at Queen's University in Kingston, but before he enlisted to go overseas, the couple became engaged. Agnes expected to marry when he came back to Canada just as her sister wed Meredith Reany upon his return. Perhaps Tucker formed another attachment overseas, but whatever the reasons, they were so painful that Macphail blotted out completely any reference to the war, and she was never to marry. The words of Psalm 85 assumed special significance as she read them:

> *Love and faithfulness met together;*
> *righteousness and peace kiss each other.*
> *Faithfulness springs forth from the earth*
> *and righteousness looks down from heaven.*

The deep-seated emotions aroused at her parting from Robert Tucker and her personal identification of war with psychological conflict only became apparent in Macphail's peace activities during the succeeding two decades.[6]

Now in her late twenties and without a romantic attachment, her discontentment with her life increased. She loved children and wanted her own, but she remained unwilling to be a farmer's wife like her mother. Marriage and a family implied a subordination, a selflessness, that Agnes was not prepared to accept. Always excelling at whatever she tackled, she could not reconcile her own immediate interests with the demands children would make. She continued to believe that she was destined for a more important role where she might make a larger contribution to society, and she extended her search for role models. She immersed herself in biographies and talked to others who had left teaching, but she could find no vocation that would allow her to support herself while serving others.

World War One and Political Antagonisms

Meanwhile, developments outside the tiny rural world of East Gwillembury were leading to changes that influenced the rest of Macphail's life. Canadian women gained the right to vote during World War One, first in the Western provinces and then to a much lesser extent at the federal level in 1917. By enfranchising women in the armed services and female relatives of soldiers, the newly formed Union government of Robert Borden hoped to influence the voters in favour of its recently adopted policy of conscription for overseas duty. In one of the most dramatic upheavals in Canadian political history, Liberal members of Parliament from across the country abandoned Wilfrid Laurier to support compulsory military service. The temporarily revamped Conservative party won handily in a bitter election that divided the country along numerous lines. French Canada was ostracized in a way not seen since the hanging of Louis Riel. Quebec returned sixty-two Laurier Liberals and Ontario seventy-four Unionists.

At the same time, increased militancy from organized labour and farmers, who also opposed conscription, testified to the bitter antagonisms unleashed by the war. The farmers had been apprehensive about rural depopulation for many years, and the United Farmers of Ontario had been formed in 1914 as part of a concerted attempt to reduce the disparities between urban and rural areas. Essentially an indigenous social movement, its goals were originally similar to those of the Grange. The UFO promoted education and cooperative buying and selling in order to increase profits by circumventing middlemen. It formed a separate cooperative company and purchased the *Farmers'Sun* as its mouthpiece. Membership swelled during the last years of the war, and the movement began to take direct political action.

Farmers and labour shared a belief that they had been excluded unjustly from political life by the two old parties. Following populist traditions emanating from the United States and influenced by the example of Britain, both groups wanted to transform the political system by electing their own representatives. The United Farmers of Ontario stressed that politics must be democratized by overturning the partyism they saw as its central corrupting influence. Farmers and labour both wanted to introduce direct legislation into the political process. Specified numbers of voters would be empowered to place concerns on the public agenda through what was called the "initiative." A referendum would then decide the question in the manner established in some American states. Proportional representation and the recall of elected members also appealed to them as ways to alter a system from which they had been excluded for too long. A more complicated proposal was called the transferable vote. By having voters indicate their preferences among the various candidates in order of priority, the selection of the winner would more accurately reflect the ballots cast.[7]

The first steps towards greater labour involvement in politics came in 1917 when the generally conservative Trades and Labour Congress of Canada called for the creation of a Canadian Labour Party to emulate its counterpart in Britain. While an Ontario section was formed the next year, initiative quickly fell to local unions and trades union councils through the Independent Labour Party (ILP) founded in Hamilton in 1917. One concern labour and farmers shared was the conscription of human beings without comparable drafting of wealth. Although the federal government had responded with the income tax, a supposedly temporary fiscal expedient that proved permanent, the ILP felt that only more labour representatives would ensure justice.[8]

Because the war had suspended the massive immigration seen before the onset of hostilities, farmers were preoccupied with labour of a different sort — that of their sons on their farms. During the election of 1917, rural voters in Ontario had received assurances that offspring who laboured in food production would be exempt from military service. During spring seeding in 1918, however, the Borden government announced cancellation of the agricultural exemptions. When military personnel requirements proved more pressing than food production, many farmers felt betrayed. Thousands marched on Ottawa with their counterparts from Quebec. This time they were unable to repeat the success they had achieved in 1910. Rebuffed by politicians and derided by the urban press, they failed to gain access to the House of Commons. Their remonstrance, following in the great tradition of appeals against arbitrary executive authority, was read into Hansard by one of the sitting members. An upsurge from the grassroots of the organization propelled the UFO into politics later that year in a by-election on Manitoulin Island. The leadership was taken by surprise but acceded to local initiative as a democratic expression.[9]

Feminizing the Political Message

While the ILP and UFO were becoming active, farm and working women were also taking up political issues for the first time. Women thus entered into the full exercise of their democratic rights during a rancorous period when the country was divided by language, region, and sector as never before. On the labour side, Laura Hughes, daughter of Toronto reformers James and Ada Marean Hughes, energetically espoused the cause of working women. Together with Gertrude Graydon, she undertook an investigation of the working conditions of women in factories receiving war contracts on behalf of the Trades and Labour Congress. The revelations subsequently published in the press attempted to highlight the problems faced by the female sector of the labour force. Hughes spoke to women's, socialist, and labour groups around the province about women's suffrage, the economic causes of war, the international arms trade, war-profiteering and working conditions. She continued her advocacy as a member of the executive of the Independent Labour Party.[10]

However, attempts to unite the female electorate proved futile. In the wake of a visit by British suffragette Emmeline Pankhurst to Toronto in 1918, individuals associated with the National Equal Franchise Union had hastily modified the program of the British Women's Party and presented it as a Canadian manifesto. Western farm women reacted immediately against the Canadian Women's Party in which they had played no role. Irene Parlby of the United Farm Women of Alberta characterized the banner of the Women's Party as "the flag of vested interests." In Saskatchewan, the first president of the Women's Section of the United Grain Growers reacted no more positively. Violet McNaughton not only agreed with Parlby that the platform was anti-labour, she also objected that more cooperation with the opposite sex, rather than less, was what newly enfranchised women needed in order to improve the Canadian political system. The Canadian Reconstruction Association, a front organization for the Canadian Manufacturers' Association, achieved no greater success than the abortive Women's Party. Journalist Marjorie MacMurchy managed to form a national committee that emitted a unity program for Canadian women early in 1919, but it too was quickly consigned to oblivion.[11]

Ontario farm women were not brought into the picture until J. J. Morrison, the secretary of the United Farmers, realized the potential of their vote. The province's agricultural traditions lacked the activist female component seen in the West. Women had been admitted to the Grange more than a half-century before, but not to the Patrons of Industry. Many rural women belonged to the Women's Institutes that had expanded rapidly during the two decades since their founding at Stoney Creek outside Hamilton in 1897. But the institutes remained under government tutelage and concerned themselves largely with women's domestic role and economic contribution to farm productivity. Full federal enfranchisement of Canadian women in 1918 made evident the need for their direct political involvement. With stimulus provided by Violet McNaughton, the United Farm Women of Ontario was formed with a view to educating women to vote and providing a female component to the farm movement.[12]

Agnes Macphail and the UFO

Agnes Macphail first became associated with the organized farm movement during this upswing in its activities. She reacted against a letter by a fellow rural schoolteacher lamenting her lot in the pages of the *Sun*. Agnes wrote a rebuttal that drew the attention of John C. Ross, the paper's erratic editor, who was interested in extending the participation of women. In 1917 Emma Griesbach, a farmer and teacher from Owen Sound, had been appointed as columnist with his newspaper, and she had turned its women's page away from exclusive attention to domestic matters in order to discuss political and social issues. Sniffing scarce female talent at a crucial time, Ross wrote Macphail and invited her to his office in Toronto. When she responded, the editor introduced her to the activities of the United Farmers and urged her to participate. Agnes Macphail had finally found a cause that could command her total commitment, and she joined the United Farm Women of Ontario shortly after it was formed. But she never limited her activities to all-female organizations because they alone could not deliver the prominence she sought.

Macphail subscribed fully to the farmers' program because she could identify personally with it. She agreed with its democratic principles and found in its populist thrust a means to make her own influence felt. Populism is neither an ideology nor a style of politics. It is a conception of the political process that seeks to overcome barriers separating those who govern from the people governed. Populist movements typically stress mass involvement and more direct accountability by officials to the voters. Generally viewing the professional politician as corrupt or corruptible, they often advocate fuller representation by a greater cross-section of the electorate. When they are successful at the polls, the complexity and variety of political issues creates inevitable tensions between those within the populist movement who comprise its base and those who get elected.

The United Farmers of Ontario were a voluntary movement that reluctantly accepted a political role cast upon it by its

membership. Their policies, which were adopted democrati-
cally at conventions held in Toronto each year, seemed ineffectual without greater political involvement. Many farmers
resented their underrepresentation in the nation's legislatures.
Agriculture was still the foremost industry in the province and
the country, but agrarian influence in public life was limited.
Government war propaganda had emphasized the egalitarian
nature of the collective struggle against a common foe and
repeatedly told the rural community how vital the agricultural
sector was to the nation's military efforts, but the UFO viewed
the Liberal and Conservative parties as captives of a business
sector grown wealthy at their expense. They reacted negatively
to the mergers and combinations that had created large industrial empires during the opening decades of the century.
That trend limited their options in selling their produce at the
highest prices while inflation ate into their purchasing power.

The great bacon scandal of 1917 galvanized popular opinion
more than any other event. The press pilloried Sir Joseph
Flavelle, pork-packer and munitions czar of fabulous wealth,
who was charged with profiting excessively from sales of
bacon to the troops and Britain. The crusty Methodist and
Conservative party stalwart was also known to have refused
fair-wage clauses in contracts for the Imperial Munitions
Board that he headed. "Holy Joe" Flavelle was just too good a
target to miss taking a pot shot at. Farmers already resented
his William Davies Company because it had gobbled up
several smaller firms and now imported hogs from the United
States, depressing prices for their sides of pork. The newspaper
charges were totally erroneous — Flavelle and company were
later exonerated by a public commission — but the scandal left
a deep impression in the public mind through popular expres-
sions such as "robber baronet," "patriotic hog," and a host of
other ingenious epitaphs that only pigs seem able to inspire.[13]
For every instance of real corruption and profiteering uncovered, greater numbers of rumours circulated. Liberal party
propaganda during the 1917 election played to popular passions by telling aggrieved farmers to "VOTE YOUR INTER-
ESTS AND AGAINST THE TRUSTS AND PORK BARONS."[14]

Agnes Macphail associated these collective resentments
with her own experiences as a woman limited by social conventions and attitudes. While teaching in York County, she

asked a shrewd old farmer why there were no women principals in schools nor on the staffs of district hospitals. "Give
women that much rope," he replied, "and they'd be taking all
kinds of men's jobs."[15] She encountered the same discrimination in the political discussions she loved so much. During one
of the perennial debates on fiscal policy, Agnes affirmed that
she was going to master the intricacies of the tariff. "Huh," one
of the men snorted, "you learn the tariff. You could never learn
the tariff."[16] There was nothing Agnes Macphail liked better
than a challenge, whether it had emanated through prejudice
or not. She concluded that women must stand together and
meet men on their own ground.

Her first ventures in the public arena were modest. In her
district she attended local UFO meetings, read all she could on
contemporary issues, and helped to organize farmers' clubs.
Word of her abilities spread. UFO president R. W. E. Burnaby
paid her a visit at the beginning of the 1919 provincial election
and took her to attend a political meeting at Mount Albert in
support of a UFO candidate. When she was asked to speak,
her immediate reaction was to refuse, but she mustered her
courage and addresssed the audience for ten minutes.
Listeners reacted well, at least to her audacity, and cheered
loudly in appreciation. In the election, the United Farmers
were again surprised when they elected enough members to
form a government in concert with representatives of the Independent Labour Party.[17]

Afterwards, Macphail continued her organizational work,
but soon her health failed again. Early in 1920 as she travelled
to Bowmanville to make a speech, she began to feel ill. At first
she thought that her splitting headache stemmed from the
bright sun reflecting on February's snows. She carried through
with her speech but spent the night alternating between chills
and fever. The doctor who was called diagnosed smallpox.
Quarantine signs were slapped on the house of the secretary
of the UFO where she was staying, and an overnight visit
extended into many months. Finally the disease worked its
course, while Agnes worried about paying medical bills from
her salary of eight hundred dollars. Fortunately J. J. Morrison,
who had suffered from the same disease, had the UFO assume
the expense since Macphail had been working on its behalf.

Health restored, Agnes returned to her political activities. She began writing a column in the *Farmers' Sun* about what she knew best — her family. Recounting the stories about the struggles of her grandmothers, she converted them into symbols of the Canadian past whose hopes would be forfeited if farmers did not sustain their memory through political struggle. "Such people," she informed her readers, "your grandparents and mine, are the real builders of this country. They were and are true patriots. They built the foundation of the country strong and true, and if we sit around and let 'captains of industry' so undermine it, that this land for which they toiled so hard, is taken out of our hands by the fiscal policy of this Dominion, we are not worthy of our heritage."[18] In 1920 her name was placed in nomination during a federal by-election in North York. Other women supported her. "It's time that women were represented in Parliament," Bill Wilmot's mother, a former schoolteacher, informed Agnes indignantly.[19] Agnes was flattered and knew that others like Emma Griesbach were eager for Ontario women to follow the example of their sisters in the United States, but she also understood that the gesture was only a compliment. She withdrew, and R. W. E. Burnaby secured the nomination as expected.

At the annual meeting of the North York UFO in Newmarket, Macphail addressed her audience in a direct, forceful manner and with all the righteous indignation that populists frequently use, particularly those who believe that they have God on their side.[20] First she savaged her opponents, Robert Borden's Unionists. They were the "trebly-hyphenated government," she said before announcing that as they had done the job for which they were created, it was time for them to depart. She pointed out the inconsistency in those same Conservatives who had opposed reciprocity in 1911 now preparing to send an ambassador to Washington. Most of all, she lampooned industrialists sitting comfortably behind tariff barriers. "Protection for industry," she pondered aloud as she approached her subject. "What is industry?" she immediately queried. "Is it limited to hogs who have their noses in the trough all the time?" A consummate actor, she continued by deftly capitalizing on Clifford Sifton's remark about Canada welcoming poor immigrants in sheepskin coats: "If those asking for 'protection' would ask for charity, we would probably give it. But when men in sealskin coats drive up in limousines and demand thirty cents on every dollar, we draw the line." Nor did she neglect the interests of her own gender. "Some say that women should stay at home," she remarked. "If women should stay in the house," she retorted with the clincher, "then men should not be permitted to stray beyond the garden gate." The audience loved her outlandish wit and shared her resentments. She was elected director of the North York United Farm Women.[21]

Provincial Recognition

Local acclaim led to provincial recognition. As one of the farm representatives chosen to appear in Toronto before the minister of finance, Sir Henry Drayton, concerning tariff adjustments prior to the 1921 budget, Agnes began her presentation innocently, charming her audience. She had never been in the presence of a real knight, she avowed. Then she proceeded with a saucy presentation that displayed all the truculent animosity of a class-conscious farmer speaking to a group of pharisaical townspeople. Farmers had been treated no better by the federal government's fiscal policy than Indians had been by the Hudson's Bay Company, she maintained. Distorting her personal experiences to play to her audience, she affirmed that marriage to a farmer appeared such an unalluring prospect that she had determined to remain single.

Fresh from this minor triumph, Macphail addressed the annual provincial UFO convention where her emerging political philosophy surfaced. The educational system was her topic, but its urban bias was her main point. She maintained that the educational train began in the country and dumped in the city without any return cargo. Reflecting her occupational background, she argued that teacher-training should prepare young people to teach in ungraded schools until consolidated school became available. She used rural schools as icons just as she had used her grandparents. They should teach "love of rural life; a class consciousness and a class pride." Only in this way could the drift from country to city be altered. The farmers' movement, she informed her audience, was "striving to establish a democracy in which each is for all and all is for each." In full rhetorical flush, she repeated the early motto of the UFWO: "Equal opportunities for all and special privileges for none." Great reforms do not emanate from governments, she concluded, "but from the people. Legislation follows public opinion."[22] Macphail now moved up within the United Farm Women of Ontario by being appointed to its executive and to the immigration committee of the Women's Section of the Canadian Council of Agriculture.

Agnes Macphail had found the spotlight she had desired for so long. She had emerged as a person with immense appeal among a community disgruntled by war and its aftermath. The farm community was her concern, but she remembered that women formed a special constituency. In feminizing the political message, she made her most original contribution. While she had worked hard to master the issues, it was her exceptional abilities as a public speaker and her gender that drew attention to her. At the podium, she prided herself on saying what she thought. Unfortunately, she did not always think before she spoke. Her democratic and cooperative ideals conflicted with her appeal to class consciousness and her rhetorical devastation of her opponents. The memory of grandparents and the education of schoolchildren were all thrown into the crusade for occupational representation despite her abhorrence of indoctrination. She soon set aside the UFWO motto once she recalled that it had been used in the anti-Catholic and anti-francophone crusades of the Equal Rights Association three decades before. Outwardly confident but inwardly insecure, her love of bombast was to make her vulnerable to her opponents in the early years of her political career.

3

History Is Made in Southeast Grey: The 1921 Election

"Shout it out aloud, do not hold back. Raise your voice like a trumpet. Declare to my people true rebellion and to the House of Jacob their sins."

Isaiah 58:1

While she had quickly become known on the broader provincial stage, when Agnes Macphail entered the political arena, she stayed on her home turf. But she did not restrict herself to local issues or emphasize women voters. Instead, she concentrated on broad agrarian and labour concerns.

Grey County was Ontario Protestant heartland in the opening decades of the twentieth century. Overwhelmingly rural, the largest number of its inhabitants were farmers descended from mixed Irish, Scottish, and English stock. By 1921, most were native born. Presbyterians and Methodists comprised over 60 per cent of the population while Roman Catholics and those of German ancestry were only found scattered thinly. In general, individual farms were small, ranging from fifty to two hundred acres.[1] As terrain and soil quality began to change markedly in the hilly southern reaches of the Georgian highland, discrepancies in wealth determined by the productivity of the land were visible in the small houses on the back concession roads. Livestock, poultry, forage crops, a wide variety of vegetables, fruit, and forest products were all produced in time-honoured ways. Full mechanization of agriculture, electrification, and indoor plumbing had not arrived.

Agnes Macphail never lost contact with the place of her birth. When she was home from teaching during the summer months, she loved to stop at the local blacksmith's or the general store to engage in conversation. She was known to speak her mind without false modesty. Friendly and outgoing, she always made a point of asking people who were walking along the road if they wanted a ride to their destination. She loved the sense of community that emanated from people who knew each other and who helped one another in times of distress. Dropping in on neighbours was a common pastime, but Macphail did not always observe the usual proprieties. Finding no one home at her neighbours, but catching glimpse of a tempting pie, she might help herself.[2] Not all shared her communal values or charity, however defined.

Campaigning in a federal by-election in the constituency of East Elgin on behalf of a Farmer candidate provided Agnes with greater experience and the exhilaration that accompanies victory. Early in 1921 her thoughts turned to her own federal riding of Southeast Grey now that four years had elapsed since the last general election and Arthur Meighen had succeeded Robert Borden as prime minister. There was clearly a chance for her to succeed if she could secure the nomination on the combined United Farmer-Independent Labour ticket. All three constituencies in Grey County had returned UFO candidates in the 1919 provincial election because their message had struck a responsive cord. The abandonment of farms and the drift to the cities were apparent in land returned to nature. The result was "an abomination of desolation where fertile fields and happy homes might exist."[3] The weeds that contaminated adjoining properties served as a daily reminder that rural Ontario had once been more vital. While Grey County had seen its population decline by 14 per cent since 1911, the effects of the trend were even greater in its southeastern section. Nearly a quarter of that riding's rural constituents had departed in the preceding twenty years. Residents in Artemesia Township, where the MacPhails lived, had dwindled from 4,442 to 2,392 during the past decade. Only nine people lived in one thousand-acre section of Proton Township, and two of them were over eighty years old.[4]

Provincial activities brought Agnes Macphail local renown, and the *Durham Review*, a weekly newspaper published by

Charles Rammage, mentioned her name as a possible candidate. Her family had been among the first settlers in that part of Grey County, her father was its best-known auctioneer, and she had worked hard on behalf of the United Farmers. Agnes was elated by the suggestion, as she always was by marks of approbation, but she decided on a strategy intended to dissemble in order not to peak too early. She avoided speaking engagements in her home riding that might draw attention to her aspirations. From Sharon, she wrote Violet McNaughton, the women's editor of the *Western Producer* in Saskatoon, seeking advice about current issues troubling the farm constituency. She read W. C. Good's lament for rural Canada and his indictment of the Canadian taxation system as well as William Irvine's call to arms, *The Farmer in Politics*.[5]

The Plunge and the Backsplash

Grasping for the ring was a huge gamble that unnerved Agnes profoundly. She would have to resign from her school and live off her savings. Her parents would not help. A proper place in the community was what they sought, not the notoriety that came from public scrutiny. In face of their opposition, she remained so determined that she projected a pyschological justification for her move. Grandmother Campbell, now in her ninety-second year, was ailing. One night Agnes awoke from sleep startled by a bad dream in which her grandmother appeared in miniature while being dragged along by another woman. The little lady protested that she could not walk any faster. Finally the two came to a halt, and the old woman exclaimed, "Aggie, come and take care of me!"[6] The next day Agnes served notice that she would resign at the end of term in June.

In the summer of 1921, Agnes returned to the Campbell farmhouse in Proton Township. There was still no certainty of an election, but the ailing grandmother with whom she lived served as a convenient explanation for her homecoming. Attending a community picnic, she heard Dr. David Jamieson, Conservative member for Grey South and Speaker of the Legislature, give a speech that criticized the United Farmers and their methods. UFO members were so infuriated that some approached Agnes to rebut his presentation. In light of her strategy, she knew that she risked overplaying her hand, but Agnes Macphail was not one to ignore a challenge. She responded deftly to Jamieson's criticisms, and her audience was thoroughly impressed that this native daughter could express herself so passionately and forcefully without preparation. They were delighted with her address, and it made her the person to beat for the nomination.

Luck was initially with her. Prime Minister Meighen announced early in September that a federal election would be held on 6 December. Many farmers were angry. Prices for agricultural commodities had begun to fall in 1919, two years before a decline in the consumer index, and the rapid descent had continued throughout 1921. The postwar recession provoked voter discontent, and questions relating to trade and tariffs assumed new relevance. The election call forced Agnes to show her colours. First she got herself elected by her local club to the joint United Farmer-Independent Labour nomination meeting that was to select a candidate. While her parents would not accompany her to the local riding convention, her two sisters and their husbands did. Lilly had only recently married Hugh Bailey, a local farmer, who bolstered her male support along with her other brother-in-law, a wounded veteran.

The excited state of the farm community was evident in the large attendance at the meeting in the Durham town hall. Over 150 men and a sole woman had been elected as delegates, but hundreds milled about outside. Twenty-five names were put forward from the floor for the nomination, including that of Macphail. This time she did not refuse. All the hopefuls were asked to give a speech, an interminable process taking over four hours. One fellow nominee stressed his involvement with Sunday School. Clearly a fine exemplar of Protestant Ontario, he was no David to slay the Goliath. Another, a high school teacher, displayed his credentials by quoting in Latin, but it soon became apparent that his audience appreciated his talents less than solutions to current problems.

Agnes was clearly the front runner. She alone among the twenty-five was applauded as she stood up in a navy blue serge dress to make her presentation. First of all she challenged the assembled for having only elected one woman to the convention. Women formed half the electorate, she said, and if the UFO-ILP did not encourage them, the other parties surely would. She then went straight to the heart of the matter. "Premier Meighen says the tariff is the issue," she maintained, "but I say it is democracy. It is a question of whether the people are to rule or the big interests. They say this is a class movement. I grant you, it is — but it is a movement to assist the basic industry of Canada, agriculture, and we are doing a patriotic duty."[7] She condemned the Meighen government for mismanagement and blamed it for the low prices farmers received for their produce. If the reciprocity agreement had not been rejected in 1911, she continued, the Americans would not have placed their new high tariffs on Canadian exports. It was no time for parliamentarians to have given themselves an increase of fifteen hundred dollars in their sessional indemnity. The UFO stood for economy in government, and the increase represented dirty money because it was voted when troops still served in Europe. She would return it if elected to set an example of the belt-tightening needed in government. Great cheers arose spontaneously from the audience as Agnes concluded her speech and resumed her seat.

Patriotism and democracy are hard to beat. Macphail was clearly superior to the other candidates. She had brains, was well informed, and expressed her views forcefully, but she was still a woman. According to the conventional rules of the political ritual, it was unseemly for anyone to appear to want the nomination to satisfy personal ambition, but this prohibition was applied even more stringently to females than males. The candidate must be a person dedicated to lifting the standard, not seeking personal advantage. Agnes sought to allay any sense that she was self-interested by absenting herself while the interminable balloting progressively narrowed the field. Outside the hall for most the time, she went into town with her sisters to buy ice cream while others did the fighting for her. The representatives from Proton Township set about convincing delegates that the risk on a woman candidate was worth taking. Four ballots were called until there were just two nominees left. By six o'clock, when the final count was made, her backers proved successful. Agnes Macphail had secured the nomination for the federal election. She had beaten her nearest opponent eighty-four to sixty-seven.

The next morning a counterreaction set in. One old farmer from Osprey Township expressed the views of many. "What!

Are there no men left in Southeast Grey?" he exclaimed in a traditional appeal to male tribalism.[8] The riding executive convened hastily, and Agnes was summoned to discuss the reservations that had emerged. The candidate stood her ground and calmed their fears momentarily, but dissatisfaction continued to seethe. One or two disgruntled losers further fed the fires of discontent over the choice. The executive eventually asked Agnes to resign, but she steadfastly refused. She had waited too long for such an opportunity to alter the course of her life. The ring was hers and she was not about to return it without a fight.

Since women had gained the franchise, seven had been elected to provincial legislatures in the four Western provinces, including Nellie McClung, and in 1921 Irene Parlby and Mary Ellen Smith became the first women cabinet ministers in the British Empire. Their example provided encouragement, but, more importantly, Agnes knew she was the equal of any man. Firm in her convictions, she summoned all her talents to demonstrate that she was worthy of the support she had received. One or two malcontents did not desist in their grumblings, but Agnes forged ahead with plans for her campaign.

The 1921 Election

The movement of provincial farm organizations into federal politics in 1921 presented the first serious electoral challenge to the two-party dominance of Canadian politics. The Canadian Council of Agriculture had set the stage for agrarian revolt by revising its farmer's platform in 1918. It demanded immediate reciprocity in natural products with the United States, the extension of the preference accorded trade with Britain, and the introduction of free trade with the mother country within five years.[9] The United Farmers of Ontario had been the first provincial group to endorse the platform before the groundswell that led to their victory in the 1919 provincial election. Many outside the movement had been sceptical about the ability of the Farmer-Labour coalition to govern effectively, but they had been proven wrong. While the ideas behind much of the government's legislation were not new, the Drury team managed to institute an impressive social program aimed at strengthening the family, and women were among the chief

beneficiaries of its legislation. The enactment of mothers' allowances broke with the nineteenth-century practice of dealing with social problems through institutionalization. Limited
relief was provided to deserted mothers, to those whose
husbands were completely disabled, and to foster mothers
with dependent children in their care. Adoption was made
easier and cheaper, the stigma of bastardization lightened,
desertion by fathers made an offence, and a minimum wage
law passed in 1920 that covered all female wage-earners in the
province.[10]

These activities verified the early prognostication of the
Financial Post that "The Farmers Will Give Ontario Stable
Government."[11] After a Western agrarian group in Parliament
declared the formation of a National Progressive party in 1920,
the United Farmers of Ontario slid into federal politics in the
same manner as it had into the provincial election the year
before. In reality there was no Progressive party outside the
the minds of the Ottawa parliamentary caucus. The rural upsurge was predicated on provincial farm organizations unclear
of their long-term goals but determined to expand farm representation to achieve immediate influence. The United Farmers of
Ontario resolved in 1919 that it would not enter an alliance
with either of the old parties, but expressed its willingness to
work with others in sympathy with the principles it affirmed.
The Farmers' platform was revised in preparation for the 1921
election, but in Ontario the United Farmers continued to let
political initiatives rest with riding organizations.[12] In some
critical aspects the political drama in Ontario after 1919 entailed a repetition of scenes first rehearsed during the Patron
upheaval during the 1890s.

Waters were tested initially in four federal by-elections won
by UFO candidates. Henry Wise Wood, president of the
United Farmers of Alberta, travelled east to bring his version
of the Farmers' message to Toronto in 1920. Agnes heard him
expound his views on group government at the annual UFO
convention. Wood believed that farmers and labour constituted the democratic forces in society but that they had been
thwarted by the rich, and therefore powerful, in the country.
Represented by such bodies as the Canadian Manufacturer's
Association, financial and industrial tycoons had used their
wealth to capture the apparatus of the two old-line parties.

Legislation creating the country's tariffs had fattened plu-
tocrats at the expense of rural Canadians. Wood proposed a
parliament in which the representatives of various economic
groups would cooperate in the formulation of legislation. Parties were anathema to Wood. Like the early conservative opponents of responsible government in the nineteenth century,
the former Missouri populist saw them as self-serving factions
rather than as instruments of the people's will. He publicly
opposed the formation of a new democratic party because it
would perpetuate a system he deplored and weaken the progressive forces he wished to promote.[13]

Agnes Macphail embraced the political outlook of Henry
Wise Wood wholeheartedly. It explained to her why the rural
community had been ignored and suggested the way in which
it might make its influence felt in the future. It gave legitimacy
to the farmers' cause and stressed the importance of the immediate campaign. Agnes agreed with the views of J. J. Morrison, the secretary-treasurer of the UFO and its cooperative
company, whose views were akin to Wood's. Her admiration
for that wizened veteran of organized farm movements from
Wellington County was unbounded. "I revere and honor that
common old soul with the bald head," she exclaimed, adding
that he was the only man she had ever praised in public.[14]
Sometimes as severe as the piercing eyes protruding from his
gaunt face suggested, the aging Morrison stood firm in his
commitment to dignity for the small landholder like himself.
Agnes shared his commitment to the ordinary farmer as well
as his view that party entanglements might end the farmers'
movement.

Not all their colleagues shared Macphail's and Morrison's
lofty ideals nor their advocacy of group government. Resting
on a naive belief in human nature and a parochial view of
national affairs, group government proposed far too great a
change from accepted practices to have any success in challenging the party system. At root, it forecast class — or occupational group — as the basis on which politics should be
founded. Once such a revolution in thinking had been enacted
in law, various groups in legislatures might decide through
cooperation what laws would be enacted without the interfer-
ence of partisan demands. Premier E. C. Drury could make no
sense of the proposal. While he believed in the primacy of rural

values no less passionately than others, he advocated that the UFO broaden its base politically to include people who shared its goals. Morrison wanted to increase farm representation only to secure favourable legislation. Although Drury remained a crypto-Liberal and Morrison might have been described as a radical democrat, their differences reflected more than conflicting political visions or ambition. They struck at the root of cleavages within the Ontario agricultural community between small farmers and larger operations. Deep fissures were apparent within the farmers' movement as it headed into the federal election.

Pundits predicted a minority government because there were three wild cards this time rather than one. Women as well as farmers and labour made the hand impossible to call with any certainty. The enfranchisement of women had nearly doubled the Canadian electorate to some three million people. A million and a quarter were first-time female voters. In preparation for the election, the National Council of Women of Canada had published a women's platform in 1920 that was remarkably prescient and reformist. It boldly supported equal pay for work of equal value, no gender descrimination in employment, uniform marriage laws, equality in divorce and the removal of financial barriers, collective bargaining, the abolition of patronage, the publication of all political contributions, the naturalization of women independent of their husbands, and political equality for men and women.[15] But these were not topics Macphail chose to emphasize in Southeast Grey.

Agnes Macphail's Campaign

Agnes Macphail concentrated on farm and labour issues; women were only considered in relation to them. Winning an election was her immediate object, although the ability of local candidates to influence the outcome, even when native to the ridings in which they run, is severely limited. Macphail ran the race in anticipation that it would be a cliffhanger where a handful of votes would tip the scales. Her chief opponent was the entrenched Conservative member, sixty-four-year-old R. J. Ball, a furniture manufacturer from the town of Hanover. Facing his fourth campaign since he was first elected in 1911,

Ball looked the very epitome of the Conservative industrialist with his manicured moustache, thinning hair, and corpulent body. Ball could afford to be complaisant in a manner that his two opponents could not, although the tide appeared to be running against the Conservatives and his hometown remained a Liberal stronghold.

The challenge posed in Southeast Grey was sufficient without the opposition that Macphail faced as a result of being a woman and representing a new political movement. The riding was large — some eighty kilometres in length — and with over twenty-eight thousand residents. Most were farmers, an advantage decidedly in her favour. The two towns in the constituency, Hanover and Durham, were home to slightly less than four thousand people. Caught in the dissent within her ranks, Agnes resorted to her personal contacts. The big guns of the farm movement were called in to blast away her opposition. J. J. Morrison came first. He assisted with her campaign kickoff in Durham, an experience that initiated her successfully into the political rite that unfolded during the next ten weeks. Her old friend from the *Farmers' Sun*, editor J. C. Ross, followed suit, and so did A. A. Powers, president of the United Farmers Cooperative Company. Other UFO members and candidates also came to Grey to support her candidacy.

Thirty-seven farm clubs in the riding's nine townships and its sole labour union in Hanover stood behind their woman candidate. Agnes and her team set about mobilizing the townships first by naming a supervisor for each and appointing a small organization in every polling subdivision. Then they moved on to the towns. Her stenographer kept an index file of the names and addresses of the chairs of all local groups. Agnes used the telephone extensively. Each week, nine newspapers in the riding carried her advertisements. Her campaign, financed one-third by herself and the rest by the United Farmers, cost her less than two hundred dollars. At every meeting, free copies of the *Sun* were distributed and the contribution of one dollar solicited brought with it membership in the provincial organization. Since Macphail did not own a car, she was forced to take the train or rely on others. Farmers extended their hospitality for overnight accommodation, and she learned to love small farmhouses because their bedrooms were not so cold. Her car broke down late one night, forcing

Agnes and her companion to walk eight kilometres. When they reached their destination at four in the morning, they found that a search party had been sent to rescue them.

While Agnes Macphail early revealed a talent for organization central to electoral success, she also excelled on the platform. So eager were people to hear her that crowds often overflowed the halls. In Hanover, she was forced to speak a second time to a throng that gathered in the rink when they could not hear her earlier. In all, she made fifty-five speeches. Here Agnes was thoroughly in her element, able to command attention for up to an hour and a quarter at a shot. Although she had a set routine, she adjusted her preliminary remarks to gain the attention of her audience. Her determined manner and the force of her convictions impressed, although she revealed her nervousness by swaying unconsciously in unison with her words and fidgeting with her belt. While her message followed the party line, she personalized it through humour, references to common experiences, and adaptation that allowed her to make the common themes of the UFO-ILP platform her own. On the perennial issue of the tariff, she declared that "I believe in the theory as set forth in the Book of Books that no nation can live unto itself, and if it does, it dies." She related the same issue to women by quoting materials previously published in the press to provide a detailed calculation of how much the tariff added to the cost of raising children.[16]

On the stump, Agnes Macphail looked every inch the Girl Guide portrayed in caricature later by the *Canadian Forum*, a small left-wing intellectual magazine that she read. During the election, Toronto newspapers dispatched reporters to interview her. She exuded the confidence in herself, her cause, and the outcome of the contest required of a political candidate. "I think we have a sure riding here," she announced at the Dundalk fall fair. Sympathetic papers repeated the propaganda, but they were surprised by the person they found. "That she wears glasses doesn't mean that there's anything of the timid, afraid-to-get-my-feet-wet school ma'am about her," the reporter for the Toronto *Star* wrote. Then, in a telling comment, he noted, "You can have lots of fun with Agnes, so long as you don't try to get a rise out of her."[17]

Agnes was far better at slinging arrows than in receiving contrary blows. The two old parties and their representatives were the objects of her attack, but she carefully avoided personal references to other candidates. Again referring to Clifford Sifton's Liberal immigration policies, she remarked that "Sir Clifford and his kind would have them continue to wear their skeepskin coat forever." To the stress laid on loyalty to Britain by the Conservatives during the campaign, she replied: "When you find a man promising his wife unduly, he needs careful watching, one sometimes finds. It is the same of those who talk too much of loyalty. There are others beside the Queen in *Hamlet* who 'doth protest too much methinks.'"[18] Following some remarks made in eastern Ontario about the British flag that flew over Canada and the national anthem, "God Save the King," the *Orange Sentinel* questioned her patriotism, but she remarked that people did not go about professing their love of mothers and wives.[19] Macphail remained a committed monarchist, and her political meetings always closed with the national anthem.

Macphail ranged broadly in her criticisms. Decrying the "big interests" pitted against farmers and other workers, she denounced the practice common before the Depression of watering stocks. Then, with an animated face and a smile on her lips, she added that if all the water were let out of them, they would create new Great Lakes. Macphail advocated that the names of shareholders in major newspapers be made public because such papers represented the voice of the few rather than the many. She inveighed against intermediaries in business and extolled cooperation between producers and consumers. She even went so far as to take note of fashionable city women whose fur coats were so long that they were dressed for the North Pole from the knees up and equatorial weather from the waist down.[20] In response to the common rumour that the farmers were communists at heart, she replied that "Farmers stand for ordered society and property rights and would be the first to kill anything like Sovietism. But in any case, I'd rather be red than yellow." She spoke in favour of limited public ownership, a position not difficult to assume in light of the creation of Ontario Hydro. Worried that state involvement in economic life might simply enlarge the infamous political pork barrel, she advocated a new morality in government represented by the Progressives. "We need something more than legal honesty, and a great deal of unselfishness, if it is to triumph," she remarked of public ownership.[21]

In the small halls of Southeast Grey, Agnes Macphail was a new style politician, determined to break with past traditions. "If there is any good point about me," she maintained, "It is that I am what I am, and I tell them what I think." Such conviction stemmed from representing her own people. She entertained no desire to belong anywhere else. To her, class consciousness was integral to self-respect. She shared with John Bright, the nineteenth-century British reformer, the belief that people's "sympathies are naturally with the class with which [they are] connected." "I would," she said, "infinitely prefer to raise the class of which I am one than by any means whatever creep above it or out of it."[22] Preaching the gospel of economy in government that figured prominently in the UFO platform, Agnes claimed that there was "one thing that I intend to do if I go to Ottawa: I will live exactly as I have always done. I won't offer any apologies for the class I represent any time or any where. My idea is to hang your hat on the peg and sit down. Most of those men when they get there live on Peacock Alley, on a plane they were never used to and in which they have no right to live at the public's expense. That's what made Canadian political life so rotten today." In her parlance, the House of Commons became the house of temptation — and she was St. Agnes sent to return it to true virtue.

The people's champion decided that she needed to look like the people's choice in order to give substance to her rhetoric. Like William Morris, the British socialist who always appeared in later years in a blue serge cut-away sailor suit, Agnes continued to appear in the same dress she had worn to her nomination meeting. She found this apparel amusing. "I must confess that this dress I wear has had quite a career," she told a friend serving as host to a gathering on her behalf. "It is my campaign dress, for I have never worn another, and it had either to take me to the house of parliament or the house of refuge."[23] Worn blue serge would confront the temptation of sybaritic Ottawa and destroy it.

Macphail made no special play for women's votes. She did not have to, just as Wilfrid Laurier had seldom tipped his hat towards Quebec before the 1917 conscription crisis forced his hand. Conservatives and Liberals on the national scene tried

to appropriate the achievement of women's suffrage to themselves, but such claims were lost on those enmeshed in the
agrarian revolt. Prime Minister Meighen pronounced pious
platitudes in his pitch for female support and came to Hanover
to support R. J. Ball, but women's concerns attracted little
attention nationally. In Southeast Grey, one of the nominees
who had lost to her cast aspersions on her church affiliation.
Not long before the election, he resigned from the UFO-ILP
riding association executive citing Macphail's religious affiliation, but neither could he support a woman candidate. Some
Protestant ministers raised the matter in their sermons. Both
the riding association and Macphail moved quickly to dispel
any hint of dissension within the ranks. "It has been a proud
boast of the UFO," Agnes declared, "that in it people of every
race, color and creed can meet on terms of perfect equality."[24]
She also had to contend with the emerging division over the
ultimate fate of the UFO protest. One old farmer asked at a
meeting if she stood for Drury, the college-educated gentle-
man farmer, or for Morrison, the man who prided himself on
representing the dirt farmer. Such divisions, she maintained in
a diplomatic reply, were largely the creations of newspapers.
Disagreements within the farmers' movement would soon be
overcome. "One man is simply on the inside of the situation
looking out, and the other is on the outside looking in," she
explained with a Solomon-like wisdom that belied the course
she would later adopt.

To Macphail, farmers and workers were united in a common determination to alter the political system by increasing
their representation. They were the primary producers of the
nation's wealth. She showed her solidarity with that section of
organized labour holding similar beliefs during a meeting in
Hanover where she shared the platform with London labour
leader Joseph Marks. Speaking on behalf of the Independent
Labour party, Marks extolled the accomplishments of the provincial coalition. Agnes was more broad-ranging in her remarks, saying that the Progressives would clean up
government through such measures as publishing the sources
of all campaign funds. Her support came in one-dollar bills,
she announced proudly, and she "hoped they would come in
fast and furious, because if they didn't, it would be hard on
her pocketbook, which wasn't very full."[25] Such a throng

greeted this reappearance in Hanover, including women and farmers, that the commotion made at the back of the hall by people who refused to move into the aisle made it difficult for Macphail to be heard despite her deep, resonant voice. That afforded her an opportunity for humour. First criticizing government policies, she stared at those who refused to budge and said they were like the Conservatives, "they won't do anything and they won't get out of the road." Developing her argument about Tory mismanagement, she noted how ships had been built at public expense for a merchant marine that had no goods to carry because of protectionist policies. "Consistency, thou art a jewel," she declared, "but thy home is not at Ottawa."

Macphail was also called upon to speak outside her riding. She added to her demanding schedule by accepting eight such invitations. She returned the favour extended by J. C. Ross by campaigning in a provincial by-election in North Oxford on behalf of his brother. She travelled over to Shelburne to appear on the same platform as Progressive leader Thomas Crerar and J. J. Morrison and narrowly escaped death when the car in which she was riding nearly collided with an oncoming train. Always the teacher, but now one for whom the province formed her classroom, she carried the plight of rural Ontario to the Labour Forum meeting at Toronto's Labour Temple. Massive exodus, an aging population, and inadequate returns on farm commodities were paraded as sad symptoms of ill-health in the countryside. Before an audience whose bosses attributed their jobs to fiscal protection, Agnes audaciously suggested that rural sacrifices had been burnt offerings on the altar erected by the tariff. Condemning both Liberals and Conservatives, she expressed grudging admiration for the former because they acknowledged that tariffs were legalized robbery. Liberals, she maintained, did not entertain even the courage of their own convictions, lauding free trade publicly but retaining the tariff wall when they were in power. The "death of the agricultural industry," she informed her audience, "means the ultimate death of the nation. We have got to make conditions better for those who work to earn their bread."[26] Despite her expressed affinity for labour, Macphail remained primarily a product of the agrarian revolt. The local opposition press perceived the disparity in her comments and criticized her for saying one thing in the countryside and another in the towns. Macphail responded simply that urban areas were dependent on agriculture for their prosperity.[27]

The Outcome

Agnes had so exhausted herself that during her last campaign speech she stopped dead in her tracks, hesitated a moment, and thought that she could proceed no further. Mustering her reserves, she finally made it to the end of her address. When voting day arrived, it was the last time that cars were able to navigate the county's roads before snows fell. Although grandmother Campbell had died during the campaign, eighty-one-year-old Jean MacPhail made it to the polls to vote for her granddaughter. All gathered at the family home to await the results amidst tremendous tension. The neighbour who had chided her so mercilessly in her youth was assigned to the telephone to tabulate the results as they were received, but his hand shook so much with excitement that he asked someone else to replace him. Gradually, when enough returns had been phoned in to indicate that Agnes had scored such large majorities in the townships that the towns could not overtake her lead, a neighbour stood up. "Friends," he announced, "we have made history in Southeast Grey. We have elected the first woman to the Parliament of Canada."[28]

Right he was. Only four women candidates ran in the election, and none represented the two principal parties. The three others had not stood a chance; they represented labour and socialist groups.[29] Agnes Macphail, in contrast, was informed that her plurality was the largest in the history of Southeast Grey. Her Liberal opponent had never really been in the running, and she had outdistanced Ball by 2,598 votes. That was cause for a jubilant victory celebration in Durham on the night of the election. The next day she learned that her plurality had been the largest of any Progressive member in the province. Her father remained remarkably restrained in reaction to her victory, but Agnes attributed his reticence in public to Scottish reserve.

As the sole female victor and someone radical in her views, Agnes became the immediate object of intense media attention. Even the American press took notice of her election. She was unprepared for the instant celebrity status she had attained at the age of thirty-one. It was not just that she was completely run down from her campaign; emotionally and intellectually she remained a novice in a larger drama where fate and hard work had given her a role. Reporters sought out the farm in search of interviews. They wanted to talk to her parents, and they stopped along the way to pick up whatever gossip might be fit to print. They looked for details about her personal life that would appeal to their readers, while she preferred to talk about the issues as she saw them. When their stories appeared in print, they were often inaccurate. They said awful things. Her victory, local newspapers wrote, had been an "Aggienizing" defeat for the two old-line candidates.[30] Rather than distributing her campaign photograph to accompany articles, she allowed photographers to snap the shutters of their cameras at will, often producing results that bore little resemblance to the real person. Because Agnes had not yet learned the value of good publicity, nor how to control it, she deeply resented such intrusions into her life.

Agnes Macphail was a novelty not just because she was the first woman to be elected at either the federal or provincial level in Ontario, but also because politics was generally thought of as men's dirtiest sport. Calgary journalist Bob Edwards captured this image beautifully in a story that he related the year before he ran in the 1921 Alberta provincial election. A father, he wrote, decided to test the future career prospects of his son through an experiment. He set out three items for the young man to choose. If the youngster took the Bible, he would be a minister; the money, a business person; and the whiskey, a politician. When the son was put to the test and rapaciously grasped all three items, the father exclaimed, "My gracious, he will be a member of parliament."[31]

What sort of member of Parliament Agnes Macphail would be remained to be seen, but for the present she hated being treated as an exotic curiosity, "a sort of bear in a cage," she said.[32] Reporters would have preferred to find "one of those petite, delightfully feminine little mothers who honour the cradle in their souls," a description applied to one of Agnes's sisters.[33] Instead they found a vibrant person who defied sexual stereotypes. Scurrilous gossip among opponents in the riding charged that Macphail was "mannish," a rival to wives, and a threat to the sanctity of marriage — the normal slander for a single woman venturing into public life. The local press, unsympathetic to the United Farmers, were also sometimes sexist in their remarks, although they never impugned Macphail's femininity. "The lady wears skirts," one newspaper wrote, "but they do not appear to be much of an impediment when she takes a notion to run."[34]

More sophisticated and detailed in their coverage, the urban national media commented on Macphail's penchant for smart dresses, but they also noted how she defied convention by not wearing hat and gloves in public. Agnes responded jokingly that hats cramped her brain and did not allow her to think on her feet. "I did not solicit a single vote," she declared openly in commenting on her win. "I told the people that I would not kiss babies, and I didn't. The men worked for me and the women all voted."[35] She avowed that her highest ambition was to be what her constituents wished and even suggested that she might not have much to say when the House of Commons convened. Otherwise, Agnes Macphail refused to interpret her victory in personal terms but cast it as an advance for all women. She thought her election was a vindication of women's struggles over the past century, and, she asserted, she would represent all the people of her constituency.

The Aftermath

The election created more pressing problems than the encounter of Agnes Macphail with the press. No party had gained a majority. The Liberals had captured the largest number of seats, but the Progressives finished in second place and held the balance of power with sixty-four members. William Lyon Mackenzie King, after successfully defeating the ruling Conservative party during his initial election as Liberal leader, hoped to avoid forming Canada's first minority government. The Progressive revolt was momentary, he reasoned, caused by particular grievances in Ontario and the West that stemmed from the Conservative administration; his government would remedy them. Progressive leaders like Crerar and Drury were simply Liberals in a hurry who might be wooed by a sweet political deal designed to satisfy mutual personal and political interests. In attempting to form a cabinet that would bring the strays back into the fold, King entered into a series of complicated negotiations that could not be fully hidden from inquisitive journalists.

King early demonstrated the adroitness that maintained the Liberals in power for so long. The National Progressives were far from united on any but a limited range of issues. The platform of Canadian Council of Agriculture camouflaged loyalties that remained provincial. Collective action had arisen from a common concern over the fall in farm prices, aversion to tariffs, and a feeling of alienation from the political process, but otherwise the West was agitated by the demise of the Wheat Board that had previously sold its grain while Ontario was more preoccupied with rural depopulation. Internal divisions within Ontario were seen at the national level where the differences between the United Farmers in Manitoba and Alberta were pronounced.[36] The Manitobans, led by Thomas Crerar, hoped to realign the country's political parties along the tariff issue, but among the representatives of the United Farmers of Alberta, the independence of members and the group government idea commanded allegiance. The former believed that cooperation with the Liberals was possible, but the Albertans insisted on remaining apart in order to secure the legislative program that they desired.

With twenty-four seats Ontario formed the largest provincial contingent among the Progressives, but not as many were elected as some had expected.[37] Although they had run under the banner of their provincial organization, many were former Liberals who had only abandoned the party to secure immediate results. King's machinations while forming his cabinet brought internal discord to the fore at the UFO annual convention following the election. While Macphail's personal victory was received warmly and a resolution expressed "the hope that the presence of a woman member will have a beneficial effect and trust that it will be a means of further breaking down the age-long prejudice against your sex taking part in public affairs," more important to the new M.P. was the prominent role she played in determining the UFO response to the question of collaboration with the Liberals.[38] The farmers, she said, were now in a position to support good legislation, oppose bad, and avoid the responsibilities of governing. This was a better way of addressing the needs of the country's agricultural communities, she thought, than falling victim to enslavement through party. "We are not longing for power as some others have," she said, "for its own sake only, because power without principle is one of the most dangerous things we can have." Recycling her old house of temptation line, she went much further in the heat of the moment and proceeded to brand Drury and others who favoured collaboration as traitors. Emotion eclipsed her judgment as she declared that "I have more respect for the man outside our movement who originates and starts the slander against us than I have for the man in the movement who believes it."[39]

Just as truculent following her speech, Macphail told a reporter that if Thomas Crerar accepted King's offer to enter the cabinet, the Progressives would look for a new leader. While her views were extreme, they were held as passionately by other farm leaders. J. J. Morrison said simply that the UFO "cannot be the discredited adjunct of the Liberal Party."[40] He felt that nothing would destroy the Farmers' position as quickly as an alliance with the Liberals. The convention affirmed this policy in a resolution advocating that the National Progressives remain intact in order to devote themselves to the platform on which they had been elected.

When the newly elected members gathered in Ottawa early in 1922, Macphail took an instant dislike to Crerar and followed the directives given her to the letter. The Progressives refused to function as the official Opposition, a role that fell to the Conservatives by default. Macphail, Morrison, the Albertans, and others whom Crerar called "the super democrats" were determined that the Progressive movement would not emulate the past practice of political parties but alter the system.[41] As a former Liberal and a minister in the Unionist government, Crerar understood only too well the independence of many in his group. Since they had been elected without party machinery, they saw themselves representing only the people who had elected them. Crerar advocated compromise as the best way of promoting their ideals, but he achieved only limited success.[42]

Agnes Macphail did not learn that lesson at the beginning of her political career. She quickly thrust herself into the thick of Progressive politics as a major player. In her first election and ensuing battles, she showed herself ready to address the main public issues by tackling men on their own ground. Life was too full for her to compartmentalize her energies or restrict them in any way. The sphere that had been carved for and by women always seemed too small for her aspirations, but she did entertain hopes for gender equality where women's province would be as large as men's one day. She had readily accepted a position as director with the United Farm Women of Ontario in 1920 and as member of the immigration committee of the Women's Section of the Canadian Council of Agriculture.[43] In 1921 and each succeeding year, she was the keynote speaker at the annual convention of the Ontario organization, but her commitments were always much greater.

Macphail was in demand everywhere, and she accepted as many invitations to speak as she was able. It soon became apparent that her views were those of the countryside. While she felt that agricultural and labour parties had sprung from the same well and hoped that they would unite to form a cooperative government, she expressed no sympathy with those who expounded socialist or communist views. "Labor would win more if they were not so radical in their views," Macphail told a Toronto audience.[44]

In the interval before the parliamentary session began, she also led the Progressive campaign against Arthur Meighen in a Grenville by-election. Taking the opportunity to visit nearby Ottawa before the session began, tears filled her eyes as she approached the Parliament buildings and read the words over the main entrance: "The wholesome sea is at her gates, her gates both east and west." Agnes was as anxious to get down to work as a child is to play with a new toy, but she knew nothing of the profound tribulations she would soon experience as she entered her new life.

PART 2

PRIME

4

Violating the Gentlemen's Club: The First Term in Parliament

And a highway will be there; and it will be called the Way of Holiness. The unclean will not journey on it; it will be for those who walk in that Way; wicked fools will not go about on it.
                                                                    Isaiah 35:8

Despite the attention she had received on her election, Agnes Macphail was not prepared for the continuing publicity, much of it negative, that she attracted in her first session in the House of Commons. But she did not allow personal attacks to deflect her from her causes like the peace movement, nor would she be bullied into aligning with the Liberals as most Progressives did.

A cold rain was falling the first morning Agnes Macphail arrived in Ottawa early in 1922, and it matched her low spirits. Once she had settled her belongings, she did not know what to do with herself. There were no trumpets or drums to greet her as she had half hoped. Having neither friends or relatives with whom to share her excitement, she sought refuge in the parliamentary library where she read until the words on the pages lost their meaning. When she emerged into the sunshine, she encountered Ted Garland, Bill Irvine, and Henry Spencer, all new members of Parliament from Alberta representing farm and labour. Deciding that the afternoon was too beautiful to waste, they hopped a streetcar to the Ottawa Experimental Farm. Returning to the city following a rollicking time filled with laughter, someone suggested they have dinner together. All were keen, but together they could not muster the cash for such an indulgence. The happy band commiserated with each other and agreed that they were faced with life's stark realities.[1]

A new governor general, a new prime minister, and the largest contingent ever elected outside the two old parties were novel features of Canada's fourteenth Parliament as it convened in March of 1922, but the reception and conduct of the first woman member attracted special public attention. Agnes Macphail immediately captured the popular imagination. Doggerel that began to appear early in the year continued throughout her two decades in the capital:

> When Agnes comes to Ottawa,
> In that old gown of blue
> That's braved the battle and the breeze
> For years that number two
> And takes her seat in Parliament
> Among the pigmies there
> Contentment will spread o'er the land
> And vanish Dull Despair.[2]

Public anticipation matched her own personal excitement. A political career was her primary goal in life. As the first woman elected, she determined to set an example for those who came after, and she understood that she needed to acquire political skills. For the first time a session of the Canadian Parliament opened with a new salutation from the Speaker of the House. After Macphail had assumed her seat in the front row of the Opposition desks, the Speaker intoned, "Madame and Fellow Members of the House of Commons." The importance of the occasion could not fail to impress, but more frivolous thoughts also fleeted through her mind. "Two hundred and forty-four men and me — and lots of them bachelors too!" she thought as she was introduced to the House of Commons.[3] One French-Canadian M.P., having read what Agnes had said of the chamber, declared its new woman member to be the chief temptation of the House.

Now thirty-one years of age, Macphail had lived in a variety of small communities that bore little resemblance to Ottawa's austere environment. Socializing with neighbours and relatives had constituted her principal recreation and provided her chief emotional support. In Ottawa those props were temporarily removed. Nor was Macphail prepared to find how sexist, racist, and anti-semitic the gentlemen's club she had just entered would be. On her first day in Parliament, flowers adorned her desk. They appeared as a kind gesture, even to a woman who had determined that her aim was equality above all. "What we women want," she said, "is not deference but equality. This old fashioned chivalry is all hollow. It means nothing except that men think women inferior."[4] Such strong views were easily set aside in the poignancy of the moment, but Agnes soon learned what had occasioned the gift: the flowers had appeared not as a tribute, but as the result of a member having lost a bet that she would not get elected. Macphail may have violated the chief gentlemen's club of the land, but the tribe asserted itself by retaliating in small, sexist ways. It stung.

Ridicule in the Press

Real hurt followed in the form of public humiliation. The Toronto *Telegram* liked nothing better than ridiculing the farmers who had converged on the nation's capitals. Barely a day passed when the newspaper did not lampoon the Ontario Farmer-Labour government with cartoons on its front page or spew invective inside. Under approving eyes, the talons of the paper's society editor extended to draw fresh blood from the female neophyte. "**Even Agnes Donned War Paint for State Drawing Room**" bannered the report of the social event of the season where the governor general and his wife greeted members and the diplomatic corps in the Senate chamber after the formal opening of Parliament. The German consul was savaged first. He had committed the grave error of wearing modern evening dress that "the humblest waiter might don." Worse was reserved for the new woman M.P. "But if Cinderella had arrived in her golden coach," the story continued,

> she would not have created more stir than the appearance of Miss Agnes McPhail, M.P. in the line of Members of Parliament and their wives. For Agnes had evidently repented of her decision to go so plain. Canada's first woman member was attired in a black lace, round neck, short sleeved dinner dress with corsage bouquet of sweet peas and one of those red feather combs in her dark hair. One mean woman remarked that it looked like a U.F.O. trademark. We might also

report that Agnes was wearing a pair of those wicked long white kid gloves which cost $7.50 to take them home from the store.[5]

A column reporting an interview several days later constituted an even more personal attack as the woman journalist stacked the cards against the unsuspecting M.P. The story began innocently with comments on the sixth floor office in the main parliamentary block that Macphail had decorated tastefully with curtains, new furniture, and pots of primroses and hyacinths. In the course of these pleasantries, Agnes had expressed her dislike of the carpet and her desire to secure a new one. "Then we knew we had got the right woman," the column continued, "for Agnes is nothing if not an objector." When Macphail averred that there was little special about her, that she was only one type of country woman, the pugilistic reporter retorted that Agnes had not been in one of her machine gun moods that day. The absence of the famous blue serge dress was a further disappointment, but the journalist wrote, it had been replaced by one "guaranteed to take ten pounds off."

Cattiness combined with trite parody to turn Macphail's best features into their opposite. When "she smiles her face is positively mask-like in its inscrutability ... as if Mona Lisa had escaped Grey County and ended up in Ottawa," *Telegram* readers were informed. No quarter was shown regarding her conduct in Parliament. Looking down on Macphail from the press gallery, the newspaperwoman observed that the country's only female M.P. "appeared to regard herself as the very watchdog set on guard at last for women in the nation's parliament." During the interview she went further and tried to goad Macphail into making comments on matters that fell within provincial jurisdiction, but the novice was too smart to leap at the bait. The article closed with a complete misrepresentaion of Macphail's personal likes and dislikes.

The *Telegram* did not desist. Two weeks later Macphail's performance on her job was questioned. Agnes was chided for being absent from her desk when the first vote in Parliament was taken. Noting that "Miss McPhail expressed her distress about the long working hours of the poor M.P.'s," this report commented that Macphail's decision to attend a conference in

Baltimore showed that "her official duties were not entirely using up the lady from Ceylon." Agnes had made no secret of her loneliness in Ottawa, but, the paper responded, "Some people may remind her that it much depends on herself just how long she will be lonely." Then in a final blow the reporter ended the column by discussing how the woman ambitious for herself rather than the common good was the one likely to get elected.[6]

The adverse press reaction that greeted Macphail's debut contrasted sharply with the reception accorded Nancy Astor as Britain's first woman member of Parliament in 1919, although Astor was an equally outspoken advocate of reform who initially displayed as much impatience with political life as her Canadian counterpart. The contrast between Britain and Canada stemmed from more than the upheaval in the latter's politics in the immediate postwar years; it also resulted from the differing social backgrounds and party affiliations of the two women. Nancy Astor was a Virginian by birth, a divorcée, and a Conservative who had married into the peerage and won her husband's seat when he went to the House of Lords. Her presence in British politics did not challenge accepted practices as did Macphail's Progressive beliefs.[7] As well, Astor advocated more innocuous reforms such as temperance that Macphail did not stress.

Anyone would have been infuriated by such journalism, but it struck at the heart of Agnes Macphail. She reeled psychologically, her hurt unassuaged by sympathy expressed in other newspapers. Bitterness swelled within her, and the wounds took several years to heal. Turning in on herself, Macphail became guarded in the presence of reporters. Her weight dropped four kilos. She got angry at little things such as the pomp and expense that greeted the opening of Parliament. With members from the old parties she was sometimes petulant, and her rude manner with cabinet ministers was noted. As late as 1924 she counselled young women at the Ottawa Ladies' College bluntly: "Do not rely completely on any other human being. We meet all life's greatest tests alone."[8] By that time Macphail was beginning to gain acceptance within the House of Commons. Such marks of approbation brought a return to her true nature. Men in ceremonial uniforms, she thought, were little more than children in dress-up clothes;

women journalists, she came to understand, had been denied the same privileges as men in that profession.

During the first year in Parliament, work provided a means to forget the barbs of society editors. Macphail was so eager to learn the workings of the House of Commons that she often listened to debates late into the night. The committees on which she served (elections, banking, and soldiers' pensions) devoured much time. As the only woman M.P., she was inundated with mail. Requests for her to speak flooded in — seventy invitations arrived in the month before Parliament opened — and she accepted as many as she could. The needs of constituents required constant attention, and Macphail was only too happy to welcome visitors from her riding to Ottawa. She began to write letters about events in Parliament that she sent to newspapers and some five hundred supporters in her constituency. All these activities reflected more than common good sense or the heart of a woman who remained an ardent educator. Macphail cherished the Progressive doctrine of constituency autonomy that placed a premium on members representing more directly the interests of those who elected them. She was determined to show that the UFO experiment would produce better government through more direct communication.

Her activities frequently exceeded that political mandate. Macphail took biblical injunctions against undue concern with material wealth seriously and was charitable to a fault. A colleague recalled her as the type of person always ready to "lend a sypathetic ear to anyone who had a hard luck story."[9] During the first session she even invited all the students at the Ottawa Teacher's College to tour the Parliament buildings, take tea, and hear her talk on the functioning of government. And since she had experienced problems in securing visual aids when she was teaching, she distributed photographs the young women could use in their classrooms. Despite these extra expenses, she returned a part of her parliamentary indemnity at the end of the first session as she had promised and as E. C. Drury had upon becoming premier of Ontario. The UFO stood for economy in government, and Macphail could not tolerate dissonance between theory and practice. Both individuals later recanted, but unlike Drury, who secured the return of his money, Macphail suffered the supreme indignity of having her donation to federal revenues taxed as income!

Entry into Parliament

Macphail's long-awaited first words in the House of Commons concerned a minor matter that she turned into a question of principle. While she was now an experienced speaker, the dignity of the institution impressed her as much as the wretched acoustics of the building made it difficult for members to be heard. She knew that what she said would be closely scrutinized, but the applause that greeted her as she rose from her seat to ask a question about civil service salary bonuses only served to make her more nervous. Why, she inquired of the government, were bonuses set so that those at the top received larger amounts than those lower on the totem pole? Where was the justice in such a distribution of rewards?

Sensing the historic nature of the moment, the Hon. Henri Béland rose from his desk and began his reply by saying that "It will be to my eternal honour ... [to] ... have drawn into discussion of this committee the first lady member of the House."[10] His last phrase summarized all that Macphail found so objectionable in the reaction to her presence in Parliament. She was a woman, not a lady, and she preferred to be addressed as "the Member for Southeast Grey" in the same way men were acknowledged. She hated the deference shown to her because it distracted from the importance of the views she expounded. "When I first came to the House of Commons," she later recounted, "and walked into the lobby men sprang to their feet. I asked them to sit down as I'd come to walk around. I didn't want them doing me favors. I was right. I found that I couldn't do my job without being bally-hooed like the bearded lady. People in the gallery pointed me out and said, 'Right there. That's her.'"[11]

Although she later learned to turn the constant public attention to her advantage, initially such scrutiny disoriented Macphail. Her least remark or the most incidental piece of her apparel was reported in the press in a way no male member had to endure. Macphail was not alone in her negative reaction to the excessive attention that plagued her. One of her parliamentary deskmates felt the same. Spying a book with the title of "Man in a Cage," fellow M.P. George Coote pointed it out to the clerk and said, "That's me. I'll buy it."[12] Not even able to escape the spotlight during meals in the parliamentary dining room, she sought refuge in the cafeteria for civil servants or took her meals in town.

These experiences quickened Macphail's desire for gender equality, the subject of her first address to the House on 29 March 1922. Macphail argued against an amendment to the Elections Act intended to give voting privileges to non-Canadian women married to citizens because it failed to treat women on the same basis as men. The changes proposed denied women's individuality by considering them as men's appendages. "I think that what women really want today is perfect equality with men," she began, "and therefore if the striking out of section 29 of the Dominion Elections Act does not confer upon women perfectly and entirely equal rights with men, then, I think, it is not going far enough. It would seem to me that if a woman were herself a naturalized Canadian it would not matter whom she married at all, because she would be permanently a Canadian, a naturalized citizen. On the other hand, if she were not a naturalized citizen herself, it would not matter whom she married, or whether she was married or not — she would not be a Canadian citizen. If that is not true then women must simply be deemed to be part of the goods and chattels of men — she is not an individual at all." Continuing her campaign against antiquated prejudices, Macphail also took issue with her future anatagonist, Hugh Guthrie, by objecting to his views that American women were more entitled to special privileges than women from European countries. "I think women just want to be individuals, no more and no less," she concluded.[13] Macphail confirmed her words by working to remove petty annoyances that served as constant visible reminders of inequality. She negotiated an agreement with the Speaker to relax the rule on women wearing hats in Parliament. Guards were asked to stop enforcing the regulation, and it slipped into abeyance.

Although some initally saw her as an acidulated schoolmarm, Macphail quickly began to gain her stride. During that first session of Parliament she spoke forcefully about the problems afflicting men and women engaged in agriculture, but it was the debate on the industrial conflict brewing in Cape

Breton that she considered as the greatest achievement of herself and the Progressives. In the face of inflation, the newly formed conglomerate called the British Empire Steel Corporation had signed a contract with the United Mine Workers of America giving significant raises to its twelve thousand members in Nova Scotia and New Brunswick. When the economy subsequently slumped, the company announced wage reductions amounting to 35 per cent early in 1922. Cape Breton, which had been paralyzed repeatedly by brutal strikes where the militia had been called in during the previous half century, appeared ready to erupt again.[14] The Progressives forced the government to debate the issue.

In the House, Macphail accused the British Empire Steel Corporation of watering its stock and spoke in defence of the miners and their children and of the suffering caused by pitifully low wages. Clearly nervous, she bored members with a long reading from Mackenzie King's pious treatise on industrial relations entitled *Industry and Humanity*. Before calling on King's government to establish a royal commission into the cause of the industrial dispute, she added a comment that stood at the core of her social philosophy: "the only thing worthwhile in industry, no matter what industry is, is humanity."[15] While Parliament would soon see much more stirring demonstrations of her speaking ability, Macphail concluded that the "debate we had in the House regarding the coal miners was to me the turning point in this new Parliament, and the most encouraging thing that has happened because it proves that if we have courage enough and are earnest enough and are determined enough we can do things even after the Government have decided that they should not be done."[16] A royal commission was later struck, but only after militia had been dispatched with machine guns protected by sandbags piled high on railway gondolas. The violent clashes involving men, women, and children that followed led to national protests with thousands of British Columbian miners walking off the job.

Macphail branched out. In the fall of 1922 she began the first of many speaking tours to the prairie provinces. Earlier, in Montreal, she had appeared on the same platform as Nancy Astor. There she made clear that she placed reform ahead of feminism. In a powerful preachment of the Progressive credo,

she declared that financial, industrial, and transportation issues took precedence on the public agenda. Only after they
had been addressed, she maintained, would women's interests
be safeguarded. Pursuing concerns exclusive to women at that
time, she thought, was akin to papering the ceiling to stop the
roof leaking. Such views did not prevent her from playing on
franchise restrictions in the British North America Act of 1867
when she concluded that since women got the vote, they could
be divided into two classes: "the woman who knows that she
never belonged to the same class as aliens, idiots and the like,
and the woman who thinks they do." Neither her attempt to
counter prevailing ideas nor her advocacy of Progessive ideas
was well received within all quarters of Conservative anglo-
phone Montreal, but lest she appear sexist, Macphail divided
men into two groups as well: "those who knew their wives
and daughters are as good as they are, and those who did
not think so. The latter group includes the grouch, but he is
not here tonight as he never attends women's meetings."[17]
Nancy Astor paled in comparison to the Canadian member of
Parliament.

In defying stereotypes Macphail made herself a target for
an opposition press that produced another example of its petty
vindictiveness shortly after Astor's arrival in the nation's capital. To mark the occasion, Macphail's UFO colleagues gave her
a corsage of three red roses and Agnes presented one of them
to Lady Astor. When the British visitor spoke at the old Russell
Theatre, she wore the blossom as her single adornment. The
Ottawa *Journal*, no lovers of the Progressives, reported that the
Canadian M.P. had been presented with a dozen roses and had
generously given a single blossom to the visitor from Britain.[18]
This was the last personal attack that greeted Macphail's initiation into Ottawa life. Thereafter, she was subjected to closer
attention than most other members, often in a critical manner,
but without the personal peevishness that had characterized
reports in her first session. While she seethed at personal slander, Macphail fully accepted disagreements on more reasonable grounds. "I desire that women have equal rights in
regard to criticism," she said, "equal rights in matters of abuse,
as well as equal rights in the bests things of life."[19]

Peace Activities

Macphail did not believe in allowing men to establish the public agenda. Women, she felt, "need to express their womanhood and not allow themselves to be restricted or diverted by the traditions of men."[20] Nowhere did this conviction express itself more fully than in relation to international affairs. Since men had waged war, newly enfranchised women would ensure peace. Macphail followed the example of the United Farm Women of Ontario who had participated in the Women's Peace Union at Niagara Falls in 1921. Organized rural women in the country sought to replace cadet training in the schools with genuine physical education. The UFWO advocated that school texts be revised to emphasize agricultural contributions rather than military exploits and opposed government subsidies to associations such as the Navy League.[21]

Of all the causes she espoused Macphail's peace activism incurred the greatest criticism from men, especially from those who thought that common sacrifice had strengthened the bonds between Canada and Britain. Macphail believed that the old imperial ties to Britain were withering as a new era of internationalism dawned, most visibly through the establishment of the League of Nations. She strove to involve women in a new citizenship based on an international consciousness. She also welcomed closer cooperation with the United States since it matched her continentalist economic ideas. "Why should we sit and accept the protection of the United States?" she queried. "Why should we not?" she replied in terms that were decades in advance of their times, "I think we should take advantage of every position that is naturally ours."[22]

The Women's International League for Peace and Freedom was Canada's major anti-war feminist organization, although it consisted of only small, struggling groups in Vancouver and Toronto. The plight of the British Columbian section was painted vividly by journalist Laura Jamieson in comparing her organizing efforts to those of a woman on the prairies. "I do not have the commercial instinct," Jamieson wrote, "nor her conservative background, which has enabled her to make her club 'the thing' in Winnipeg. The fact that I am known in

Vancouver as a Radical, and even to many as a 'dangerous woman,' mitigates against the popularity of my club."[23] The International League in Canada remained a tiny band that emphasized the economic causes of war, a position that Macphail supported.

At a "No More War" rally in Toronto in 1923, jointly sponsored by the United Farmers of Ontario, Macphail appeared with people like churchman George Pidgeon and Jimmy Simpson, Toronto labour leader and politician. To prove the farm women's contention that school texts were biased, she provided a detailed listing of references to war. Pidgeon argued that the rally was not a peace at any price campaign, but banners denouncing the Boys Scouts and Girl Guides as militaristic did not go unnoticed. It was too much for the *Telegram*. Once again the newspaper saved its special wrath for the person whom it mocked as that "noteworthy stateswoman, Miss Agnes Macphail."[24] Undeterred, Agnes returned to the city the following spring to criticize other elements of the provincial school system before the Ontario Educational Association.

In 1924 Macphail travelled to Washington with Lucy Staples Woodsworth, wife of new Labour member James Shaver Woodsworth, to attend the International League's fourth congress and the first held in North America. Given a room in which she loathed the wallpaper, she insisted on another, her pique causing her more retiring companion discomfort.[25] At Washington Macphail made her grand entrance onto the international stage. Delegates from twenty-six national sections attended along with observers from many other countries. There were sessions on eduation and calls for tariff reductions, control of raw materials to regulate armaments manufacture, and efforts to counteract destructive male tendencies by bringing the influence of men and women into a new equilibrium in the conduct of foreign affairs. American social reformer and peace activist Jane Addams addressed the congress on recent positive developments such as Gandhi's assertion of the self-determination of the Indian peoples without violence and the Geneva Protocol on arbitration, security, and disarmament that had been presented to the League of Nations.

Macphail's childhood dreams of conquering a larger world were first translated into reality at the Washington congress. The experience of meeting so many eminent women who shared her social concerns and hopes that women would attain a place in foreign affairs left a lasting impression, and an impulse to serve on a larger international stage quickened within her. She was chosen as the only Canadian delegate to the next congress in Dublin in 1926, and she invited the delegates to visit Canada when they travelled to several American cities aboard a train called the "Pax Special." The dignified reception they received in Toronto contrasted with the opposition they encountered in a few American cities, but some of the press attacked the visit, and the Board of Education denounced the event as "a sinister attempt to undermine British patriotism."[26]

In Parliament, the debate on the National Defence estimates afforded Macphail an opportunity to air her views because a subsidy was provided to provincial schools for cadet training. Although various women's groups opposed military instruction as part of the curriculum, the number of cadets had continued to expand in the postwar years, partially because military instructors were paid according to the number of boys they enrolled. Since only a few formalities had to be observed in order for them to get paid, practices varied, but boys who dissented were often subjected to ridicule and humilation.

Macphail began an annual campaign to end cadet training by reducing federal expenditure to one dollar. Military training in the schools conveyed the very opposite of what she thought education should instil in young people. To her, education was sacred and it should be child-centred. The "ten-cent tin-pan jingoism" taught to children stressed competition and the use of force rather than the mind. The system's emphasis on memorization did not teach children to think for themselves. "The schools are hollow like a cup," she concluded, "in every hole the sea comes up till it can raise no more. I am convinced that we can make no progress towards a co-operative democracy where human life, human development and human happiness are supreme until we raise the school to a higher level."[27] As a teacher, she knew how impressionable young people were. "War is not glorious. The object has been to associate in childish minds these three things — soldiering and honour and glory — but retrogression rather than progress results from wars in terms of waste of human life, lowering moral standards, increase in disease, and assertion of brutality." She offered an alternative to traditional loyalties. "If getting ready to kill somebody in some other country ... is patriotism, I want to say quite frankly that I am no patriot.... If living each day cleanly and striving to the very last ounce of our ability to help our community, our province and our Dominion, to help you see a vision of service to humanity — if that be patriotism, then I want to be a patriot."[28] Cadet training was a cowardly corruption of youth designed to teach boys to strut with guns so that they would later kill for their elders. The money would be much better spent on providing pensions for the aged. Government priorities were wrong.

The strong words reflected the intensity of Macphail's concern for education and her hopes for a better society in which "the world is one." Her stand was greeted with profound admiration and equal hostility. "I worked very hard for my vote," one woman wrote, "so you may forgive how glad I was when you were elected to Parliament, and I can't tell you what joy I feel when I read your speeches.... I have taught my own children from kindergarten to high school and *know* what you mean."[29] Some elements in the Toronto Board of Education thought differently when they debated whether a member of Parliament holding "absolutely perverted ideas on cadet training" should be allowed to speak at the Central Technical School.

Disruption in the Farm Movement

The country's fragmented farm movement was the other main object of Macphail attention. In a manner that resembled debates within Britain's Fabian Society during the 1890s, the Progressives could not decide whether they represented their constituents better by remaining apart or by influencing the Liberals. Although they assumed the trappings of a political party, they did not become one. A caucus was created, but its decisions were not binding on members in the House. Progressives were free to vote as they wished because they considered that their constituency, often broadly conceived as the class or provincial organization they represented, commanded their first loyalty. Independence was conditional, but to Macphail it reflected the hope of replacing partisanship with a new form of cooperation in the workings of Parliament. She condemned parties as "probably the greatest enemy of good citizenship. Partisanship puts your brains in cold storage and asks you to use somebody else's that are not as good as your own. Of course, some people like to treat their brains that way — they think they'll keep longer — but that is not good citizenship."[30]

Macphail fiercely opposed attempts by Progressive leaders at the national and provincial levels to turn the farmers' crusade into mechanisms for party expression either through alliance with the Liberals or through the creation of a People's Party in Ontario. During a meeting of Progressives in Winnipeg in November of 1922, she figured prominently among those who opposed changing the character of the Progressive revolt as she and the majority in the United Farmers of Ontario saw it. Thomas Crerar argued for compromise. "Political parties in Canada founded upon a class or occupational basis" he wrote, "will never achieve anything. I think it is a tribute to the good sense of the Canadian people that it is so."[31] When Crerar lost the battle at Winnipeg, he resigned, invoking business commitments, and was replaced as leader by fellow Manitoban Robert Forke.

At home Macphail stood firm with J. J. Morrison to thwart E. C. Drury's desire for a populist party in what was called the "broadening out" controversy. The showdown came late in the year at the UFO convention in Toronto where Macphail maintained that "the broader one gets the flatter one gets until finally there is nothing left but a large expanse of polished surface."[32] Before Drury spoke and while he was absent from the convention, Macphail railroaded through a motion that called for no change in the Farmers' political platform and reaffirmed constituency autonomy. When those with contrary views prolonged the discussion, Macphail secured a motion closing debate.

In Ottawa Agnes Macphail distanced herself from most of the other UFO members, who had become increasingly friendly to the Liberals because they believed an alliance constituted their only hope.[33] The die was cast and the result foreshadowed when Howard Ferguson and the Conservatives routed farm and labour in the 1923 provincial election. The United Farmers recoiled, eschewing political activity totally and declaring themselves an occupational organization dedicated to economic and social goals.[34] W. C. Good, who represented Brant for the UFO, concluded that the "'Progressive Party' was never born; or, if so, it was still born. It never had any real existence. It was a project; it was a plan; it was an appellation given to the supporters of a certain group at Ottawa by those who thought of political action only in terms of political parties."[35]

The principal political battles in the Western world during the past two centuries have not involved its major parties or the challenges to their hegemony. No matter how deadly the confrontations between liberalism, conservatism, and socialism have sometimes appeared, the fundamental political division in the West basically derives from two irreconcilable strains in its thought. One tradition advocates inalienable human rights, as outlined first in the American Declaration of Independence; the other follows ideas formulated by thinkers like Jean-Jacques Rousseau during the eighteenth-century Enlightenment and transmitted through Jacobinism to Marx, Lenin, and Mao Zedong. Asserting the primacy of the nation or one section of the nation, the latter opens the door for the state to trample individual rights. Populism overlays this unbridgeable chasm in political traditions and transcends both in multifaceted ways.[36]

Firmly planted within the rights tradition, Agnes Macphail was a staunch democrat fond of invoking Abraham Lincoln's dictum that democracy is government of, by, and for the people. Yet populism, with its sharp people/government dichotomy, was also deeply embedded in her outlook. Macphail believed that the democratic process in Canada had been subverted by political parties that had divorced people from more direct involvement in their own governance. Group government appealed to her as a reform that would address people's real concerns and economic interests more fully, but it needed to be combined with a number of other innovations as proposed by the United Farmers. When they formally withdrew from political action, Macphail reverted to being a delegate of her riding association.[37]

Macphail held on to her hopes for political reform until the electoral process, unfavourable court decisions, and World War Two finally made it clear that they were ideas whose day would never arrive. Aimed at replacing competition with cooperation in the political arena, Progressive ideals were a frontal assault on the Canadian notion of politics as a battle between the "ins" and the "outs" — with all its patronage implications. To some, including the judiciary, they smacked of unwarranted American intrusions into the country's political system where Parliament, not the people, was sovereign. While most of these ideas were too complicated or imprecise for voters to grasp, those who promoted reform failed to comprehend that tinkering with the political system was less important than governing in the short term or fundamental alterations to the party system through legislation. Macphail thought that the Progressives should not form a government at the national level since it was no more fair for the agricultural community to rule than for others to govern them. She followed William Irvine, who had established the Non-Partisan League in Alberta, in maintaining that under group government cabinet positions would be awarded proportionally, an idealistic assumption predicated on the spread of cooperation, but a clear prescription for paralysis other than in national emergencies. As these strategies failed, she retained a glimmer of another alternative to the party system that she shared with J. S. Woodsworth and W. C. Good. "I look forward to the time," she said, "when the idealism we have in the Farmer's party and the idealism you have in the Labor party are united to form a co-operative government."[38]

The Search for Coherent Beliefs

While she was disappointed with the slow pace of reform, Agnes Macphail was content to work for specific items appealing to her agricultural constituents and to Canadian women. Agriculture remained the country's most important industry and farmers constituted the "bedrock of the nation," she believed, but it had been treated "like a step child in Canada."[39] Seldom missing an opportunity to bring the concerns of rural Canada before the nation, Macphail quickly emerged as one of agriculture's most eloquent advocates. She professed her admiration for all people who worked by the efforts of their hands and sweat of their brows and chided other members for speaking only of young men when the problems of the country's farms were under debate. Girls left the farms even more readily than boys, she pointed out, and the problem of rural depopulation needed to be addressed from a feminine point of view.

After the resentments that embittered her first days in Parliament had passed, Agnes Macphail began to develop a network of friendships that allowed her personality to re-emerge. Muriel Kerr, an Ottawa schoolteacher and president of the Business and Professional Women's Club, became one of her closest associates. The two women spent many happy hours together, often in the company of Macphail's Progressive friends like W. C. Good and Albertans Ted Garland, George Coote, Robert Gardiner, and H. E. Spencer as well as Bill Irvine, the Alberta Labour M.P., and A. R. McMaster, the Liberal member from Brome who crossed the floor to join the Progessives. Relaxed social evenings with animated conversation among four or five people in Kerr's apartment or stepping out to go to a dance remained Macphail's principal forms of entertainment. In such informal settings she was herself. Her earlier mischievousness resurfaced. Spotting a hat in Kerr's apartment that the teacher had bought for a meeting at which she was to preside, Macphail donned it in her friend's absence and appeared at the function revelling in her own stylishness. Later, Macphail sought the company of other professional women by joining the Ottawa Zonta Club.

In Preston Elliot, a fellow Progressive and M.P. for Dundas, Macphail found a person with whom to renew her love life. The affair could not be kept a secret after the couple appeared together on a shopping expedition in Owen Sound, and the local press delighted in pondering Macphail's matrimonial prospects. One newspaper took exception to this undue attention to personal matters and affirmed that Macphail should suit herself in her choice of companions.[40] She did just that, ending her involvement with Elliot when she decided that she did not love him. Gossip flourished about other romantic entanglements, involving such men as Howard Graham, a farmer her own age from Vandeleur, and a French-Canadian M.P. Agnes swore that she would learn French, but she never mastered the language.

She also soon found friends among members of the opposition parties. Witty, intelligent people without airs were those she associated with, individuals like Jean-François Pouliot, who represented Témiscouata, and Sam Jacobs, the brilliant constitutional lawyer from Montreal whom she often met in the afternoons for tea. C. G. Power, the gregarious ward politician from Quebec City who later became minister for air during World War Two, was another, except when he was drinking. The debate on the formation of the United Church of Canada in 1924 provided one opportunity for Chubby Power to hit the bottle. Since he was clearly drunk, Macphail attempted to avoid him in the corridors, but when they met unexpectedly, she had to face him, though she was afraid to take him to her office. As they walked the halls together, Power asked if Macphail were interested in church union. "No, not very," she replied. "Neither am I," he continued, "they're going to hell anyway and if they want to go together, why should you and I stop them?"[41]

Macphail's political education was fostered most genuinely through her associations with the Alberta Progressives and the two members of the Independent Labour party. Her flights of rhetoric declined as her thought extended in new directions. J. S. Woodsworth, the former Methodist minister and Labour M.P. from Winnipeg, elicited her greatest admiration and constituted the most formative influence on her development. Macphail acclaimed Woodsworth as a man of the deepest integrity, the greatest vision, and most formidible industry despite the frailness of his body. He reciprocated by displaying her portrait along with photographs of four British and American socialists that adorned his office. Their working association blossomed into a friendship that extended to other members of the Woodsworth family.

Macphail and Woodsworth had their disagreements, especially as Macphail attempted to reconcile old viewpoints with new ideas in her decade-long transition from radical to social democract. While she agreed with many of Woodsworth's innovative ideas, Macphail initially refused to adopt his socialism. Farmers were not interested in any ideologies, she asserted, with a traditional agrarian aversion to big government. Social programs were needed, she believed, but aggregates such as government and industry could best be balanced by people voluntarily forming cooperatives to further their own economic self-interest. "The very last thing the farmer should ask for in politics is government paternalism," Macphail maintained. "The greatest gift that life holds out for us is our freedom. To lose that is to lose all. The way to freedom is not slavery to the State. The way to freedom is the straight highway of voluntary cooperation. We grow strong by doing for ourselves, not by leaning on the Government."[42] Agrarian radicalism expressed itself as the ideology of the small producer, but such views so clashed with Woodsworth's socialism that the Labour M.P. threatened to remove her picture from his office.

Macphail did not step far beyond the policies of the United Farmers of Ontario, although they proved an inadequate guide to the complex issues she faced. When Woodsworth and Irvine advocated the eight-hour day for labour, Macphail had no trouble dissenting because farmers worked much longer hours with equally meagre financial rewards. Their advocacy of old age pensions and the abolition of capital punishment, on the other hand, met with her complete accord. "It is true that the taking of life is wrong," Macphail said in Parliament, "but two wrongs do not make a right. To me life is sacred, and because it is such a sacred thing that I could not take the life of anyone, even though that one had taken the life of another."[43] She also supported William Irvine in his unsuccessful attempt to have the Bank Act examined more frequently than every ten years even though a majority of the Progressives were backing the King government. Rising from her seat in the House of Commons, she spoke without a prepared speech about the need for a central bank and a national currency to replace that issued by private institutions. "Of course," she maintained, "bankers ever have been moral cowards, they have always been afraid."[44]

The attempt to sort out her contradictory ideas was dizzying. Enamoured of one viewpoint, she would argue for it vociferously until the weight of the counterposition forced her to concede. She wished that she had gone to university but worried that what was then a bastion of middle-class privilege might have lessened her populist impulse.[45] The flux in her thoughts during these years reflected her search for an integrated set of beliefs. Her experience in helping former soldiers secure veterans' benefits helped her to move beyond the agrarian call for minimal government. Slowly she began to believe that the role of the state could be expanded without loss of individual freedom, that labour's views deserved greater respect, that protection of civil liberties was an essential safeguard of democracy, and that new social programs were needed to provide a buffer for the hard edges of the capitalist economy for all Canadians, not just the class she represented.

A few other UFO members in the House shared these concerns along with a smattering of Western Progressives, especially those from Alberta. The position they assumed fomented dissension within the Progressive ranks that appeared most forcefully during the budget debate in 1924.[46] In providing tax and tariff reductions, Mackenzie King had courted Robert Forke to secure Progressive support even though the changes in customs duties were minimal. Woodsworth manoeuvred adroitly by proposing an amendment to the budget that was essentially the same as the Progressives had proposed the previous year. His motion called for a substantial reduction of the tariff on the necessities of life, a graded income tax that would bear more heavily on upper incomes, taxation on unimproved lands and natural resources, and a graduated inheritance tax on large estates.[47]

The Advent of the Ginger Group

Macphail and her associates were caught between the principles they professed and the desire of the majority of Progressives not to defeat the government on an issue they would have difficulty explaining to the electorate. Fourteen voted for the Woodsworth amendment, which failed, but the negotiations over the issue served to complete an irreparable breach within the Progressive ranks. Shortly afterwards Macphail, four Albertans, and one member from Saskatchewan seceded from the Progressive caucus.[48] Later they were joined by four others, including Elliot and Good from Ontario. The strains created by those stressful days had combined with more fundamental disagreements about the party system to create a new bloc in the House. The ten secessionist Progressives began to meet together in an informal caucus with the Labour members and an Independent. Someone knowing that the application of ginger or other peppery substance to a horse's ass brought new life to old nags, and recalling the name given to the Tory M.P.'s who opposed the Military Service Act of 1917, dubbed them the Ginger Group. The provincial associations of

United Farmers in Ontario and Alberta concurred with their conduct. J. J. Morrison went so far as to say that "the establishment of a body of independent electors desiring to overcome, if possible, the domination of our government by partisanship" had been the principal reason for the UFO entering politics.[49]

Woodsworth preferred the term "co-operating independents" to describe the Ginger Group. Sharing common viewpoints on many issues while retaining their right to disagree, these members aspired to transform the political system in order to expand the people served by government. They tended to vote together to further forward-looking measures such as Macphail's motion for prison reform, J. T. Shaw's bill to establish equality between the sexes with respect to the grounds for divorce, Good's attempt to secure the transferable vote as a prelude to proportional representation, and Irvine's amendment to the Elections Act that would have allowed labour unions to contribute political funds. Although the Ginger Group was merely transitional, it provided Macphail with an essential support at a crucial time in her political development.

The postwar years marked a significant change in Canadian politics and society. World War One had confirmed traditional beliefs in some quarters but stimulated new values in others. The old shibboleths that conveyed the mental constructs governing the collective psyche were assaulted from all sides. The Ginger Group was but the political expression of more potent forces working internationally. Increasingly, social science and the example of other countries would relegate to the graveyard outmoded thinking that divided all life simplisticly into private and public spheres.[50] The growing complexity of Canadian society required new responses outside the parameters of the limited areas that had been allotted to governments. Macphail's pragmatic response to these issues and her more rigid adherence to UFO policies contributed to that development.

Agnes Macphail had arrived in Ottawa when national political affairs were more confused than ever before. Jumping headlong into the hurly-burly world of federal politics, she championed reform with tenacity as she grew in the job and proved quickly that she was no ordinary member of Parliament. Accepted distinctions in public life were beginning to crumble, a development that she did her utmost to promote. Her first term had been trying emotionally and politically, but she had gained confidence in herself and her role. The lessons she had learned prepared her for a larger role along the more arduous road ahead.

5

Equality Rights: The Campaign for Women's Rights, 1926–1930

But the commander replied, "Was it only to your master and you that my master sent me to say these things, and not to the men sitting on the wall — who, like you, will have to eat their own filth and drink their own urine?"

Isaiah 36:12

The family home in Grey County, which provided Agnes Macphail with respite between sessions of Parliament, became her refuge during the latter half of the 1920s as she turbocharged her campaign on behalf of women's rights and entered the world's arena in Europe. Relaxed among familiar surroundings with the people she loved, Macphail was able to engage in the political bridge-building that came naturally to her. The public attention she attracted never influenced her character or conduct. While her time became more regimented, she always found occasion to socialize with friends and constituents. Her days tended to divide into reading and speech-writing in the morning, a walk or chat with friends in the afternoon, and political meetings in the evening. During her first term in Parliament she had given eighty-three addresses in her constituency, but as time went on and the security of her political position increased, she reduced her local speaking schedule.

Relations with the UFO

Macphail was especially interested in fostering the farm movement in her riding through the extension of its clubs for women and young people. The United Farmers of Ontario aimed at self-improvement and enhanced self-esteem among its supporters. To further these objectives it blossomed into an integrated organization with several branches. Its excursion into politics beginning in 1918 had represented only a momentary reaction to specific conditions following the war. Membership swollen during the political advance shrank with its retreat back to its original social and economic goals. Reaching a high of forty-six thousand members in 1921, ranks declined to eighteen thousand members in 1925.[1] Leaders like Agnes Macphail rationalized that those who had fallen by the wayside had only been fellow travellers without commitment to the movement's basic ideals. Renewed emphasis on educating the farm community was undertaken as part of the return to its original purpose.

Macphail viewed the United Farm Women of Ontario as a more valuable vehicle for educating women than its rival, the popular Women's Institutes. Once the federal government had revealed the shocking extent to which women died during childbirth in Canada, she appeared with Toronto public health nurse Eunice Dyke to urge the United Farm Women to undertake a campaign to bring the country in line with others in the Western world.[2] In Ceylon the local UFWO group called itself the Holdfast Club, a name that stuck long after Macphail had died. Here the M.P. also introduced the first iodized pills to counter goitre. While she was adverse to involvement in her daughter's political life, Etta MacPhail doggedly participated in the Holdfast Club. Sometimes the materials studied proved so difficult that she had to seek assistance from neighbours, but Etta MacPhail was only one of many rural women who made the effort to expand their horizons. For her part, Agnes Macphail was too wise to let her involvement with the United Farm Women of Ontario prevent her from attending meetings of the Women's Institutes when she was invited.

The United Farm Young People of Ontario served as the other branch in the network filtering through the countryside. Macphail had never lost her love for youth, and she took a special interest in promoting their activities to help them compete with the Junior Farmers promoted by government-appointed county agricultural representatives. The UFYPO sought not only to foster education but also to improve the ability of farm young people to speak publicly and debate intelligently in the manner of their urban counterparts. Each year Macphail brought the winner of the local public-speaking contest to Ottawa, and she later donated a trophy. A young woman won the first year, but a youth named Farquhar Oliver quickly became known as the star debater among the members of the UFYPO club.

So successful was Macphail in the eyes of her supporters in Southeast Grey that she was asked to find a running mate to carry the UFO banner provincially. Macphail chose Oliver despite his age and limited education. Barely twenty years old, he had been born in the riding at Priceville. He had passed the high school entrance examination but chose to leave school to work the family farm, which was located near the MacPhails'. Agnes admired his empathy for people, dedication to the farmers' cause, prowess on the platform, and desire to improve himself. "F. R. Oliver will go far," she predicted. "He has native ability. He seeks knowledge. He is modest and loves work."[3] A nephew of "Honest John" Oliver, who served as British Columbia's premier for nearly three decades, the fresh-faced young farmer with the cleft chin seemed a younger male mirror image. Macphail assumed direction of Oliver's informal education by supervising his reading in history, economics, and politics.

Cape Breton

While she thus looked after the interests of her constituency, Macphail was also broadening her knowledge of other Canadian problems. A trip to Cape Breton early in 1925 convinced her of the validity of the views she was in the process of forming. Strikes had continued, with the violence between strikers and police sometimes involving women and children. Union leader J. B. McLachlan, a communist, had been imprisoned but released by the Privy Council in Ottawa.[4] Following Woodsworth, Macphail travelled to Glace Bay and surrounding towns to see for herself the conditions of the miners and their families. She was shocked and indignant at what she discovered. A place so devoid of beauty in spring she had never seen, although it recalled the description of Scottish mining towns that her grandmother had related. There were no trees or other vegetation; roads were simply immense mud-holes, paralleled by open sewers, and black as pitch at night. She visited schools and hospitals and met some thousand miners at a meeting in the town.

Carefully avoiding a conducted tour, Macphail went to see people in their homes. Few company houses enjoyed running water, and most lacked sanitary conveniences. Normally so impatient that she refused to knock at a door more than once, Macphail was forced to allow time for people to cover their bodies with ragged clothing. Often the the door jambs sagged so badly that that it was difficult for her to gain entrance. In many of the houses she found people of Scots ancestry like herself living in conditions worse than those in her grand-parent's generation. Children without shoes or adequate clothes were forced to stay away from school. Macphail knew of deprivations experienced by her own family, but confronting the human face of appalling poverty jolted her. Such conditions, she told her sisters, were "something we should all be ashamed of."[5]

In one of her most moving speeches in Parliament, Agnes Macphail related the utter destitution she had observed. Workers and their dependents were so chained by an insidious wage slavery to the company that after several weeks of unemployment families were forced into hunger lines to survive. Above all, Macphail's heart was smitten by the plight of young children suffering from malnutrition and its attendant diseases such as rickets. The bodies and faces of toddlers appeared aged beyond their years, like famine victims in developing countries. Macphail expressed admiration for the pride displayed by Cape Bretoners faced with such adversity, but she questioned the wisdom of their refusal to accept five thousand dollars in relief from the Soviet Union in order to remain respectable in the eyes of other Canadians. After two days in Glace Bay, she said, "nobody looked red to me. I think if I lived there long I would be a lot redder than anything I saw." She lamented that the country put "the commercial value of making dollars above the value of making human life and creating comfortable conditions of living." "We are indeed a smug, self-righteous people," she concluded.[6]

Macphail, Woodsworth, and other members of the Ginger Group pressed for action to help gainfully employed people living below the poverty line, but the King government hid behind the constitutional convention requiring a request from the province of Nova Scotia first. Although restrained in her report, Macphail was criticized by opponents in Parliament for being ill-informed and for having failed to consult the right people on her visit. Others found her courage inspiring in the way recorded by one aspiring poet:

> One lone woman in Parliament
> 'Twas Agnes Macphail
> When the miners were hungry
> She never did fail
> To fight for the starving
> With their empty dinner pail,
> God give us more women
> Like Agnes Macphail.

Chorus

> God give more women
> Like Agnes Macphail (repeat)
> When the miners were hungry
> She never did fail.
> God give us more women
> Like Agnes Macphail.[7]

The Politics of Confusion

Cape Breton served to extend Macphail's education and prepared her for the battle that ensued in the 1925 general election. Progressive politics had continued to be characterized by dissension, and there were so many defections back into the Liberal fold that the fractured movement was clearly in serious difficulty well before Progressive leader Robert Forke decided not to conduct a national campaign. With no challenge from the Liberals locally this time, Macphail's Conservative opponent, L. G. Campbell, took to the podium in Southeast Grey to attack the record of the United Farmers in the federal House. Macphail leapt to their defence, reciting positive legislative accomplishments and blaming the old parties for their failure to support other measures on behalf of the farm community. She frankly admitted her error in returning a portion of her indemnity during her first term because she had learned that the expenses of an M.P. were far greater than those in private life. Declaring herself free of any party, she said she was accountable solely to the United Farmers and her constituents.[8] Her constitutency machine again rolled into high gear, and she gave forty-one speeches during the campaign. She sported a new Starr automobile that she drove along with her new lieutenant as he cut his political teeth with brief speeches opening her meetings.

Agnes Macphail's campaign style remained unaltered, although at the outset she officially changed the spelling of family name to make it easier to write. She continued to refuse to ask people for their vote but ended her addresses by saying that "I have tried to be true to a noble ideal and have valued and trusted the goodwill and trust of the people above all things. I have been happy in serving you and I leave you to judge whether or not I have been a worthy servant of the people."[9] While she professed her love for the community, a small turnout at a political event suggested a lack of interest in public affairs that would lead her to castigate those present for the sins of those who were not. Bad weather on 29 October when the polls opened prevented some of her supporters from navigating the roads on the back concessions, but her personal popularity carried her through, though her majority was sliced in half to 1,407 votes. The absence of a Liberal contender had saved her by increasing her vote in the towns and villages.

Nationally, the Progressive ranks were decimated, especially in Ontario where only Macphail and J. H. King succeeded under the UFO banner. Despite receiving only 9 per cent of the popular vote and electing only 24 members, Progressive leverage was actually increased since neither Liberals nor Conservatives could command a majority in the House without their support. The Conservatives returned 116 members and the Liberals 99, but King determined to carry on with Progressive backing. Macphail had no more confidence in the Liberals than many of her colleagues, seeing them as hypocrites who had adopted a forward-looking platform in 1919 which they refused to implement, but Mackenzie King danced nimbly to lure the dissidents. Arthur Meighen, temperamentily unsuited to pandering, stuck with the protectionist platform that had brought the Conservatives 46 per cent of the popular vote. As ever, the Progressives were sorrily divided, with a majority eventually seduced by the promise of lower taxes, reduced tariffs, and rural credits. In order to secure the support of A. A. Heaps and J. S. Woodsworth, the two Labour members, King also agreed to introduce noncontributory old age pensions and to amend the Criminal Code, changed in the aftermath of the Winnipeg General Strike, so that British subjects might no longer be deported without trial. Another olive branch invited the Progressives to help formulate the legislation for this program. As a member of their executive, Macphail met regularly with a committee of the government to work out the details of the legislative program and helped to devise the Old Age Pensions Bill, the country's first significant federal social assistance law.

In the uncertain aftermath of the 1925 election, King dangled the prospect of a cabinet post before Macphail as part of his continuing efforts to secure Progressive participation in his government. Macphail was eager to pursue new ideas but smart enough to know when to back down, the prime minister was informed. Beaten in an argument, "she merely stopped, and seemed to reflect: well, I'm up against it."[10] King was advised to follow Arthur Meighen's conduct by securing her favour, which he did by having an intermediary suggest that she might expect a cabinet position if the Progressive group changed its mind about entering the government. Macphail blushed and did not respond directly, but she did comment that all her correspondents warned her against defeating the government and precipitating another election. While Macphail refused to be courted by the Liberal party, her most formidable journalistic adversary also swung around in her favour. The women's editor of the Toronto *Telegram* lamented the sad decline in the standards of evening dress at the opening of Parliament in 1926 — as Canada finally moved away from aping British practice — but she waxed eloquent about Agnes Macphail's stylish attire.

Political realities instilled in Agnes Macphail the fine line between diplomacy and compromise in principles. When the government moved early in 1926 to lower duties from 35 to 20 per cent on imported cars in an effort to reduce domestic prices and increase Canadian content through a series of tariff adjustments, General Motors closed its Oshawa plant for a day, and three thousand workers descended on Ottawa the next week to protest. Women formed part of the delegation — perhaps the first working women to demonstrate before Parliament. Some one hundred met with Agnes Macphail while their male colleagues spoke with the Mackenzie King and the minister of finance. Because she agreed with the reductions, Macphail exercised great tact, sympathizing with the workers' concerns while explaining why they had nothing to fear from the measure. She assured them that she would would work to have the tariff on imported parts reduced so that more cars would be assembled in Canada and condemned the manufacturers' practice of laying off workers and closing plants without seeking alternatives. The women emerged from the hour-long meeting in better humour. "I think she's just lovely," one commented. Another said that "she made it so clear."[11] Later, when the Liberals gave into pressure from manufacturers by repealing excise taxes on cars that met Candian content standards and thereby increased the industry's protective margin, Macphail approached Mackenzie King with "a very friendly and reasonable attitude" that convinced him that the move had been a mistake.[12] Increased experience had imparted a greater measure of tact — but always within limits!

After corruption in the Customs department was exposed, the session degenerated into a welter of motions and amendments, rulings and challenges, where the fate of the King government hung in the balance of a single vote. In the tricky parliamentary manoeuvring, Macphail found it difficult to adhere to principles that seemed easier to expound than to demonstrate through consistent practice. Lobbies and parliamentary corridors were abuzz with discussions. At one critical juncture during the four days and nights of debate, her office became the centre where King vied for Progressive support. While she normally sided with her colleagues from the Ginger Group, the complexity of the agenda found her praying for guidance about how to vote. The day that Mackenzie King informed the cabinet that he intended to ask the governor general to dissolve the House and call an election, Macphail had left Ottawa to catch a ship in Montreal for the Women's International Congress in Dublin. When she heard the news, she rushed back to the capital.

Twice Governor General Byng, a career soldier in the British army who had commanded Canadian troops in Europe during

World War One, denied King's request for a dissolution. A motion in the Commons threatened to censure the Liberals as well as the prime minister for their handling of the Customs fraud, and the Conservatives commanded the largest number of seats in the House. The royal prerogative exercised by the governor general allowed him to determine which among the parties was best able to govern based on their representation in the House. Believing that King's actions were not in the best interests of the nation and that another election was unnecessary, Byng rejected King's advice for a third time. Convinced that this response was unconstitutional, Mackenzie King took the unprecedented step of resigning and refusing to remain in office during the transitional period. When Byng called Arthur Meighen to form a new administration, an infuritated Mackenzie King determined to defeat the Conservatives and force the election that had been denied by the royal representative.[13]

The House continued its extended sessions early in the mornings before rising with raucous singing to relieve the tensions. A motion challenging the Conservatives' right to govern came on 1 July, although the proceedings of the previous day had not ended until 1.30 A.M. Mackenzie King knew that a cliffhanger stood in the offing where every vote would count. At 3.00 A.M. he sought out Macphail at the Chelsea Club where he found her in the company of Dr. Alexander Young, a new M.P. who had been mayor of Saskatoon. Macphail desperately wanted to leave the capital, but the prospect of an election determined her priorities. She told King that she might remain.[14] The following day she assumed her seat in the House and voted with the Liberals; the Conservative government was defeated by one vote. Europe had to wait.

The 1926 Election

The Progressives had defeated two governments in one year, but they had furthered their own fragmentation and compounded their failure to realize their program. The session had clearly shown the futility of such ideas as group government and cooperative cabinets, but its lessons were slow to sink in. J. J. Morrison and W. C. Good contined to denounce the evils of partyism during the election when they spoke on behalf of Macphail in Grey County. As a provincial election was also about to be called, Farquhar Oliver was nominated at the same time, and both candidates fulfilled UFO policies by signing recall notices where they agreed to resign if requested by a majority in a riding convention.[15]

Macphail again ran unopposed by the Liberals, but she knew she had a fight on her hands in defending what most people could not understand. Aware that UFO popularity had slumped badly and now more familiar with constituency politics, she resorted to pork barrel claims, stressing that she had got the riding money for a post office, an extension of rural mail delivery, improved railway crossings, electric lights in a railway station, and pensions for veterans, as well as providing services for innumerable individuals. Thinking her vulnerable in this and the next election, the Conservatives dispatched their top performers. Arthur Meighen and Hugh Guthrie both spoke in Grey. Guthrie was clearly befuddled by the unorthodox farm representative who was totally unlike any other women he had met during the twenty-six years the good burghers of Guelph had re-elected him. He branded Macphail a Bolshevik of the same stripe as J. S. Woodsworth — which she might have interpreted as a compliment had it not been for the bad press.[16] Vicious electoral attacks would continue for the next two decades until they reached their crescendo during the 1940s.

In this election Macphail was able to call on the resources of the women's and young people's organizations she had assisted. Women were seen at political events in numbers equal to men, and young people participated in what were essentially social occasions with music and singing. Macphail and her team spent voting day surmounting partisan challenges to their supporters at the polls, and she emerged from her third victory with a larger majority. She then moved into the Oliver house for the provincial election where she engineered the triumph of her protégé. In 1926 F. R. Oliver became the youngest person elected to the Ontario legislature.

The King government returned to power with the support of Liberal Progressives and Progressive Liberals. Macphail displayed no sympathy with either political hybrid sprouted during the election.[17] After Parliament convened, she sat with the United Farmers of Alberta to the left of the Speaker. In 1927 Macphail was appointed as the sole M.P. to the national committee to organize celebrations for the sixtieth anniversary of Confederation. Initially she declined because no representative of organized labour had been selected, but she relented when the oversight was rectified by the appointment of Tom Moore from the Trades and Labour Congress. Her riding association marked the occasion by initiating annual UFO picnics on 1 July. They attracted thousands with sports events, big bands, games, and dancing, but Macphail and Oliver were always the featured speakers. Macphail rivalled John A. Macdonald in her ability to work the grassroots, but even so the UFO picnics did not match the extent of the annual Orange parades that drew up to seven thousand people to Hanover each year.

Women's Equality

This attention to local affairs showed that Agnes Macphail was an astute politician, but they had not been her only concern. Initially she had assumed that other women would follow her into Parliament; she could even see them coming in her mind's eye, she later said. The elections of 1925 and 1926 ended that delusion. Seven women were nominated, but only one each for the Conservatives and Liberals, and Macphail concluded that she was the only woman who had stood any chance of election. Macphail urged women to become more active in political life, but it was her friend Nellie McClung who exposed some fundamental barriers to their full participation. The contrast between the prevailing images governing the conduct of women and politics, McClung wrote, stood at the root of the problem. Women were "supposed to find the highest delights of the soul in mixed pickles, eyelet embroidery, charity balls or teas for for these are considered eminently respectable and safe; while politics is disturbing and disquieting." Common sayings reinforced this impression by maintaining "that women and children should be seen and not heard ... that men must work and women must weep; quietly too, and with becoming aloofness, for loud weeping is hysteria, and much to be deplored."[18] From her experience as a Liberal M.L.A. in Alberta, McClung had learned that most men deeply resented working with women as equal partners or allowing them public service employment, which they guarded as a lion his preserve.

Enfranchisement had created interest in politics among women, but generally they were only active in small socialist parties or in subordinate roles in separate party organizations at the local or provincial level. Macphail's success in Ottawa had spurred a shrewd politician like Howard Ferguson in Ontario to find at least one token female candidate for the provincial Conservatives before the election of 1923, but generally men reacted against nominating women, let alone electing them. Mackenzie King exemplified the negative attitude that McClung had pinpointed when Ottawa Liberal women met with him to discuss the national organization. "I dislike too," he concluded with distaste, "having women talk of party funds etc."[19] Despite the leader's comments a National Federation of Liberal Women of Canada, led by heiress Cairine Wilson, was created in 1928, but the Conservatives had no equivalent position until after World War Two.

Agnes Macphail continued to encounter the fears of misogynists. When J. S. Woodworth tried to woo French-Canadian nationalist Henri Bourassa following his return to Ottawa in 1925, he invited Macphail to join them for lunch. Bourassa then declined the invitation. Undeterred, Macphail travelled to Montreal to assist Thérèse Casgrain and others in the long battle for suffrage in Quebec. Premier Louis-Alexandre Taschereau dismissed her speech as the foolish utterance of a young girl. Maintaining that she was spreading herself too thinly among 244 men, the premier offered to act as her matrimonial agent.[20] Such comments Macphail took in her stride, particularly since they emanated from a culture unlike her own, but her temper was dynamite set to explode in the face of men like the pugnacious Mitchell Hepburn. Following his election to Parliament in 1926, the future Ontario premier remarked that men would never have any trouble with women doing work for them as long as there were wedding rings. Macphail blasted him, but she derived greater satisfaction when she learned later in life that she had been a plague on Bourassa's house. "I still don't think that a woman has any place in politics," the anti-feminist confessed, "but I must admit that you have done all the right things. Now my daughters are always throwing you at me."[21]

The right things entailed speaking out for women's equality wherever and whenever she could be heard. During her first term in Ottawa, Macphail had largely restricted herself to involvement with farm women's groups. Even there she assumed a broad view that integrated her feminism with her other beliefs. She upheld the dignity of all beneficial labour and advocated that rural women be more aggressive in satisfying their needs. Following her statements about women's rights, reporters often emphasized her feminism to the exclusion of all her other concerns. In still fashionable purple prose, one eminent journalist pictured her as an native warrior queen. When he asked if politics did not tarnish feminine character, Macphail replied unequivocally that "public life broadens, not blunts, a woman's makeup." Probing further by inquiring if she thought women's influence might temper the asperities of public life, she responded: "I'm not much for tempering. I'm no gulf stream in the cold ocean of poltical life."[22] Macphail promptly disabused the press of the erroneous notion that she represented only women, but since they were the majority of the population they became a primary concern.

With three electoral victories, Macphail had greater self-confidence, and she came to believe that few would promote interest in public life among women if she did not. As a result, during the late 1920s Agnes Macphail emerged as the country's foremost advocate of women's equality based on fundamental human rights. From the great classics — Mary Wollstonecraft's *Vindication of the Rights of Woman* and John Stuart Mill's *On the Subjection of Women* — she developed an argument for women's equality that assailed the dominant assumption of her age that women were destined only to be wives and mothers. In adopting this course Macphail followed in the tradition of earlier radical feminists like Flora MacDonald Denison of Toronto, but she expounded her views more fully, frequently, and forcefully than any other Canadian during the first half of the twentieth century.[23]

The assertion of women's right to full equality was no more popular in the decade of jazz and flappers than before. Postwar normalcy implied a reassertion of prewar values. Women returned home from the positions in the workforce they had occupied temporarily, a movement abetted by government policies.[24] Rising standards of living also afforded more women the middle-class luxury of not having to seek paid work. In 1928 the average male manufacturing wage finally reached the point where a Canadian working man might, for the first time, support a family of four without other members holding jobs. Figures produced the next year showed that 82 per cent of working women and 60 per cent of labouring men earned less than $1,000, while $1,200 to $1,500 were needed to keep such a family in relative comfort.[25]

In coming to grips with her role as women's only direct conduit to Parliament, Agnes Macphail did not hide her single status or her feminism. "I am a feminist," she told a rally in Toronto in 1927, "and I want for women the thing men are not willing to give them — absolute equality. We will not get it this year, but will get it next."[26] She never abstracted feminist commitment from her other beliefs; the advance of women was intimately connected with the struggle of all disadvantaged people for human dignity and social justice. To Macphail, feminism implied a willingness to place human rights first, to tackle women's special concerns as well as the questions that men confronted, and to challenge stereotypes with humour. She never believed that women embodied any superior morality or that they were any more united than men. The differences between men and women developed out of differing life experiences rather than inherent biological factors. Ultimately, when men and women shared equal partnership in all areas of life, each gender would acquire some characteristics from the other with humanity the chief beneficiary.

Macphail thought that "whereas men naturally place business values, economic values, first, we women naturally place the emphasis on human values. So I wish to push human values to the forefront of politics. I believe this to be the fundamental effect of the political enfranchisement of women. But eventually this will not be limited to women. Has not women's most difficult task been, since the race began, to humanize men in order to make civilized life with them possible?"[27] Although pooh-poohed as naive by a later generation of feminists, Macphail's faith in the power of women stemmed from her assessment of legislative accomplishments since female suffrage. The social program of the United Farmers of Ontario, although implemented without a single woman legislator, reflected the concerns of the rural women who formed part of the larger social movement. Macphail's contemporary, Helen Gregory McGill, also concluded that as "naturally as day follows darkness, with the recognition of the rights of women as citizens came justice to the married mother in regard to her children."[28]

Agnes Macphail acknowledged that women faced special problems resulting from centuries of enslavement that too often produced female submission in the face of male aggression. Marriage compounded the problem by denying women economic freedom; too many women retired into homes devoid of dynamic female companionship and lost their ambition. "Women give over too much time to pleasing men," she thought, "but they please them most when they try not to. I found that out.... Women should be like themselves and avoid artificialities of speech and manner. Now, men don't usually assume to be something they aren't. They don't have to; you can't add to perfection."[29]

Macphail advocated that women abandon some of their past and criticized marriage ceremonies for their lingusitic anachronisms. As the first woman admitted to debate at the University of Toronto's Hart House, she rebutted the prevailing view that women belonged in the home by contending that "woman's place is wherever she wants to be — as is man's," but she added that women's emancipation would remain incomplete as long as society was based on property rather than human rights.[30] The prejudice against women in business and public life survived only from the rule of force, which civilized society would end, she believed. Women required equal pay, equal opportunities, and equal honours.

In the long process of adjustment needed for women to reach social equality, Macphail did not envision that females would become male clones. She herself was far too vibrant and appealing as a woman to believe that. She liked the sexual attention that men lavished on her, including R. B. Bennett, the wealthy bachelor with an eye for women who was the new leader of the Conservative party. He and Macphail were very fond of each other in a personal rather than an intimate way, although some believed otherwise. Approaching her desk one day, Bennett commented to Macphail in a tone of discovery, "You have very nice ankles, Agnes" — the only part of the female anatomy that males could see or were allowed to compliment when dresses were long and bust lines high. One of her male Alberta friends wondered along with his fellows, "Who does he think he's kidding?"[31]

Agnes Macphail never had any difficulty attracting men sexually. Her attractiveness was conveyed in political gossip circulated in Liberal circles following the incident in 1926 when she returned to Ottawa as the fate of the Meighen government had hung in the balance. That particular version of the story had a timorous and indecisive Mackenzie King climbing the dark stairs to Macphail's apartment very late one night only to find her alone with one of his own M.P.'s whom she was supposedly dating. The account was wrong in detail, but it testified to the perception of Macphail as a desirable woman with an active sexual life.[32]

In public Agnes Macphail drew a strict line between her political and personal lives. Like most politicians, she believed that her intimate life was not for publication, a pact respected at the time by the Ottawa Press Gallery. But she never minded commenting on her single status. Introducing herself at Queen's University as "thirty-seven years old, unmarried, with no apologies," she counselled female students simply to be themselves.[33] Mutual support and networking also figured among her prescriptions for a fuller life. So strongly did she emerge as a role model that the University of Toronto's Women's Union declared during a debate in 1926 that it would rather be Agnes Macphail than film star Mary Pickford.

In Parliament Macphail fought for equality to end legal discrimination against women. With other members of the Ginger Group, she succeeded in 1925 in modifying grounds for divorce in the four western provinces to establish gender equity. Making a ringing speech, she declared:

> I believe it would be a good thing to make marriage harder instead of easier, for there is too great a tendency on the part of people to rush into marriage without realizing either its hardships or its binding nature. It is a fact that all women contribute more to marriage than do men; for the most part they have to change their place of living, their method of work, a great many women today changing their occupation entirely on marriage; and they must even change their name. They then work continuously for years until death happily releases them and that without wages at all. No one can claim that a married woman

is economically independent, for she is not; apart from some very rare exceptions, married women are dependent economically, and that is the last remaining bond on women.... When I hear men talk about women being the angel of the home I always, mentally at least, shrug my shoulders in doubt. I do not want to be the angel of any home; I want for myself what I want for other women, absolute equality. After that is secured then men and women can take turns at being angels."[34]

She then drew laughs by recalling how one member, who had called women angels in one breath and claimed men superior in the next, led her to conclude that men "must therefore be gods."

On another occasion Macphail assailed the double standard that governed familial roles: "I believe that the preservation of the home as an institution in the future lies almost entirely in the hands of men," she said. "If they are willing to give women economic freedom within the home; if they are willing to live by the standard that they wish the women to live by, the home will be preserved. If the preservation of the home means the enslavement of women, economically or morally, then we had better break it ... when we have a single standard for men and women, both morally and economically, then we shall have a home that is well worth preserving, and I think we can be quite sure that it will be preserved."[35] In 1929 and 1930 Macphail supported William Irvine and J. S. Woodsworth in their successful campaign to obtain a divorce court for Ontario. The system of petitions for divorce to Parliament had proven inadequate as well as costly, effectively restricting access to the wealthy. On this issue, Macphail found herself opposing Ernest Lapointe, the great bear of man who served as Mackenzie King's minister of justice. She often found herself in accord with the lovable French Canadian but not on this issue; she accused him of having been born five hundred years too late.[36] Men were always fair game as butts of Macphail's sarcasm, but in public she never speared other women.

International Affairs and Civil Rights

Macphail's feminist views were applauded in some quarters but denounced in most. In Calgary the opposition press dismissed her when she spoke to the United Farmers of Alberta in 1927. "Her addresses," one newspaper declared, "composed largely of a mixture of socialistic dogma, feminism, peace-at-any-price theories, and the Bolshevik brand of world brotherhood, no longer attract much attention."[37] Macphail accepted such criticism as the price she paid for speaking out against what she saw as antiquated traditions, and it did not deter her from challenging the blatant British chauvinism that remained strong among Canadians. She proposed an alternative vision of Canada based on multiculturalism and racial tolerance that the majority was equally unprepared to accept.

In one of her regular newletters to school children in 1927 Macphail attempted to clarify the unrest in China that followed the death of Sun Yat-sen. During strikes and protests against foreign intervention that were abetted by Soviets present, British and French troops stationed in Shanghai and Guangzhou had killed and wounded hundreds of Chinese, many of them students.[38] Macphail's letter tried to reveal the negative effects of British foreign policy. Warning her young readers about the disastrous effects of narcotics, she dug into history to show how Britain had forced the opium trade on China through wars in the nineteenth century. While acknowledging Soviet complicity, she sympathized with the desire of the Chinese to run their country free of foreign involvement and thought Canadians should not condone murder. Drawing an analogy to the 1926 Balfour Declaration that had announced an end to colonial status for Canada and other self-governing British colonies, Macphail asked why Canadians could not accept the same for the Chinese people. The glaring contradiction between the presence of Canadian missionaries in China and Canada's failure to treat Asians with respect did not escape her attention.

Macphail's letter was a model of informed analysis that challenged prevailing assumptions and stood in advance of contemporary opinion. Since only selections from it appeared in the metropolitan press at first, her views were distorted and a storm gathered. The Toronto *Globe* declared her letter to be "a specious tissue of half-truths and untruths, and a despicable attempt to discredit Great Britain and British policy in the eyes of school children." Premier Ferguson, who held the education portfolio, reacted as negatively. He contemplated measures to prevent such information reaching the schools in the future. "I think it is a crime against the country, and particularly against the youth of the country," Ferguson declared, "that their minds should be poisoned with statements that do not represent the facts."

Since facts are often illusory in the modern world, one smart reporter headed off for Grey County to investigate. Macphail was in Ottawa, unnerved by the intensity of the counterblast. Questions were raised in Parliament that could not go unanswered. J. S. Woodsworth lent her his file on China and provided support by having dinner with her while she waited for her defence that evening. When she had completed her justification, Woodsworth chided her. "Now will you be good?" he asked, knowing full well the answer. In this instance Macphail did not have to be, for independent corroboration established the validity of her case. A Chinese instructor at McGill University confirmed her account, and the reporter discovered that her interpretation of history reflected a textbook written by two American progressive historians that had been approved for use in provincial high schools.

Macphail went further in explaining her conception of what it meant to be Canadian. She felt that Canadians had been too ready to force newcomers to assimilate and too unprepared to accept the contributions they might otherwise have made to the country. "The idea of people of British stock that they are superior is absurd," she maintained. "We have not allowed people from other countries to make contributions which would make Canada, not a little England or a little Great Britain, but Canada. We have imposed our thoughts and our culture on the newcomer and have stopped him from making the contribution he desires to make, and which he is capable of making."[39]

Macphail's personal friends included individuals of various nationalities, and she travelled to Montreal to address a conference on interracial friendship. While she was convinced that ethnic prejudice would eventually disappear through better understanding, she advocated active concern, not simple goodwill. And when Howard Ferguson was appointed High Commissioner to Britain, she informed her colleagues that "It is hard on the Court of St. James, but it is a relief to the province of Ontario."[40] She loved to have the final say.

Coupled with her internationalist outlook and sensitivity to ethnic diversity went a belief in the importance of civil liberties. During the late 1920s a new wave of repression swept Ontario as it had following the war. Toronto police forbade public meetings in any language but English and announced that halls allowing communists to speak would have their licences rescinded. In Sudbury the editor of a Finnish-language newspaper was convicted of sedition for some frivolous anti-monarchist remarks and later deported to Finland. When Woodsworth provoked a debate in the House of Commons about the trampling of civil liberties, Macphail defended fundamental freedoms by arguing that their suppression spread the very things they were intended to avert. "I think that the more opposition there is to freedom of speech and assembly," she said, "the more opposition to decent standards of living ... the more communism there will be. Suppress that and you bring about the thing you fear — communism.... I believe in free speech, free assembly and a free press. I believe the more freedom there is in those respects, the greater will be our happiness and self-respect."[41] Since Macphail believed that the appeal of communism was rooted in economic deprivation, she urged the acceptance of unemployment insurance and served on the parliamentary committee that examined the issue in 1928, more than a decade before it was implemented.

Addressing this wide range of topics during her third term in Ottawa, Agnes Macphail emerged as a skilled parliamentarian acknowledged as one of the best orators in the House of Commons. She represented a new wave that avoided the long-winded pomposity previously admired. Her speeches were researched and written in advance, but she delivered them in a style that appeared extemporaneous. Often peppering her remarks with cutting comments, she spoke in a terse, epigrammatic manner. She frequently included self-deprecating humour that even pervaded such unlikely topics as commodity imports. Apples were bought on the basis of appearance, she told the House, "just like wives. That is why I have been so unlucky."[42]

She also continued to visit her home between parliamentary sessions. In 1926 her parents sold their farm and moved into Ceylon where they brought a small brick residence that Agnes Macphail referred to as the "dollshouse." Her father kept busy with a small flock of chickens, which a sexist press portrayed as Macphail's because it conformed to stereotypes. Macphail also travelled when the House was in recess. She parlayed her speaking skills into additional income by working for Chautauqua tours that featured speakers like American firebrand William Jennings Bryan. One Toronto newspaper warned the West in advance of what to expect by relating how Macphail had handled a front row heckler who had shouted,

> *"Aw, why don't you get a husband."*
> *"Stand up,"* Agnes *retorted, but when the man appeared reluctant, the crowd insisted and he rose from his seat.*
> *"You are married, of course,"* she *continued, receiving an affirmative reply.*
> *"Now I'd say this man has been married about ten years. He wasn't like this ten years ago. How could I be sure that someone I married might not turn out like this?"*

The crowd roared with laughter as it did on another occasion when some man in the audience bellowed at her, "Don't you wish you were a man?" "Yes," she shouted back, "don't you?"[43]

Touring extended Macphail's experience in Western Canada and the United States, while the two hundred dollars a week she earned allowed her to indulge in clothes and to entertain on a grander scale. At home and in Ottawa, Agnes Macphail loved nothing more than throwing catered dinner parties for up to three dozen people with all the little touches that make such occasions memorable.[44] Believing that money was an instrument to be used, she remained a generous spendthrift who sometimes found herself in financial difficulties. She hated soliciting donations even for worthy causes. When caught short herself, she could not countenance calling in old debts, but she did not refuse her secretary's offer to canvass her friends.

The League of Nations

Macphail's commitment to internationalism also assumed new forms. A fervent admirer of Jane Addams, the American social reformer and president of the Women's International League, she secured the agreement of Mackenzie King in 1928 to have Canada support her nomination for the Nobel Peace Prize, an honour Addams received three years later.[45] Believing that governments only moved when pushed, Macphail proposed that emphasis on the military be offset by a government department to promote peace and international understanding. She also argued for nationalization of munitions manufacturing and government control of armament industries.

Macphail's interest in international questions brought her publicity and esteem in some quarters, but the only positive outcome of her efforts was her appointment as Canada's first woman delegate to the League of Nations in 1929. Mackenzie King's views on women in politics were beginning to moderate, and in that year he also appointed former Vancouver M.L.A. Mary Ellen Smith, the British Empire's first woman cabinet minister, as a delegate to the International Labour Conference at the League of Nations. In accepting, Agnes Macphail asked the prime minister to appoint a Conservative so that the delegation would be truly non-partisan. Sir George Foster accepted King's invitation and won Macphail's admiration for his diplomatic skills.

Macphail's appointment to Geneva coincided with her previous plans to attend the congress of the Women's International League in Prague, a trip she managed to finance through the generosity of a wealthy Montrealer and a writing contract with a newspaper in Ottawa. She sailed from New York aboard the *Mauretania*, landed in Cherbourg, and travelled to Paris where she renewed her wardrobe prior to proceeding through Germany to Prague. Macphail was exhausted and grumpy when Violet McNaugton and Laura Jamieson met her train, but a convivial café meal alleviated her foul humour before their women retired to their billets at a college owned by Czechoslovakia's agrarian party.[46]

President Jane Addams presided over a stunning assemblage at the International League's Prague congress. Six members of parliament, Germany's first woman lawyer, and Hungary's first female ambassador stood among the more than two hundred attending from twenty-six countries. The clamour of so many powerful women speaking in so many different languages at the opening session led the always impetuous Macphail to mount a chair and call for order, but the more experienced president promptly admonished her for her presumption. Disarmament commanded centre stage in the aftermath of the Kellogg-Briand Pact renouncing war and the publication of Erich Remarque's *All Quiet on the Western Front*, an angry denunciation of war's effects on the young that had broken publishing sales records. Even among this group of eminent women Agnes Macphail shone. She addressed the congress twice, spoke over the radio, and was elected to the international executive as well as two important committees. Later Macphail became president of a paper executive created for the Canadian organization.

When she arrived in Geneva from Prague, Macphail refused to sit on an inconsequential committee concerning women and children that was usually reserved for her gender. Arms reduction was the foremost international question of the hour, and Canada's only woman delegate secured a seat as the first female to sit on the League of Nation's disarmament committee. The Canadians formed part of the British delegation headed by J. Ramsay MacDonald, whose statesmanship Macphail had heard Addams laud at Prague. She took an instant dislike to him; his stiff manner and rigid formality reminded her of Thomas Crerar when he had first met the Progressive caucus in 1922. MacDonald kept insisting imperiously that the position of his government represented everyone, a notion that unified the Canadians and led more than one country to disagree.

Macphail enjoyed the good fortune of participating in one of the League of Nation's most productive sessions, and those in diplomatic circles thought few Canadian men had matched the quality of her performance. She won kudos from the British press as well. One journalist commented that "if I lived in her constituency she could rely on my vote. She strikes me as a fine type of woman in public life, enjoying it but first and foremost for the causes she has at heart; human enough to appreciate popularity but quite prepared to do without it and champion alone, if need be, a policy in which she believes."[47] Hugh Keenleyside, a brilliant but arrogant young officer with Canada's Department of External Affairs, noted the favourable impression that Macphail had created, but he was less complimentary when he met her for the first time. She struck him as "a rather hard looking woman but one who keeps herself well, dresses appropriately and possesses a clear, effective voice."

He concluded that Macphail's instincts seemed better than her brains, but the redoubtable M.P. had an answer for such male prejudice: "You know when men have intuition, it is wonderful, but when women possess it, it is a weakness."[48] Keenleyside later became one of Macphail's many friends.

When she returned to Canada, Macphail was invited to dine with Mackenzie King at Laurier House. She impressed upon the prime minister the need for better preparation of delegates before they went abroad, improved language training so that they could participate in both French and English, and a new League of Nations section in an expanded Department of External Affairs. The following year Macphail proposed in Parliament that one dollar for every hundred spent on defence be devoted to establishing chairs in international relations and scholarships at Canadian universities. The Women's International League attempted to gain popular support for the initiative, and the House committee on international relations invited distinguished academics to give evidence, but without result.[49]

Macphail spoke in Washington and twice in New York City in 1930 despite the federal election that year. Although she enjoyed the company of Americans, she was becoming even more impressed with the calibre of British women in public life. "British women have the faculty of losing themselves completely in their subject. I suppose all great people have it, but a large number of them seem to be British," she wrote.[50] Appearing in Manhattan at a conference on the causes of war, Macphail was upstaged by Carrie Chapman Catt, the venerable suffragist and peace worker, who prefigured flag burners by denouncing the American national anthem for its aggressive spirit. "She does not compare at all with Jane Addams," Macphail thought. "She is popular and gifted, but Jane Addams is truly great." In New York Macphail fell ill from exhaustion and was forced to rest for three weeks at the home of a wealthy American friend, Katherine Blake.[51]

Prior to her European trip Macphail had been sceptical of the League of Nations, seeing it as an instrument controlled by the major world powers. Her experience changed her mind, and she remained a devoted supporter for many years, advocating a role for Canada as an interpreter of the United States since it was not a member. Towards the League of Nations

Society in Canada Macphail was less well disposed because she thought it too exclusive in membership.

But her heady optimism disappeared, and Macphail considered the prospects for peace work bleak once countries began to scramble to erect tariff barriers following the onset of the Depression. Nevertheless, under the auspices of the Associated Canadian Clubs, she toured in 1931 from Thunder Bay to Victoria speaking about arms reduction. Collecting signatures for the Women's International League's mass petition prior to the first World Disarmament Conference, Macphail also spoke frequently on the radio.

She gave five talks in one day in Saskatoon, but in Vancouver she was excluded from the Women's Canadian Club. Macphail had charged H. H. Stevens, a Conservative who represented one of the city's ridings, with displaying loose ethics in using House of Commons information when seeking investors for a railway venture. His wife saw that Macphail was not allowed to appear before the Canadian Club, but Laura Jamieson found an alternative venue in the Vancouver Women's Buiding. During this trip she became ill again. In Winnipeg she succumbed to tonsillitis and had to be carried on a stretcher from the train to hospital. After her recovery, she completed her commitments, but she underwent surgery later in the year.

With all these activities Macphail had distinguished herself nationally and internationally by the end of the 1920s. While the press had joked in 1926 that the only woman in Parliament might as well try her hand at governing since men had proven themselves incapable, greater attention was paid to Jean-François Pouliot's suggestion in 1929, the year the British Privy Council declared that women were "persons" under the terms of the British North America Act, that Macphail become the country's first woman senator. The reformer in her baulked at the idea. "I would certainly hate to see a good woman wasted there," she replied tongue in cheek. "It is a useless institution, and appointment to it would be like being placed on a shelf, prior to burial."[52]

As Agnes Macphail reached the pinnacle of her career, she would be forced increasingly to make decisions that were both more painful and more momentous than her opposition to a Senate appointment. Her father fell ill late in 1929, and she and her mother cared for him until his death early the next year. His passing reminded her of her own mortality and heightened her anxiety about motherhood past the age of forty. In the next decade she ruled out marriage for the last time. She also found she had to question some of her most cherished political principles. In doing so she made the most crucial choices in her life.

6

The Great Divide:
The Depression and the
Creation of the CCF

*In that day the deaf will hear the words of the scroll, and out
of the gloom and darkness the eyes of the blind will see.*
Isaiah 29:18

As the Depression of the 1930s deepened, Agnes Macphail
grew increasingly restive with her inability to effect legislative
change, and she gradually came to believe that a new political
movement was required. It was all very well to be right most
of the time, but it did little good if reforms were not embodied
in legislation. The parliamentary session of 1928 she found
especially frustrating because every measure she championed
on behalf of farmers was voted down. The 1930 federal election
brought R. B. Bennett and the Conservatives to power, but
Progressive forces were cut in half to twelve members. In
Southeast Grey, Macphail was forced to defend the continued
existence of the Independent group, as the Progressive rump
had become known. The election proved a soul-searching
experience from which she emerged with a bare majority
of several hundred votes over her old Tory rival, Dr. L. G.
Campbell.

Provincewide, union membership experienced steady decline, and the United Farmers of Ontario slumped to seven
thousand members by 1932. Consolidations in industry continued unabated with farmers particularly concerned about
the near monopoly in the meat-packing industry in the eastern
part of the country that had resulted from the formation of
Canada Packers in 1927. The Beauharnois scandal over large

corporate donations to the Liberal party in 1931 revealed once again the corrupting influence of big business on the party system when large government contracts were involved. Ten years seemed to have come to naught apart from the introduction of pensions, changes in divorce legislation, and minor adjustments in taxation. Even then, the Old Age Pensions Act passed by the Liberal government in 1927 was niggardly. It imposed a means test for qualification and afforded a meagre payment of only $240 a year.

Women and Politics

Most of all Agnes Macphail was disillusioned with the sorry showing of women in the 1930 federal election. Most Canadians were still unreceptive, if not hostile, to women politicians. Societal values conveyed by the press contrasted women's domestic and reproductive roles with the ruthless demands of public life. The emphasis that suffragists had placed on women's familial responsibilities was inadvertently strengthened by the new health drive sponsored by government and voluntary organizations to reduce infant and maternal mortality. Women like Violet McNaughton knew full well the forces that blocked political aspirations. When an American friend in the Women's International League encouraged her and Laura Jamieson to seek nominations, both declined. Neither wanted to be a sacrificial lamb. "The progress of the Women's Movement in Canada," McNaughton wrote, "is more apparent than real."[1]

Only six women secured nominations in 1930, and only Macphail was successful. After her fourth election, the role of pioneer was wearing thin, but Macphail faced her situation with a jocularity that showed she was more relaxed. When she was asked about women in politics, she retorted sarcastically, "What women? Where are they? Show me some women who take part in politics. I would like to see them." The blame lay with both women and men — the latter, she said, were "not bad fellows really, but one should not take them too seriously."[2] While men naturally refused to forfeit their privileged position, Macphail could not understand why women refused to challenge male hegemony. As the bearers of children, women possessed greater courage than men and a genuine belief in the superiority of human values. "In addition to all this," she maintained, "women have in an unusual degree the gift of intuition — in women called 'jumping to conclusions'; in men, called 'genius.'"[3]

Women were invaluable to political parties, but they had accepted subordinate status through segregation. "How long," she asked, "are women going to do half the work for men, swallowing platforms and not digesting them? Was that what resulted from Mrs. Pankhurst's effort? If women are exclusively interested in private life and not in a place in the world, then they are not worthy of the franchise."[4] The solution lay in beating men at their own game. Macphail urged women to form effective lobbies within their parties and to withhold their services if they were denied equal treatment. "I'm fed up with auxiliaries," she concluded. "Join with the men. Be adults together."[5] While Macphail continued to encourage women, other problems moved to the fore.

The Early Years of the Depression

As the first year of the Great Depression rolled into a second and then a third, the economy dominated all discussions, although those who saw only as a cyclical adjustment intrinsic to capitalist economies thought prosperity to be just around the corner. Such optimism did little to console farmers in areas of the prairies who had suffered from years of drought in the preceding decade. Since Ontario agriculture had prospered during that period, the effects of the economic collapse there were even more devastating psychologically. Real agricultural income in the province dropped 40 per cent between 1929 and 1933. Farmers earned less cash on average than a family of four on government relief in Toronto received for subsistence.[6] The rural community was convinced that it shouldered a disproportionate share of the country's financial catastrophe. "The brunt of the economic blizzard has been borne by the Canadian farmer and other primary producers," journalist Wilfred Eggleston concluded.[7]

The most visible discontent occurred in the cities as Agnes Macphail was reminded daily when she passed the unemployed milling about the Chateau Laurier hotel next to the Parliament buildings. To some, communism appeared as a panacea through which a collective response might solve their personal crises. Organizations such as the Worker's Unity League and a host of others denounced the evils of capitalism and worked to defend workers' rights. An equally confrontational government determined, as Prime Minister Bennett said, "to put the iron heel ruthlessly" to their efforts. The Conservatives spotted subversives behind every foreign accent, although at the federal level they were more sensitive to Canadians who spoke French than their predecessors had been during World War One.

Two official weapons stood at the government's disposal to arrest the communist menace. The Immigration Act provided a means to deport thousands suspected of being agitators, while Section 98 of the Criminal Code could be invoked against native Canadians. The latter amendment had been formulated hurriedly in reaction to the Winnipeg General Strike in 1919. It outlawed any organization or individual advocating the overthrow of government or the economy by force, but the law was vague, and it presumed that the accused were guilty until they proved their innocence. Provincial and municipal governments in places like Toronto cracked the whip for their federal colleagues, using tactics that included the banning of parades and restrictions on freedom of assembly. Woodsworth, Macphail, and the Independent group led the campaign in Parliament for the repeal of this unjust law that subjected legitimate dissent to the whims of police.

Macphail herself was prevented in 1931 from speaking at a public meeting in Toronto, although she abhorred communism. Others were more unfortunate. Eight leaders of the Communist party of Canada, including its leader Tim Buck, were rounded up, convicted, and sentenced to prison. The Canadian Labour Defence League, a communist front organization, rallied to their defence. Headed by A. E. Smith, a former Methodist minister, the league intensified its activities when guards shot only into Tim Buck's cell during a prison riot in Kingston penitentiary in 1932. The situation in Saskatchewan was even more appalling. During a strike at Estevan in 1931 involving the Workers' Unity League, the Royal Canadian Mounted Police opened fire on a parade. Three strikers were killed. Their collective tombstone said simply: "Murdered by the RCMP."[8]

Agnes Macphail considered the Depression as a catacylsm announcing the end of the old economic and political order. The human suffering she witnessed quickened her desire for social change and a redefinition of the role of government. During the depression years her radicalism matured into a quest for economic rights and social justice. The right of all Canadians to work for fair wages and to enjoy decent standards of living appeared more prominently in her thought. During the first phase of Roosevelt's New Deal, she watched closely events in the United States and saw that central planning agencies such as the Agricultural Adjustment Administration could use government creatively to get the country moving again. She also read widely in the works of innovative thinkers like John Maynard Keynes, G. D. H. Cole, and Harold Laski. There could be no lasting political democracy, she concluded, without economic democracy. People reduced to mimimal subsistence did not enjoy the fruits of democratic life. "Our economic system," she said in 1936, "has caused economic and social slavery."[9] There could be no fundamental happiness until fears about destitution were replaced with economic security for all Canadians, including the disabled. During the thirties, social democracy supplanted radical democracy in Macphail's thought, but even so it retained a distinctly populist hue.

Macphail reassessed her stand on the country's two old political parties, which she thought had come to differ in attitudes rather than policy. Conservatives were dominating, she said. "They rule with a rod of iron — at least the head does, and the others through him. I think they assume a very superior attitude, which, I suppose, accounts for the superiority of Toronto the Good. For a long time the Conservatives had a corner on superiority and, for a long time, a corner on patriotism. I mean that one's devotion to one's country was always an open question, unless one is a Conservative and an Anglican. If you are a Conservative, a Methodist and an Orangeman, you can get by." The Liberals were flailed for lacking the courage of their convictions. They became conservative through their own inertia. "The Liberals put great store on personal liberty," she told the Canadian Club in Toronto. "I would ask how much liberty have the destitute? Liberty to have two slices of bread and coffee or not to have them!"[10]

Poverty was everywhere, including Southeast Grey. Macphail was sickened to learn of a war veteran so poor that he and his family were reduced to making their clothing out of discarded flour sacks. She provided them with money to buy some clothes and made sure that the ex-soldier secured a pension from the government.[11] The elderly were especially hurt, sometimes selling their meagre possessions for a few pennies. Unable to maintain their life insurance, many people forfeited their future financial security. Robbed of hope, too many youth sank into disillusionment. Most labourers and farmers were tied to unrelenting toil in order to survive or sometimes reduced to destitution. Macphail feared that such people were prey to demogogues of the right and left who promised a better life through dictatorship or communalism. "I sometimes wonder," a close friend wrote her, "if the Russian and French revolutions were not the right method after all. Sometimes it takes violence to oust some elements."[12] Agnes Macphail did not agree. To her the time was ripe for a new political coalition that would achieve more than the old parties. During the years from 1930 to 1934 she worked tirelessly, despite persistent bad health, to create a socialist alternative within Canada.

As measures were discussed in Parliament to provide the needy with mimimal assistance, her voice was frequently heard asking the question, "What about the women?" The contraction in employment forced women from their jobs, created underemployment, and led others to stay at home to free up jobs for men. Women "are suffering greatly," she said in 1932. "They will not get into queues for meals. No shelters, or very few at any rate, have been provided for them.... Many women who were formerly in offices are now willing to work in homes for pitifully low wages, in some cases almost just for shelter and food."[13] When the question of relief camps was raised, she challenged the minister of labour: "If men are not capable of taking care of themselves during periods of stress and unemployment, does Parliament think that women are more capable of taking care of themselves? If they are not, what provision has the government made, or what provision does it propose to make for single, unemployed women?"[14] Apart from a token woman on the National Employment Commission, the minister was forced to admit that the matter had not been considered.

A Last Romance

The increasing emphasis that Agnes Macphail placed on the importance of meaningful work reflected more than the sorry state of the world economy; it had a major personal component as well. The competing demands of career versus marriage and family, with which she had wrestled during her entire adult life, finally moved towards resolution. She had become involved in a relationship with Robert Gardiner, the leader of the Independent group in Parliament and president of the United Farmers of Alberta after Henry Wise Wood. A taciturn Scots immigrant who had moved to Canada in 1902, Gardiner had acquired a homestead in Saskatchewan, but three successive crop failures forced him to move to Alberta where he took an interest in municipal matters and then was elected to Parliament in 1921. So ensconced was he politically that in 1930 he won election by acclamation. A life-long bachelor, Gardiner was infatuated with Macphail. She was the love of his life.

The couple shared similar backgrounds and a close affinity in political outlook, but those very commitments divided them as much as their personal differences. Gardiner was little better at caring for himself than Macphail's father had been. In Ottawa he lived in a shabby boarding house that she encouraged him to leave. Macphail, in contrast, devoted time to her own appearance and that of her surroundings, however much she regretted that men got off so easily in such matters. Marriage implied that one spouse assume responsibility for the other in a way that Macphail was unprepared to accept, although when Gardiner was hospitalized, she visited him every day. More importantly, Gardiner was as devoted to the farm movement in Alberta as she was to the United Farmers of Ontario. Neither could reconcile public service with personal allegiance.

Sometime before Gardiner was trounced in the Social Credit surge during the 1935 federal election, Macphail broke off the affair. She wanted a space of her own, but she knew, she said, as she was formulating her decision, "that when I am sixty that I shall probably look back at this life I have chosen and regret every bit of it, dust and ashes, because I will wish I had married and had children and had been a happy country woman. Sure I will!"[15]

Her decision left Gardiner crestfallen. Macphail continued to show concern for his well-being, learning from correspondents in Alberta about his increasingly miserable and isolated existence plagued by sickness. Gardiner displayed no further interest in women during the last decade of his life, but he made his former lover the principal beneficiary in his will.[16] Nor is there any record of further personal entanglements concerning Macphail.

During this turmoil Macphail was also suffering from gynecological problems. Her menstrual periods were frequently preceded by intense lower back pain for which she had to seek therapy. Returning from a speaking engagement in Halifax in 1933, Macphail realized that she was seriously ill and stopped to see a specialist in Montreal. An operation was necessary, she was informed, but she persuaded the doctor to travel to Ontario and the surgery was performed in the little hospital in Markdale near her home. She suffered intensely during the first four days of recovery, but the support of her many friends and relatives heartened her. Two years later she returned for a hysterectomy. Since hormone treatments following such operations were not yet available, surgeons normally left a small portion of the ovaries. Macphail amused her friends by converting this medical necessity into a story about her insistence that the doctors not remove everything so that she would retain her fatal sexual attraction.[17]

These emotional and physical changes in her life had profound effects on Macphail's social outlook. More than ever she became convinced that nothing prevented women from contributing to social betterment in the same way as their male counterparts. While the ability to procreate separated one sex from the other and contributed to female uniqueness, she believed each gender to be equally diverse. Some women found contentment in family life, others in careers.

> But [as] I love children and have always had dear men friends, it was deep a sorrow to me that I couldn't do all I expect women to do; to be a wife and mother and also an UNTRAMMELED ACTIVE PERSON....
>
> Deciding on such matters can never be final; the whole question has to be thrashed over again and again, according to the success of one's work, the attraction of one's men friends,

the lure of children. To have part of life can never be enough; one must have all. That is what I want for women. There are some women who only want a husband, children and a home. For them there is no problem. Keeping the house is enough. But for others it is not.

One of the outstanding features of this age is the number of outstanding women who do not marry. Some old-fashioned and stupid people may say they never had the chance; any normal woman has had the chance, but for some reason she hasn't married the man she could have married. It may be the marriage was grossly unsuitable. But I have talked to hundreds of these fine, alert and capable women in business, the professions and the arts, and their reason was the same as mine. THE PERSON could not be subjected....

Unless man grows up to want an intelligent companion with all the rights and privileges of an equal, the race will increasingly lose as mothers [those] women who would help him raise the standard of his life and that of their children. The easy way is seldom the best way one finds.[18]

The Origins of the CCF

Agnes Macphail resolved her life's personal dilemma at a critical point in Canadian history. Like many agrarian radicals, she believed that fundamental changes were necessary if the country were to be lifted out of the quagmire into which it had fallen, but most of her solutions remained essentially pragmatic. Her interest in economic matters was converted into a campaign for currency reform that lasted for nearly a decade. Money became a public passion while it remained inconsequential personally. "We all know it matters, don't we," she told an international women's conference at Montebello in 1934. "The less we have, the more it matters."[19]

Since the United States had sealed itself off by higher tariffs, Britain appeared the prime outlet for Canadian agricultural produce. Macphail advocated that Canada free its trade by removing the shackles of the gold standard. The tyranny of accepted monetary standards sacrificed the majority "so that those few, sleek fatted favourites of the god of gold may be especially cared for," she said.[20] In its place she proposed a currency based on the volume of goods and services produced and suggested that the dollar be placed on par with the British pound.

> *"What shall we do with our gold then?"* Macphail queried before the United Farmers of Alberta.
> *"Use it for wedding rings,"* someone in the audience retorted.
> *"Or for dental requirements,"* replied Macphail, *"a less painful method."*[21]

Agnes Macphail was convinced that because deflation stood at the root of the Depression, a more liberal monetary policy was necessary. The inflation needed to relieve rural debts could only be achieved through the creation of a central bank and a national currency under public control. The problem lay not in a lack of production but in lessened consumption. She criticized the country's agricultural colleges for pursuing increased productivity singlemindedly when undersupply was not the problem. "What's the use of making two blades grow where one grew before," she said colourfully, "when you can't sell either?"[22]

Economics is not reduced to aphorisms so easily. While elements of these proposals saw fruition when the Bank of Canada began to operate in 1935, Macphail seemed unaware of inflation's adverse effects on foreign investment and disadvantaged groups on fixed incomes. Association with the young university faculty who formed the League for Social Reconstruction led her to moderate her views, and she grew to admire intellectuals. Advanced economic thinkers, she told her constituents, "are not the wild-eyed extremists and visionaries we are painted, but are actually much closer to reality than those who are attempting to solve 20th century problems with 19th century solutions."[23] Convinced that Canadians needed to develop a new social consciousness where success would not be measured by property but by service to fellow human beings, she stopped short of advocating socialism, which she identified as anathema to Ontario farmers. "They would be frightened out of their wits by the word *Politics* — and indeed more frightened by 'Socialist,'" she wrote.[24]

Events were about to lead Macphail on a campaign to change the mind of rural Ontario. The severity of the Depression fostered new initiatives to unite urban and agrarian radicals with socialists throughout the country. Organized labour, which had begun to shed past differences over the preceding three years, amassed a thousand workers in the spring of 1932 to protest in Ottawa. Prime Minister Bennett agreed only to meet a small delegation of them on the steps of Parliament, and they were even more insulted when an armoured car careened around the Hill, city police marched on Wellington Street in front of the Parliament buildings, and detachments of R.C.M.P. were stationed behind each block — with the one in the centre on horseback.

In May, members of the Ginger Group met in William Irvine's parliamentary office with academics from the League for Social Reconstruction to formulate a noncommunist socialist political response. They made plans for what was called a Commonwealth party, although it was essentially an expanded version of the Progressive upsurge inspired by a broader theoretical perspective. Woodsworth was named temporary president, and Agnes Macphail was accorded responsibility for Ontario. She responded by increasing her speaking engagements around the province, and it was a sure sign of the times that urban businessmen came out to listen to the only woman member of Parliament. One meeting she closed in the self-mocking manner of a schoolteacher: "There will be no more questions. You are dismissed." In Windsor, where the political star of Paul Martin was rising, the speaker thanking Macphail mentioned that Martin stood with Mackenzie King and R. B. Bennett as one of the country's most eligible bachelors. "Mr. Healey," Agnes immediately piped up to forestall the inevitable question about her single status: "let me interrupt you to say right now: I'll take Paul Martin."[25]

Following their past practice, the United Farmers of Ontario planned their own show of strength before the Imperial Economic Conference in July of 1932, a demonstration where their Quebec counterparts joined them. Four thousand men, women, and children descended on the Coliseum in Ottawa. While Bennett's advisers had learned that overkill provoked negative fallout in the press, the response of the hapless government to the farmers proved its most sorry exercise in public relations. Macphail handled the initial contacts, but Bennett had made it clear to UFO leaders that their appearance was a waste of time and a burden to his government. He requested a written statement of their recommendations and said that he would meet only a delegation of a half dozen representatives. When he learned how many people had invaded Ottawa, Bennett was dumbfounded. He had met with business leaders for four hours shortly before, but only one hour was scheduled for the farmers and that was all they got. A request that he speak to the assembled throng was denied. After refusing to delegate the task to a cabinet colleague, Bennett rushed off to his next appointment.

The crowd in the Coliseum went wild when they heard the news. As shouts of protest rose, Agnes Macphail stepped to the podium and attempted to channel their indignation in a positive direction. "Prime Minister Bennett has made some big political mistakes," she said, "but this is the biggest. It seems to me simply ridiculous that a Prime Minister declares that it is more important to meet a single person than to appear at a meeting like this."[26] She advised her listeners not to storm the Parliament buildings but to formulate their grievances into resolutions. Two Conservative members of Parliament who had formed part of the small delegation tried to offer excuses, but they were laughed down.

While the purpose of the demonstration had been frustrated, Agnes Macphail had helped to prevent it from degenerating into a mob scene. All hope for effective action was crushed at the ensuing Commonwealth parley, known lightheartedly as the Mickey Mouse Conference since the only substantial tariff reductions involved Mickey Mouse noisemakers. The Bennett government scrambled to restore its tarnished image in the press, but tremors emanating from the prime minister's ineptitude with the farmers were felt during an Alberta by-election. Bennett himself did not change. He greeted representatives from the Workers' Economic Conference the following month with a lecture on civil disobedience: "You break those laws and I say that, sure as the sun rises, you will pay the price for it."[27]

Events in Ottawa prevented Macphail from attending the meeting in Calgary where further plans were laid for the new political movement. Robert Gardiner figured prominently in the discussions that agreed on a brief program and an impossible name: the Cooperative Commonwealth Federation

(CCF). Macphail supported the initiative fully because it did not contravene her beliefs. The CCF would not be a political party but a federation of provincial coalitions based on a mutually agreeable platform. In estabishing common ground among groups, the new federation would project onto the national stage the electoral strength seen in Ontario during the Farmer-Labour government. Affiliation with the United Farmers in Ontario was as crucial to Macphail as Alberta agricultural support was to Gardiner.

In giving expression to the principles professed by the Ginger Group while retaining a loose organizational structure, the suit of clothes being offered was not entirely new. The CCF advocated a country where the principle regulating production would not be profits, but human needs. The Calgary platform also guaranteed "equal economic and social opportunity without distinction of sex, nationality or religion."[28] Other than in its sweeping aspirations, the CCF cloth was clearly frayed even as it began, but it was scarcely more tattered than that of the United Farmers. Plagued with financial difficulties, the UFO had lost its newspaper to Alan Plaunt and Graham Spry, two sympathetic young idealists who championed public broadcasting through the Canadian Radio League. UFO leadership was aging badly. Poor health forced J. J. Morrison to resign as secretary in 1933, and he was replaced by H. H. Hannam, a soft-spoken bachelor whose family had lived near the MacPhails in Grey County.

Agnes Macphail was an acknowledged leader of the United Farmers, but the Ontario agricultural community was severely fragmented both in politics and by economic specialties. The Depression deepened antipathies to political parties; only a federation of groups seemed to offer any possibility of acceptance. Since the United Farmers of Ontario were known to be more conservative than their Western counterparts, William Irvine was assigned to assist Macphail in in her home province. Prior to sweeping across the countryside in a whirlwind speaking tour, the pair met with the UFO executive to secure affiliation to the new movement, but all they received was assurance that the matter would be considered at full convention in the same way as other policies.

Only a combination as powerful as that of Agnes Macphail and the Alberta spellbinder — her equal in oratory — stood a chance of selling the new movement. Their tour was intended to enlist mass support before the first Toronto rally for the CCF and the UFO convention took place at the end of November 1932. Macphail returned to the provincial capital to assist the UFO in adopting a broad-ranging reform program. The farm convention then adjourned temporarily to attend the CCF meeting. The crowd overflowed the hall to hear Macphail, Woodsworth, Gardiner, Irvine, and social gospeller Salem Bland. Agnes Macphail showed some hesitancy. She told her audience that if they had trouble saying the word socialism, they might try repeating "British socialism" to themselves. Over a thousand people signed cards indicating they would join the CCF, but the fact that almost all were white collar workers was a portent of future difficulties.[29]

Macphail knew that the principal drama would unfold on the floor of the UFO convention during the debate on affiliation. Irvine and Gardiner gave addresses, but they were Westerners. The time arrived for Macphail to deliver. Mustering all her talent, she successfully countered an artful attempt to have the UFO cooperate with the CCF rather than affiliate. In an emotional address during which her voice broke, Macphail projected the lessons of the past decade into the future. Traditional ideas about the political role of agriculture had failed to effect the changes needed. The stress on educating rural residents was laudable, but education was "only a means to an end, and the end is the setting up of a new social order and better living conditions for the people." The eight policies affirmed at Calgary earlier in the year were tentative, she noted, and could be shaped with UFO involvement in light of its own newly invigorated program.

Even in the emotion of the moment, Macphail tried to relieve tension with humour. The CCF, she told her audience jokingly, stood for "Come, Comrades, Forward." She also put her neck on the line, telling delegates that "I'll put everything I have into this venture." She then closed her heartfelt address in her customary populist manner by telling the delegates that they were the people who must decide their future course: "I leave that to you. Do what you like about it."[30]

Agnes Macphail's masterful performance swayed the convention, but affiliation succeeded only after a compromise resolution suggested by W. C. Good proposed three caveats: the

UFO was to retain its separate identity; constituency autonomy within the organization was to be respected; and the affiliation was limited to the declared policies of the Farmers' organization. When the vote was taken, no more than six among the three hundred delegates were opposed. Agnes then joined Woodsworth and others in speaking to the United Farm Young People of Ontario. Some of its members created the New Canada Movement that was to sweep through southern Ontario in the last brush fire of agrarian discontent before being extinguished just as rapidly.[31]

The Christmas holiday provided rest Macphail needed, but she resumed speaking on behalf of the CCF early in 1933. To the rural electorate she emphasized that the new movement stood for voluntary cooperation and low-interest loans to assist farmers and establish new ventures. Financial institutions would be nationalized, the great monopolies brought under government control, and utilities publicly owned. Social services would be extended but private property would not be abolished; it only would be eliminated when it was overgrown or harmful to human rights. Since this was a sensitive point with the farm community, Macphail contrasted the difference between a company such as Canadian Pacific and a grocery store or family farm. The "new order of things will in some respects resemble capitalism," she predicted with her liberal reformist outlook, "but it won't be capitalism as we understand it today."[32]

Speaking in the towns Macphail was forced to be more direct. At Kitchener, some sixteen hundred people crammed into the hall to hear her but almost as many were turned away. "I'm socialistic," she affirmed in the Ridgetown opera house, "I'm not Marxian. Anyone who is not a socialist is not thinking. Mr. King says the CCF would nationalize all private property. If he doesn't know more than that I don't have much respect for his intelligence, and if he doesn't believe what he is saying, I haven't much respect for his integrity."[33] Within a month Macphail was back in Ottawa to second Woodsworth's motion in Parliament proposing the creation of a Cooperative Commonwealth.

In some quarters Macphail was viewed as rivalling J. S. Woodsworth in political appeal. For the first time the prospect of a woman prime minister was considered seriously. "With a saltier speech than Mr. Woodsworth, and his equal in courage," an opposition newspaper maintained, "she is potent on the platform, eloquent in the Commons, ready at all times to tongue-lash what she and her comrades call 'capitalism.'"[34] Her lack of pretention and deep understanding of human nature were Macphail's most attractive features politically. One journalist maintained that she possessed more political common sense than many of her colleagues combined. Yet her courage was more a quality of temperament than character; being fearless, she was often tactless and did not always foresee the consequences of her actions. She grasped ideas readily, but details bored her. As a result, she lacked the discipline required in organizational work.

The press had as much fun with Macphail as her admirers. One paper satirized her campaign for parity of the dollar with the pound by recasting Lewis Carroll:

> "Will you move a little faster?" said Agnes to the Banks.
> "I've the CCF behind me to kick you in the shanks."
> See how eagerly the Debtors and the Farmers will advance!
> They but wait for Jimmie Woodsworth to lead the merry dance.
> Will you, won't you, will you, won't you, won't you join the dance?[35]

Macphail's failings became apparent during the next six months, although it is difficult to see how anyone could have prevented the collision that occurred. The new CCF had to compete for support with front organizations of the banned Communist party. For Macphail, the distinction between democratic socialism and communism was clear, but it was not to most Canadians. Political opponents and their newspapers contributed to the confusion. Macphail was unequivocal in distinguishing between legitimate and illegitimate dissent. "Those of us who call ourselves radicals — constitutional radicals — should stop apologizing for ourselves and give up caring whether we are called pink or red or any other colour," she told supporters in the West. "I think the only people who are going to be much use in the ten or fifteen years coming are radicals, those willing to study and think and do a good job at mental house-cleaning and then keep the place — I mean their heads — in order, and then use their energy in service of the whole community of Canada."[36]

The Ontario CCF

Although some of the best orators in the country spearheaded the CCF, the organization of the movement placed it at a great disadvantage in trying to get its political message across. It was neither a full-blown political party nor even a union of disparate groups forced together through mutual alienation from the political system. The CCF was a league of independents, a warring coalition of farmer, labour, and socialist organizations. There were no leaders with final authority, only a system of federal and provincial councils. Nationally, the CCF was fragmented along provincial lines, and in Ontario it was splintered even more. The provincial CCF did not allow individual membership but required people to belong to the United Farmers, the CCF Clubs created to provide mass involvement, or a Labour Conference constructed from a fractious combination of splinter socialist and labour parties.

The Labour Conference was the most problematical because there was no working class equivalent to the United Farmers, even if they had shrunken to represent only 5 per cent of the farm population. National unions competed with the internationals, and each had its own tiny political party to represent its interests. Other equally ineffectual groups such as the Socialist Party of Canada (Ontario Section) responded to the cords of the *Internationale* by vying for the support of all on the ideological left willy-nilly, but without much success. Working with the League for Social Reconstruction, the Socialist Party brought together the Toronto Labour Party (American Federation of Labor unions) with the National Labour Party (All Canadian Congress of Labour unions) in a meeting in Toronto that Woodsworth and Macphail addressed and that advocated affiliation with the CCF. Although the Labour Conference that resulted was supposed to represent some sixty-six labour and socialist parties, the Socialist Party of Canada, which had only several dozen members in Ontario, came to control ten of its twelve seats on the provincial council.[37]

Not only was the farm community suspicious of organized labour, but also many in the splinter parties distrusted each other or anyone outside their own tiny circles. Some objected that the new CCF was "as Socialistic as Mussolini, Hitler and [Ramsay] MacDonald. Strange bed-fellows for Socialists 'tis true and methinks unless the former element change very radically the CCF will be shortlived."[38] Internal resentment at the intrusion of new blood worsened the situation, as did the instransigent stance of individuals like J. M. Conner and Rose Henderson, who attempted to discredit J. S. Woodsworth.

That threesomes seldom make a good love affair was apparent at the first informal meeting of the Ontario CCF troika, which Macphail attended in Toronto on 5 February 1933. The only substantive matter on the agenda provided each group with turf protection by ensuring that one would not organize the constituency of another without consultation. In May a second meeting established a provisional provincial council composed of twelve representatives from each group and a tripartite executive. Macphail became president since she had the most political experience and could serve as the pipeline to Ottawa in the absence of a national office, while E. A. Beder of the CCF Clubs was elected vice-president and Bert Robinson from the Socialist Party became secretary-treasurer.[39]

The battle lines were established well before the fractured Ontario contingent marched off to Regina in July of 1933 to formalize the program for the new federation. Farmers and labour were unaccustomed to working with each other and made no effort to conceal their animosities. Marxist jargon and Trotskyite rhetoric infuriated the farmers because it conveyed a revolutionary intent at variance with their reformist ideals. Macphail was as determined as Woodsworth that the CCF be a made-in-Canada solution to Canadian problems; little else stood a chance of success in the face of negative press and the attempts of Toronto police to obstruct their meetings. When the labour representatives harangued or called her "Comrade," Macphail recoiled and went red in the face.[40] Elections were not going to be won by speaking in the codes of foreign texts. Labour responded by needling apparent sensitivities. In June the farmers threatened not to attend council meetings because they were held on Sunday, but a compromise was reached before the meeting degenerated into a major procedural wrangle.

Regina Interlude

Macphail arrived in Regina for the CCF's founding convention in 1933 with eight other delegates of the United Farmers of Ontario. She had not previously seen a draft of the new platform written by the League for Social Reconstruction. Greatly disturbed by it, she paced the floor the entire night trying to decide if the United Farmers should pull out. Like W. C. Good, she thought the manifesto a long way from the Calgary program. She worried that what she had fought for so hard might be in jeopardy because it would not wash with the public. The eastern and western farm delegations worked separately on revisions to the agricultural plank and then amalgamated their efforts with the help of academics like University of Toronto economist Joe Parkinson. The final document began by guaranteeing the security of farmers on their land, while another clause expanded on the need for cooperation.

The launching of the CCF was intended as a new beginning for women as well as men, but at this point in her career Macphail still associated affirmative action with special privilege rather than equality. Throughout the convention one redoubtable feminist warrior popped up to demand female representation on every committee. When Macphail was formally introduced at a luncheon women had organized, she stood up and blurted: "All I can say is this. I'm sick and tired of all this 'woman business.' In all the time I've been in the House of Commons, I've never asked for anything on the grounds that I was a woman. If I didn't deserve it on my own merit, I didn't want it."[41] With that she flung her trademark cape over her shoulder, swirled around, and stalked out of the room.

The main convention floor was Agnes Macphail's forum. She shepherded through the meeting the section concerning finance and public taxation and was elected to the national council along with Elmore Philpott, the president of the CCF Clubs, and Thomas Cuden, president of the Socialist Party of Canada. Macphail entered debate after S. C. Johnson of Winnipeg moved deletion of a clause offering fair compensation to industries nationalized. During a heated exchange, she threatened that the United Farmers of Ontario would dissociate itself from any movement that advocated confiscation without adequate compensation. "The CCF is in no sense a political party," she reminded delegates, "it is a federation."[42] The amendment was lost.

While the Regina Manifesto remained a radical document — at least in the Canadian context — it methodically set out constitutional means to transform the country. "We aim," the preamble stated, "to replace the present capitalist system, with its inherent injustice and inhumanity, by a social order from which the domination and exploitation of one class by another will be eliminated, in which economic planning will supersede unregulated private enterprise and competition, and in which genuine, democratic self-government, based upon economic equality will be possible." When the some one hundred and fifty delegates voted approval of the platform, only W. C. Good objected. He continued to believe that electoral reforms were more important than nationalization and government planning.

Mackenzie King couched his reaction to the founding of the CCF in personal terms. "Do you think I want Miss Macphail to tell me what to do and how I am to do it?" he joked with a Western audience as he mocked the possibility of the country's only woman M.P. being minister of finance.[43] The choice facing the voters was clear to him: "Tory autocracy, CCF bureaucracy" or the principles of Liberalism — however they shifted. Many Conservatives were less kind, branding all to the left of the Liberals as communists.

Conflicts over policy and personal animosities aroused at Regina took time to heal. At a meeting in Toronto at the home of CCFers Alice and Bernard Loeb, Macphail delivered an indignant lecture to J. S. Woodsworth for some sin of omission or commission she thought he had committed. In Ottawa she refused to speak to Vancouver Labour M.P. Angus MacInnis until one day when Bob Gardiner was ill in hospital and MacInnis slipped into a seat beside her in the Commons to express his concern. Several days later, Agnes spotted MacInnis in the halls and called to him to wait for her. "I didn't think we were friends," she said as she slipped her arm into his, "but I want you to know that I like you."[44]

Collapse in Ontario

Soon the divisions within the Ontario CCF deepened into intransigent positions. CCF Club's president Elmore Philpott determined at the Regina convention that the provincial organizational structure was fundamentally unsound. It was holding on to antiquated ideas about group representation while the Saskatchewan CCF forged ahead with a constituency organization. In order to build on existing associations, the CCF had created the Labour Conference and the CCF Clubs. Failing to find a way to involve labour unions directly, the conference became a vehicle for a secular sect to strut as the voice of the working class. While the Socialist party that dominated the Labour Conference failed to expand, the CCF Clubs grew rapidly to more than a thousand members, and they were unhappy that their representation on provincial council was not increased.

The expressed desire of communists and communist front organizations such as the Canadian Labour Defence League to infiltrate the CCF aggravated the situation.[45] The early CCF attracted all sorts of opportuntists, cranks, and secret agents such as Stalinists, Trotskyites, anarchists, and Lovestoneites (followers of an American communist) who threatened to tarnish its image beyond repair. With backing from Agnes Macphail, Captain Elmore Philpott and Clubs secretary D. M. LeBourdais determined to rid the association of its alleged communist influence, but Philpott's tactics raised fundamental questions about party discipline, freedom of speech, and guilt by association.

Philpott was an enigmatic journalist who had become disenchanted with the Liberal party. Leaving his job at the Toronto *Globe*, he attempted to act as catalyst in forming a coalition between the emerging CCF and the provincial Liberals under its new leader, Mitch Hepburn. When that initiative failed, he joined the CCF and found himself president of the clubs. A war veteran crippled in combat, Philpott's style was populist even if his methods were not. A rousing speaker who paced the platform on crutches, his face revealing the pain caused by his contorted body, Philpott quickly showed that he denounced communism as passionately as unbridled capitalism.

With UFO support, Philpott secured the provincial council's approval to recommend to convention that it be restructured to ressemble more closely a one-person, one-vote model. At the same time a shortsighted resolution prohibited even former members of the Communist party from joining the CCF. The debate over such discrimination became so heated, and Agnes Macphail so rattled, that she objected to the use of the word socialism in reference to the CCF. She also informed Bert Robinson that he was too closely associated with communists to be secretary of the provincial council.[46] About to enter hospital for surgery, Macphail agreed to appear with Philpott at a rally attended by sixteen hundred people in Massey Hall where the changes were announced. Her remarks were temperate. In contrast to communists with whom violent confrontations were associated, she emphasized that only the ballot was needed to secure the victory of the CCF.[47]

The counterreaction from Socialist party members in the Labour Conference was immediate and intense. Because they had so few supporters, they stood to lose immeasurably by restructuring. They decided on bluff and bravura as their only recourse. Referring to the UFO and the CCF Clubs, Bert Robinson maintained that "we must put the fear of god in them about *the mighty mass strength* of our trade unions, who would swamp them under such an arrangement. Tell them of the thousands in the National Union movement, and thousands more in the A.F.L. (We don't have to tell them that we have more to fear from these unionists than they do.)"[48]

While Macphail struggled to recuperate from her operation and attended to her parliamentary duties, a series of mass meetings were held in Toronto that led to the arrest of A. E. Smith, the leader of the Canadian Labour Defence League, after he charged the prime minister publicly with authorizing the shooting at Communist party leader Tim Buck during the Kingston riot. The Labour Conference was as sympathetic to Smith following his indictment as its members were hostile to their reception by the other two factions in the CCF. A provincial council meeting — which Macphail was unable to attend — brought the revolt of the labour representatives into the open.[49] Attempting to censure Macphail, Philpott, and J. S. Woodsworth, they declared their intention to bolt party discipline by supporting Smith, whatever the ruling of council.

The UFO appointed its president, R. J. Scott, and Herb Hannam to determine whether the UFO should secede from the alliance.

The following day, when the press reported that Smith had accused Woodsworth of being responsible for the charge laid against him, the counterreaction from the labour representatives in the CCF Ottawa caucus was immediate.[50] They had been conducting their own campaign against unjust laws and were only too well aware of the pitfalls of cooperating with the Defence League. The "Labour Party in Ontario has been split before by the tactics of the Communists," J. S. Woodsworth wrote, "and we do not propose to have our Dominion-wide movement imperilled by a small section of one of the constituent members."[51] The four Labour members of Parliament asked Agnes Macphail to see that provincial council exercised its disciplinary powers to rid itself of individuals or organizations not in sympathy with the CCF program.

Macphail was stuck in Ottawa by more than her physical disability. Her motion to establish a royal commission into the country's penitentiaries was about to appear on the order paper of the House of Commons. On 26 February 1934 both the CCF Clubs and the UFO asked the national council to expel the Labour Conference for consorting with communists in defiance of established policy. Macphail tried to persuade Scott and Hannam to remain steady until the bloodletting freed the Ontario CCF of its noxious lesion, but to Hannam the gesture seemed futile.[52] The CCF had been discredited in more than rural Ontario by the adverse publicity it had attracted. Three days later Scott and Hannam pulled their organization out of the CCF, but they agreed at Macphail's urging to keep the move secret until the next provincial council meeting.

The imminent showdown forced Macphail to let others in the caucus try to repair the damage. Ted Garland, Angus MacInnis, William Irvine, and Woodsworth arrived in Toronto to attend provincial council, but UFO representatives chose to make their withdrawal public rather than be present. The Socialist Party members proved totally intransigent. "I can only say that we will fight to the last ditch to stay in the CCF," wrote its secretary, "but if we are forced we will go out with our principles intact and the Red Flag of the working class flying to the last."[53] Unable to find any common ground among the two remaining factions, J. S. Woodsworth disbanded the Ontario council in order to undertake a complete reorganization.

Macphail had been unable to avert the catastophe, but neither had her conduct helped moderate the conflict. Even if she had been able to devote her full attention to provincial affairs, Macphail was incapable of healing divisions that stemmed from deeply rooted antipathies, a fundamentally unsound organizational structure, and the willingness of too many people, including herself, to air differences in public. She identified with her own faction in the fight and supported Elmore Philpott too readily in the vain hope that order and discipline would return to the CCF once the alleged communists had been expelled. While Philpott had been confident that his attempts at reorganization would not lead to a split, his tactics and the support extended by Macphail had only made a bad situation worse.

Once the United Farmers had withdrawn from the CCF, Agnes Macphail had little alternative but to leave as well. Elmore Philpott also sought shelter in the wake of the storm he had helped to create, and he re-emerged in the 1935 general election as a Liberal candidate. Robbed of its two most popular leaders and cursed with the adverse publicity it deserved, the shattered Ontario CCF was ignored by an electorate that swept Mitch Hepburn and the Liberals to power in the 1934 provincial election. The greatest electoral strength of the fiery Essex County onion farmer came from those areas where the UFO derived its own support. UFO leaders who had risked their reputations on the CCF experiment clearly stood in advance of the general membership. Knowing Hepburn and his personal weaknesses, Macphail commented only that "Strong governments are not good governments; a large and servile majority makes a government feel independent of the people."[54] It was an accurate prediction of the stormy course in Ontario politics pursued by the hard-drinking gutter-fighter. Despite the dismemberment of the CCF, Agnes Macphail still believed that an Independent could make a difference in the life of the nation. Now she threw herself with even greater intensity into her crusade for prison reform.

Prison Reform:
"The Boss wants to
get Aggie"

"Arise and attack a nation at ease, which lives in confidence," says the Lord, a nation that has neither gates nor bars; its people live alone.

Jeremiah 49:31

Macphail's involvement with the fledgling CCF had not deflected her from other issues with which she had been concerned since she had first entered Parliament. Among the most important of these were conditions in the nation's prisons and the lack of programs for rehabilitation. In the first half of the 1930s she increased her efforts to promote changes. This time her work was almost undone by her trust in a single individual.

One night early in 1929 Agnes Macphail was working late in her sixth-floor parliamentary office as she often did. Her accomplishments had become so singular that people from many walks of life frequently sought her assistance. As she liked to have time alone to complete her work and as the parliamentary corridors were shadowy at night, she had asked the commissionaires not admit people seeking her in the evenings.

A handsome, educated, and well-dressed man managed to evade the restriction that evening. He looked to be in his early forties, just a little older than Macphail. Introducing himself as Charles Baynes, a native of Antigua whose father had died leaving a family of seven children, he told Agnes how he had migrated to Canada when he was eighteen years old. He had begun work in a bank in Toronto and quickly risen to be its manager before moving to Manitoba to establish his own business. During World War One, he had served in France with the Canadian Expeditionary Force and had received a full war veteran's pension.

The object of the visit was to discuss the death of an inmate named Lloyd at Stony Mountain penitentiary in British Columbia where Baynes had completed a prison term. The inquiry into the death had claimed it was an accident in which a derrick crushed its victim, but Baynes believed there were reasons to question the official version. The evidence given by the dead man's wife and family stood at variance with the inquiry's report and so did the condition of the body when it arrived at the undertaker. Unsound scaffolding seemed the more likely cause, one that prison officials did not wish to acknowledge. The warden of the penitentiary, a political appointment whose brother was prominent in Canadian life, was well positioned to hide what had really happened.

Macphail was already familiar with the Lloyd death. His family in Winnipeg, forced onto government relief, had come to the attention of a local service club whose members believed an injustice had been rendered. Some of its members had travelled to Ottawa where they met with Stewart Edwards, the deputy minister of justice, and when he refused to reopen the matter, they had sought out Macphail, who had agreed to explore the death further and question the minister in Parliament if she was satisfied that there were irregularities.[1]

The good manners, cultivated intelligence, and apparent sincerity of Charles Baynes impressed Agnes Macphail. She talked with him at some length because he professed a desire to make amends for past offences by assisting former prisoners in their adjustment to civilian life and by helping veterans battle the bureaucracy to secure pensions owing. Macphail did not bother to ask how such a person ended up in prison because, like criminologists, she found she never got a satisfactory answer. She accepted Baynes for what he appeared to be and worked with him on many individual cases over the next four years. Macphail noticed that her new coworker read extensively and was committed to reform of the country's prison system. Little did Macphail realize that Charles Baynes would one day prove her nemesis.

Early Initiatives

Agnes Macphail had become interested in prison reform during her first term. On the surface, it seemed a strange issue to involve the only woman in Parliament, but her concern grew out of her Progressive beliefs, her peace activism, and her desire to help women and children who faced deprivation when the family's principal wage-earner was removed. The federal prison system was not large — only about twenty-five hundred men and a very small number of women in 1925 — but it continued to be governed by legislation dating from just after Confederation. A royal commission had reported in 1914 on the need for reform, but its report was shelved by the war and not picked up again until a limited inquiry in 1920 that also went nowhere. The contrast between the treatment of male and female prisoners, the construction of a new women's federal penitentiary, and concern for their families led Macphail to concentrate solely on the welfare of male inmates.

Macphail objected to the Canadian penitentiary system because it had failed in its essential purpose: reformation of criminals so that they might lead productive lives after they had served their sentences. She firmly believed that prisons were needed to protect society, but she felt they had degenerated into institutions where the severity of punishment perpetuated a criminal class. Incarceration was used as an act of raw vengeance rather than as an opportunity to transform individuals so that they did not become repeat offenders. These views placed Macphail on common ground with prison reformers like John Howard, Elizabeth Fry, and Dorothea Dix whose efforts stretched back a century and a half, but the essential similarities ended there. These British and American reformers had believed in the power of science to transform humanity, while Macphail drew on the fruits of the emerging disciplines of criminology and psychology to inform her critique. As Macphail sought to drag the Canadian prison system into the twentieth century, she met with mammoth bureaucratic inertia and emotional public resistance.

Macphail's initial efforts at provoking change were modest. Following disturbances at Kingston penitentiary in 1923 and a demonstration the next year when four prisoners had gone on a hunger strike, she introduced a motion into the House of

Commons in 1925 to provide productive labour in federal penitentiaries. Work would impart skills that prisoners could use upon return to civilian life, she maintained; it would transform embittered victims idling away grim years behind bars into patients transformed through positive experience. The money they earned would be used to support their families, and it would aid the transition to normal life by providing them with more than a suit a clothes and ten dollars upon release.

The idea was hardly novel nor as beneficial as the member claimed. Previous investigations of the Canadian penal system and numerous organizations, including the United Farmers of Ontario, had advocated the introduction of work for prisoners because it seemed such an eminently sensible way to save the government money. Yet convict labour evoked the image of chain gangs, and some feared it would displace free workers through unfair competition. Only after extensive investigation did the Trades and Labour Congress of Canada drop its long-standing opposition to convict labour in 1924. Prison-produced goods would not be available on the open market but limited to use by government. Macphail's motion was therefore timely, but it was talked out. She sought more information from Minnesota where some prisons had become self-supporting, and the following year she reintroduced the proposal. It carried unanimously because it pleased the entire ideological spectrum by costing nothing.

Macphail's associations in Parliament fostered her interest in penal reform, especially that with the venerable minister of railways, George P. Graham, who served as honorary president of the Prisoner's Welfare Association in Montreal. A visit to Portsmouth penitentiary in Kingston quickened her desire to assist the unwanted, but an invitation to speak to female prisoners proved to be a seminal experience. Until this point the men behind bars had been like the Cape Bretoners, but when she faced members of her own gender, she realized that she was no different from them except that she had enjoyed better fortune in life.

Macphail did not take up prison reform again in a dedicated way until Charles Baynes entered her life. She detected an injustice that had reduced a family to destitution through no fault of its own, and nothing aroused in her such passion. Her own experiences as a woman and her family's background led her to believe there were three great things in life: "the endeavour toward understanding, the hunger for beauty, the urge for justice, and the greatest of these is justice."[2] Institutions such as prisons, run under the dictatorial rule of untrained officials whose authority could not be challenged, failed to provide either justice or dignity. Penitentiaries, she thought, were "very much like absolute monarchy. In other words, the warden is practically in control of the whole institution."[3] Offences against prison discipline — over seven hundred rules with thousands of interpretations — were tried in a warden's court, which some likened to the infamous Star Chamber in Tudor Britain.

The death at Stony Mountain seemed suspicious, and Macphail sought information from the dead man's relatives. The cover-up she discerned raised larger questions about prison administration and the role of penitentiaries. Macphail began to read widely in criminology and to peruse the reports of prison officials now that they had been brought under the protection of the Civil Service Act. This perspective allowed her in 1929 to expand one unfortunate death into a more penetrating indictment of the prison system. She criticized the lack of educational opportunities for inmates, the absence of training for officials, and the corporal punishment she had abjured as a schoolteacher because it had proven ineffectual. Arguing that inmates needed to be respected as human beings, she proposed medical and psychological assessment upon admission so that individual programs might be devised. She wished to break the strict prison hierarchy by introducing self-government through a board of governors composed of the warden, guards, and the best-behaved prisoners — a preposterous idea to most but one that Elizabeth Fry had advocated. Just as importantly, Macphail proposed that transition to civilian life be assisted by a parole board.

Sympathy with the plight of criminals never wins a politician any votes, but crime makes big money for the media. As prison populations burgeoned during the Depression, newspapers and magazines cultivated their readership with a blitz of sensationalized crime stories about bank robbers and prison escapes. Shoot-outs between gangsters and G-men fed the public's fascination with crime in an era that witnessed the

Lindbergh kidnapping and saw some five thousand people murdered in Chicago. And in the new talkies, Hollywood provided vicarious thrill which further mitigated against serious attention to the problems of prison reform.

Macphail was villified by those who opposed her ideas, and most members of Parliament shared the public attitudes. They were less concerned that prisoners were lashed with the cat-o'-nine-tails than they were with the timing when it was administered. Only a few questioned the customary practice of imposing part of the sentence upon admission to prison and reserving the final whipping until just prior to release.[4] Nor was there widespread doubt about the wisdom of enforcing prison discipline by shackling men to the cell bars with arms stretched high in the air or administering welts to the buttocks with an eighteen-inch leather strap known euphemistically as the paddle. Most Canadians believed in corporal punishment, even if they hid in horror behind Newspeak when it was inflicted on other than children.

Exposing the Rot

The rise in the prison population, the conviction of political prisoners, and the increased frequency of prison riots impelled Macphail to press for a full investigation of the sources of crime and the role of penitentiaries. She was convinced that the proposed reforms had been delayed too long. The number of inmates in Canadian penitentiaries increased 60 per cent between 1923 and 1933. Recidivism swung dramatically upwards. Seventy-three per cent of federal first offenders returned to the penal system, while the proportion reconvicted on a third offence doubled. An upheaval at Stony Mountain in 1932 had resulted in several guards being injured and the death of one convict. Riots followed at St. Vincent de Paul and Dorchester penitentiaries, but the "great riot" at Kingston in October of 1932 created the hottest political potato for the government. As the Conservatives had been challenged for indicting people whose only crime had been to exercise their right of free speech, the shots fired into Tim Buck's cell caused a particular embarrassment.[5] The warden at Kingston was removed and replaced temporarily by a soldier, William B. Megloughlin, who had been awarded the Military Cross for action at the Battle of Passchendaele. Megloughlin quelled the disturbance only by agreeing not to submit the offenders to prison discipline and to permit unprecedented trials in criminal court.

Whether inspired by political prisoners or not, the Kingston riot served to bring Canada's gulag to public attention. Defence lawyers W. F. Nickle of Kingston, a former Ontario attorney-general who had served on the 1920 inquiry into penitentiaries, and Frank Reagan of Toronto made sure that the trial of the some thirty accused became a forum that not even the government could ignore. The revelations were sickening and the public reaction immediate. One poor, broken individual, who was reported in the press to have been subjected to solitary confinement for twenty-three years, could hardly speak loud enough to condemn all humanity.[6] The old question of who guards the guards figured prominently. Systematic personnel training had ceased in 1889, and most guards were ex-military men. Witnesses characterized their keepers as petty tyrants who persecuted inmates and severely censored their correspondence and reading materials only to sell back the portions that they had officiously withheld. Shaved heads served as visible symbols of degradation, but even greater objection was raised to the indiscriminate mixing of laundry and dishes between those who were healthy and those afflicted with various diseases. Prisoners were kept in their cells for inordinately long periods of time on weekends. Silence was required at all times in the presence of other inmates, and the only exercise allowed consisted of parading dumbly for fifteen minutes on workdays. Talking was punished with the leather strap, sometimes soaked in water overnight when guards wanted to settle personal quarrels with inmates they disliked.

Press coverage was so extensive that the published confessions of former inmates found new respectability. The government had little alternative but to respond. General D. M. Ormond was appointed as superintendent of penitentiaries, and guards from Kingston were fired following the testimony of prisoners in open court. When the newspapers raised the imperative of an impartial commission into prison conditions, Macphail placed a motion on the order paper of the House of Commons, proposing as well a complete investigation of the sources of crime in the country. In taking this initiative, she became the centrepiece in a national campaign to drag the penal system out of the nineteenth century. Harry Anderson, the editor of the Toronto *Globe,* emerged as her principal ally outside Parliament, although some other liberally minded newspapers supported her as well.

While the testimony by inmates was sufficient to shake even the complaisant, Charles Baynes was arrested at the Chateau Laurier hotel early in 1933. At his trial, a lawyer provided him with an alibi by testifying that Baynes had been playing bridge with him at the time of the alleged crime. He was released but later rearrested and charged with indecent assault concerning an incident in his room at a boarding house. Macphail believed that the authorities were engaging in a petty vendetta. Baynes assured her that he was innocent, and she was informed by an official with the Canadian Legion that Baynes had been framed after finding irregularities in the administration of soldiers' pensions.

Baynes was convicted nevertheless. When he was sentenced to Kingston penitentiary, he wrote Macphail requesting her assistance in getting transferred to another institution where he could obtain more air and exercise. He suffered, he said, from tuberculosis contracted during the war, and his most recent confinement had led to hemorrhaging. She responded to his request for help, as she had done for many others, by asking her old adversary, Minister of Justice Hugh Guthrie, for a transfer on medical grounds. Conditions at Kingston would worsen his condition and contaminate others. At the same time she requested the file on Baynes from the ministry, but it was never made available.[7] The scent Macphail provided put Hugh Guthrie onto the trail of her relationship with a prisoner whose offences were greater than she knew.

Personal Mortification

When her motion advocating prison reform in Canada finally arrived in the Commons early in 1934, Macphail was still recovering from surgery and feeling unwell. Guthrie courteously had the rules of the House bent so that her motion might reappear on the order paper when she was better. It was an unexpected act of gallantry. Her health restored, she rose from her seat two days later when the Speaker allowed her motion. In a gracious introduction she thanked the minister for his kindness and affirmed that she was not one to request special privilege, but since it had been granted, she said, "there is no group to which it could better be extended than those who are hidden away in a little world of their own, a world that I think is sometimes too hard and too difficult."[8]

Macphail reviewed the reasons that a thorough investigation into the Canadian penal system was needed. She criticized existing conditions as intolerable. Corporal punishment was inhumane, and discipline cases were consigned to cells below ground, a dungeon. She advocated the expansion of parole services and other changes, but the core of her argument rested with the need to prevent recidivism. "While the prisoner must be punished, and must understand and submit to discipline if he is mentally able," she said, "and if he is not he should not be in the institutions I am discussing, yet while people are beginning to see that all that is true, while society must be protected against the offenders punished, unless they come out with a social consciousness, society is really punishing itself rather than punishing the criminal."[9]

In lamenting the lack of attention to preventive health measures in the prisons, Agnes Macphail alluded anonymously to the experience of Charles Baynes at Kingston where, despite his tuberculosis, he was not separated from other inmates. Always attracted to the personal element, she referred to Baynes as "a man with a fine social outlook and very much better than a great many people I know who are not in penitentiary." Her friend Sam Jacobs could not let the moment pass without interrupting her, as he frequently did, to ask if Macphail could provide the names of people she knew who were not in prison, but Macphail returned quickly to her main point.

It was Valentine's Day, but Hugh Guthrie was poised to deliver the very antithesis of a love note. A tall, impressive figure with a commanding style, Guthrie had more than three decades of experience in politics. As a result of a campaign by the Canadian Labour Defence League, he had received petitions from some fifty thousand people advocating the release of Buck and the others, but he affirmed that as he saw "nothing but the names of foreigners, unpronounceable names for the most part," he had referred them to the R.C.M.P. to be recorded.[10] What Guthrie did not say publicly was that he believed weak-kneed sympathizers like Macphail and Wood-sworth, who spearheaded the campaign against Section 98, only abetted the communist/foreigner/criminal conspiracy by stating their case publicly.

Journalists were tipped off in advance that Guthrie was going to get Agnes that day. Always appearing as the gentle-man in bearing and natty attire, the minister of justice wanted to expose Macphail as a frail object whose sympathies had clouded her reason. After acknowledging her positive at-tributes, Guthrie proceeded to read the criminal record of the man Macphail had just commended. Baynes had been con-victed nine times, once for theft and once for forgery, but mostly for sexual offences, including such "a bestial crime which I will not mention in this chamber." In a word, Charles Baynes was a homosexual.

Agnes Macphail was mortified. Homosexuality was not only illegal under the Criminal Code, but also the subject of deep emotional antagonism. "I am the only woman in a House of 245 members," she wrote while trying to find out more information on Baynes after the event, "and it is particularly distasteful to me to be attacked on this sexual matter."[11] The exposé contained the potential to end her career, although true to the code of the male press gallery, most papers related the debate without mentioning the incident. Even her mother ex-pressed her sympathy with her daughter's plight for the first time in her adult life. All seemed in ruin, but Macphail's in-dignation was reserved for Hugh Guthrie. She resented bit-terly his rapier blow masked as an act of kindness.

How was Agnes Macphail to respond? In assessing the possibilities, she did not choose the easy route. Macphail had read about homosexuals, and although she continued to use the term "inversion," which was progressively obsolete after the decade of her birth, she concluded that "our method of dealing with them is cruel and useless." Baynes, whose sexual orientation she had recognized for some time, was "no more to blame for his condition than we are for ours."[12] Instead of engaging in denunciations or attempting to clear herself, Mac-phail confessed her own culpability in a forthright account sent to her constituents and newspapers in Southeast Grey. She acknowledged that she had erred in not checking Baynes' criminal record, although she did not add that she had been denied access. Instead, she related the many joys she had experienced in assisting former inmates and their show of affection once their lives had been righted. "If one is to keep warm-hearted and helpful as life goes on," she concluded stoically, "one is bound to make mistakes. I think it is inevitable and so, when such a time as this comes, one must be willing to pay the price in suffering."

Retaliation

Agnes Macphail confronted her compromised position squarely, licked her wounds, and returned to the fray spirited by her contempt for a man she despised. Often so singleminded that she forgot little things like birthdays, she devoted herself completely to prison reform from 1934 to 1936. The government moved to repeal some of the pettiest and most vexing regulations governing prison life, but the major issues remained unresolved.[13] Retarded inmates, with mental ages as low as eight, still fell prey to hardened criminals, and the more than three hundred young offenders aged sixteen to twenty-one were not separated from the general prison population, although England had practised such segregation for more than three decades. The warden at Kingston revealed that one man had been kept in solitary confinement for nearly two years. "It would have been more humane to stand him up against a wall and shoot him," Macphail replied in Parliament with the same indignation that Elizabeth Fry had shown.[14] The government continued to promise more than it delivered and to place the glossiest light on the most meagre action. Wages were introduced for work in the prisons, but the minister of justice kept silent about the fact that they were five cents a day minus deductions for luxuries.

"Privileges are now granted to the prisoners — some people say we grant too many privileges," Hugh Guthrie maintained during one debate, "which in former days they never dreamed of. We allowed what they demanded in the riot of 1932, cigarette papers, and we now give them an allowance of two ounces of tobacco a week which seems to satisfy them. We now give them pay."

Agnes Macphail could take no more. "Do they pay for that tobacco out of their five cents a day?" she interjected.
"They pay for that out of their wages," Guthrie replied. "We pay them now; we did not do so previously."[15]

Macphail took no pride in such displays for they only revealed that her efforts had again been in vain. No attention had been given to the kind of work provided, and the rate of remuneration was so pitiful that it caused greater resentment among inmates. Thirty cents a week minus deductions provided no support for an inmate's family.

Prisoners at Kingston responded with a demonstration early in 1934, but the two sides on the issue easily interpreted such events from totally different perspectives. Guthrie reacted by changing personnel at Kingston again and rescinding privileges.[16] A fire was started at the penitentiary later in the year, and a demonstration was held at Stony Mountain. Macphail and others hammered away in the Commons, but opportunities were limited and the effects mimimal. Agnes Macphail was also sometimes as badly served by her allies within Parliament as by her opponents. General Alexander Ross, the Conservative M.P. for Kingston, appeared in the press as an essential part of the opposition on the issue. He willingly tackled the government's actions regarding prisons, but Tory insiders knew that he was piqued by having been excluded from the cabinet. Yet Ross did confirm how vindictive the ministry of justice was in seeking to discredit its critics. His house was put under surveillance, and he heard that some of his informants were dismissed from the penitentiary service.[17]

Early in 1935 Macphail learned that an attempt had also been made to put the screws to her in the previous year. Inspector J. D. Dawson of the penitentiary service in Ottawa had first kept tabs on her movements and then arrived in Kingston in April of 1934 with a view to squeezing her apparent prison mole. "The boss wants to get Aggie" was the rumour circulating among the guards.[18] The inspector intended to get a confession from Charles Baynes that could be used against Macphail.

At Kingston, Dawson had Baynes called in. First he tried to cajole the inmate into signing a statement that he had supplied Macphail information concerning the death at Stony Mountain penitentiary, and when that failed, he turned to threats and ultimately had him banished to a punishment cell. Next he called in another inmate known to Baynes named Alfred G. Hall. During an interview that grew more tumultuous as it extended in time, Dawson asserted that "Agnes made a — fool of herself in the House of Commons, but when we are finished with her she will never be able to lift up her head in the House again."[19] In a foul mood at achieving so little, Dawson went to have tea with Warden Megloughlin where he confessed that he had lost his temper and behaved foolishly. As a further indication of the pressure put on Baynes, he informed the warden that he intended to report to Ottawa that Baynes had never been tubercular.

These secrets remained safely locked behind Kingston's walls where prisoners were not allowed to read *Hansard*. Finally Baynes managed to get a heavily censored and partially coded letter to his brother, a civil servant who had recently been acting governor of the Leeward Islands. The brother contacted Macphail, and she determined to visit the penitentiary at the beginning of 1935. There she had herself locked in a punishment cell. "They might as well be dungeons," she told the press. "There was no light but that which came through three small holes about the size of a fifty-cent piece in the thick wooden door." She challenged the right of the state "to deprive any living soul of light and air."[20]

When she met with Charles Baynes, Macphail was told about the official attempts to collect information to her detriment, but the matter was not pursued since Alfred Hall was about to be released. When Macphail next went to speak in Toronto, Hall found her and related what had happened. A government official had impugned the reputation of a member of Parliament, but, more importantly, Dawson's actions provided a pretext for Macphail to keep the larger issue of prison reform alive.

The Daly Inquiry

Macphail was too much a realist not to understand fully the perilous course she was about to embark upon. She had found that Baynes had been less than forthright with her, and William Megoughlin, while still warden at Kingston, had shown that Baynes had amassed aspirins to induce fever and bleeding. She had Hall swear a signed affidavit attesting to his allegations.

Alfred Hall was a fantastic character, the consumate con artist. A presentable, slim man whose formal clothes conveyed the air he wished to impart, Hall generally styled himself as the "Reverend Doctor" because he found that religion provided the easiest ruse by which to separate people from their money. Other times he appeared as a psychologist, frequently with two male secretaries wearing striped pants who warmed up the audience prior his lecture. He had any number of tricks in his bag, including phoney schools he established throughout the Commonwealth as part of his international operations. When Hall attempted to create the National Order of Canada, he rented the ballroom of the Royal York Hotel in Toronto, but he was unable to pay the bill and ended up back in prison.

Despite the lack of credibility of her witnesses other than ex-Warden Megloughlin, Macphail had a case that served her larger purposes. The atmosphere in the Commons was tense on 20 March 1935 when Macphail rose to repond to Guthrie's defence of Dawson. Conservatives tried to shout her down with cries of "Order, Order" while the minister of justice slumped silently into his chair. CCF and Liberal members rallied to her support. Macphail turned her address towards the fundamental rights of an M.P. and argued that the matter "reflects not alone on myself. It reflects on the honour of every member of the House." As she read Hall's affidavit, one man shouted that "She knows all the convicts." "Shame," bellowed back Ernest Lapointe, the former minister of justice.

After again making her case for a larger inquiry, Macphail sat down, but Lapointe urged her on. "Why not continue?" he said, "It is all right. Go ahead."[21] So encouraged she did continue, but she did not win the day, bringing only a few Conservative members over to her side.

When the subject came up again two weeks later, following yet another fire in what was called "the Kingston inferno," Guthrie paraded Superintendent Ormond onto the floor of the Commons where the general assumed a seat in front of the minister. The debate lasted through the afternoon and into the evening with Guthrie's own supporters attacking him.

Eventually he relented and agreed to appoint a commissioner to investigate the charges against Inspector Dawson, but Hugh Guthrie was too smart to play into Macphail's hands as she had fallen into his. He appointed a county court judge to head the inquiry, but he carefully limited its terms of reference to include only the allegations of Alfred Hall, and he firmly refused to pay the costs of Macphail's counsel.[22]

For advice, Macphail turned to Gerald Beaudoin, whose law partnership had represented Hall. Beaudoin suggested that a noted Toronto criminal lawyer, J. C. McRuer, be brought in to serve as junior counsel. McRuer was a Liberal sympathetic to reform causes and he admired Macphail, so he accepted the case. Moreover, since he was standing as a candidate in High Park in the forthcoming federal election, additional publicity would not hurt. Going through records maintained by the ministry of justice in preparation for the trial, McRuer became convinced that the penitentiary system was full of intrigue and spite. The file on Macphail contained all the editorials against her but none in her favour.[23]

Tensions frequently ran high during the hearings in Ottawa and Kingston when McRuer clashed with government counsel, Richard Greer, a well-known Conservative. At one point, Greer drew the attention of the presiding judge to the level of McRuer's voice. "Is there any rule governing the tone of voice to be used?" McRuer retorted. "Can't I roar if I want to?"[24]

On the witness stand, Macphail made her case for government payment of her legal fees. Citing precedents from 1926, she argued that to do otherwise was to put the whole weight of a government department against the meagre resources of an individual member of Parliament. Defence counsel replied insultingly: "It is seldom that women are not able to ask any necessary questions," said Richard Greer, "to which they desire answers."[25] Even courts of justice provided no barrier against male prejudice.

The testimony of ex-Warden Megloughlin heartened Macphail, even if Judge Daly emphasized that the ex-soldier held that position no longer. She admired Megloughlin for his efforts to change a seemingly immovable institution and provided him with a photograph on which she wrote: "To Colonel Megloughlin who, if allowed, would make a prison what it ought to be — a defence for society and a hope for broken men. Agnes Macphail."[26]

Throughout the inquiry Agnes Macphail remained light-hearted despite the negative publicity generated by the opposition press in Grey County. When she greeted the tall McRuer and the diminutive Beaudoin for a walk before breakfast to review events, she began by saying, "Well, what's the long and the short of it this morning."[27] The testimony of the Roman Catholic chaplain at Kingston also buttressed her case against Dawson. The inspector, W. T. Kingsley said, was "full of conceit, self-opinionated, and believed that experience wasn't necessary in the conduct of a penitentiary."[28]

As she awaited the verdict, Agnes Macphail was invited to speak to the National Council of Women of Canada. Acknowledged as the spearhead for prison reform, Macphail had developed important allies and received encouragement from many women. Nellie McClung, for one, wrote to commend her campaign. "Surely we are sufficiently civilized now," McClung concluded, "not to want to make people suffer for 'the good of society.'"[29] Macphail therefore chose to portray herself as a lamb that might have been saved from slaughter by more women being involved in politics. "If there had been a group of fifty women in the House of Commons," she queried, "would the inquiry now taking place have been necessary?"[30] A chorus of "No's" arose from the audience, but the results of the 1935 election belied the response.

Unable to get the government to cover her legal expenses, Macphail could only pay through instalments. J. C. McRuer waived his fees and told her to pay Beaudoin, who kept his charges to a minimum. Macphail returned the favour by campaigning for McRuer in High Park.

The 1935 Federal Election and the Royal Commission

In her own riding, Agnes had a new, young campaign manager in 1935. She changed her local strategy and held two all-women meetings after her opponents attempted to pitch to the electorate in this way. She also brought in *Globe* editor Harry Anderson to speak on her behalf. Macphail was vulnerable as a result of her slim margin in 1930, the Daly inquiry, redistribution of her riding into Grey-Bruce, and confusion in the political situation. The Reconstruction party created by breakaway Conservative H. H. Stevens combined anti-big business sentiment with an appeal to the small entrepreneur in a way that attracted many farmers. It was erroneously reported that Macphail intended to stand under the new banner, but she again ran as a Farmer-Labour candidate. This time she had two opponents, both doctors, because the Liberals, sensing a kill, also fielded a candidate.

Macphail chose as her issues the need to avoid Canadian entanglement in the war that loomed, progressive income taxation, currency reform, and a national health plan emphasizing the eradication of disease. Attacked personally, she replied in kind. When her Liberal opponent maintained that she did nothing in Parliament, she responded by pointing to a three-foot stack of Commons debates on the table. "Dr. Hall, I am told, said to an audience in Chesley that I had received funds from the Liberal party," Macphail informed one gathering. "I would like to throw that back in his teeth too. To say the least, I don't think that Dr. Hall should use such tactics."[31]

L. G. Campbell ran against Macphail for a third time. When it was his turn to speak at the meeting and he referred to the sitting member's evident dislike for the absent Liberal candidate, Macphail muttered from the back of the hall loud enough for everyone to hear: "I'll say I don't." Campbell tried to continue by saying, "Do you know..." when someone from the throng shouted, "We know better."

The increased plurality that Macphail received in 1935 proved the old adage that any publicity is better than none at all. Nationally, the Liberals were greeted with such an embarrassment of riches that Mackenzie King was forced to stop communing with the spirits in order to get to know a greatly expanded caucus. Macphail took delight in informing her electors of a story that saw the prime minister chatting in the corridors of Parliament with some rookie M.P.s and asking their names at the close of the conversation. "And would you mind telling me who you are?" one of the novices replied.[32]

Shortly after re-entering the justice portfolio, Ernest Lapointe appointed the royal commission into prison conditions that Macphail had worked so hard to obtain. Several months later an armed robbery in Sarnia led by Red Ryan, in which two men were killed, one of them a police officer, almost scuppered the inquiry in the public's opinion. Ryan was the country's most infamous criminal, as close as Canada could come to Al Capone. He had shot up banks, broken out of jails, and then served twelve years at Kingston where he had ostensibly reformed and was accorded special treatment before being released on parole. The ever obstreperous Mitch Hepburn publicly accused R. B. Bennett, Agnes Macphail, and a senator with being responsible for Ryan's freedom to maraud.

Venom was spewed on Macphail in one letter where she was addressed as "you wretched woman." In order to protect herself, she made public a statement she secured from the ministry of justice saying she had no involvement with the Ryan case. The tempest only subsided when Ryan died from wounds inflicted during his arrest. In this context the report of the Daly commission proved totally anti-climatic when it was released the following month. Strictly adhering to his terms of reference, Judge Daly had reduced the case to one that pitted the credibility of an official against that of a professional confidence man. Macphail and her team considered the whole proceedings a complete government whitewash.

The royal commission into the Canadian penal system, headed by Mr. Justice Joseph Archambault of the Quebec Superior Court, experienced start-up problems after one of its three members, Harry Anderson, died suddenly. When J. C. McRuer replaced him, it got underway in October of 1936. During the year and half before its report was published in 1938, the commission exposed conditions in Canada's prisons worse than any of those revealed in the preceding years. When convict after convict filed before the inquiry to complain about Inspector Dawson's boss, General Ormond, R. B. Bennett addressed the subject in Parliament and glanced at Macphail. "Are they in my direction?" she shouted in reply. "My right honourable friend always looks this way for the convicts."[33]

The Archambault report created an impressive blueprint for the reform of the country's penitentiaries and its chief inspiration was presented with a copy bearing the inscription: "To Agnes Macphail, M.P, courageous pioneer and untiring worker on behalf of prison reform in Canada. Joseph Archambault."[34] The appearance of the report saw an immediate housecleaning of officials like General Ormond, but war again interfered with implementation. A new penitentiary act passed Parliament in 1939, but it was not proclaimed. Macphail kept the problem before the public's attention until parts were put into effect in 1945.[35] The inmates of the country's prisons, whom she had done so much to help on an individual and collective basis, continued to admire her arduous campaign for decades afterwards, but Agnes Macphail turned her attention to the problems that were leading the world to war.

Henrietta and Dougald
Macphail with Agnes, 1890.

Agnes Macphail (left) and
her sister Gertha, 1890's.

Dougald Macphail auctioneering.

Agnes Macphail and a friend at the Stratford teacher's college, 1909-1910.

EIGHT HOURS A DAY
ON THE FARM

MISS GOTROX HELPS IN
THE UNIVERSAL UNREST

DRAWN BY VIOLET KEENE —

A contemporary view of the farm woman's life in 1920.

Agnes goes to Ottawa, 1920.

"Fighting Aggie" Macphail

First and only woman member of parliament. Fiery co-leader of a new political party, the Co-operative Commonwealth Federation. The woman who has been variously hailed as a radical, an impractical dreamer, and the saviour of her country.

Who is this woman?

Gregory Clark, clever wit-snapper, in more serious mood, gives a clear-cut, brilliant interview with the Scotch-Canadian daughter of the farm, whose loyalty to her ain folk brought her under the floodlights.

MISS AGNES MACPHAIL, M.P., A LEADER IN THE C.C.F.

This revealing life sketch of one of Canada's greatest women is one of many entertaining features in this week's issue of the

Star Weekly

Sketch in 1932 of Agnes Macphail by Grant Macdonald at the time she led Ontario into the C.C.F..

Robert Gardener, president of the United Farmers of Alberta, Macphail's intimate friend (1932).

Mr. Robb—"There'll be no back-seat driving while I'm at the wheel."

Agnes Macphail and the Conservative leader of the Opposition, opposing the Liberal tariff of Finance Minister Robb in 1928.

Agnes Macphail at the League of Nations, Geneva, 1929.

First national convention of the C.C.F., 1933. Macphail is
seated seventh from the right in the front row.

Agnes Macphail following her fifth election in 1935 with
supporters Mrs. E. C. Murray and Mrs. Fred McTavish beside
her, and mother Henrietta in foreground.

"Agnes," Premier Bennett said, with an eff ulgent smile. "You are an angel of peace."

Caricature of R.B. Bennett, prime minister 1930-1935.

Agnes Macphail when she was a member of the Ontario legislature, 1943-5, 1948-51.

Edward Joliffe, first leader of the Ontario C.C.F., and Agnes
Macphail in the Ontario legislature, 1940's.

8

A Rare Vintage:
The Drift towards War
and Defeat

*The fields of Heshbon wither, the vines of Sibmah also. The
rulers of the nations have trampled down the choicest vines
which once reached Jazer and spread toward the desert.*

Isaiah 16:8

A mature Agnes Macphail reflected with amusement on the
sombre opening of Parliament two weeks after the death of
George V. The frequently tumultuous political battles of the
last decade and a half had moderated her ardour without
blurring her critical eye. She objected that the extreme formality of the occasion had kept some people away who could not
afford to dress to standard, but she chuckled at the contrast
presented between the black gowns of the women, called
"court mourning" by the press, with the colourful attire of the
men. "If black was mourning for women," she asked her constituents, "why was scarlet and ermine mourning for the
judges of the Supreme Court? Why, too, was the gold en-
crusted Windsor uniform of the Prime Minister an adequate
expression of the grief of the first citizen? It was said that
judges had 'weeping cuffs,' and I dare say they had, but from
my position at the bar of the Senate I could not see them."[1]
Such jocularity contrasted darkly with the cloud of war that
drifted over the world in the years leading to World War Two
and Macphail's defeat in the federal election of 1940. By the
end of Macphail's last term in Parliament the international
situation superseded all other concerns as the Depression had
in preceding years. In the intervening years, however, she

continued to promote improvements for farmers through cooperative and lobby groups and economic independence and personal fulfilment for women.

Mackenzie King had returned to office in a Liberal landslide in 1935. R. B. Bennett remained at the head of the Conservatives until 1938, but he then left political life to retire in England. Macphail could not find two personalities who contrasted so dramatically. She loved the way in which Bennett, whatever his politics, willingly displayed the full range of human emotion as much as she despised the loathsome way in which King could not let any social occasion pass without reminding her that he, too, was a radical at heart. Macphail invented a story to show the difference between Bennett and "the fat man full of words," as she referred to King. When R. B. Bennett had looked out of his office window and observed some unemployed people, he ordered the R.C.M.P. to remove them. Mackenzie King would never have done that, Macphail maintained, he would have just pulled down the blind.[2]

In 1936 Agnes Macphail had a chance to see socialism and communism in action when she visited Scandinavia and the Soviet Union with a group headed by McGill University sociologist Leonard Marsh. The opportunities for new experiences provided the type of vacation she thoroughly enjoyed. In the Soviet Union she visited a mother and child clinic, an electrical parts factory, and a collective farm, but apart from the cleanliness of the streets and the availability of birth control information, she was unimpressed with the results of communism after two decades. "I would not like to live there," she concluded. "There are no smiling people, no gaiety, no whistling in the streets. If the people have any liberty, there is no sign of it apparent." In marked contrast to British socialists Sydney and Beatrice Webb who visited Russia at the same time and panegyrized Soviet communism, Macphail was not duped. "While the people are dirty, the men unshaven, the food unappetizing and the bed bugs prolific," she wrote upon her return, "the thing I disliked most about Russia is its dictatorship."[3]

Denmark and Sweden were entirely different. For some time the Ontario farm community had been interested the rural renewal underway in Scandinavia, especially in adult education, but Macphail found that folk (volk) schools for adults in Denmark provided the basis on which their cooperatives had expanded. She also lauded the policies of the social democratic government elected in Sweden in 1932, the beginning of the love affair between the Canadian left and that remote country that few in Canada knew or cared about. Macphail believed that Denmark and Sweden had managed a middle course responding much more successfully to the Depression than had Canada.[4]

Cooperation and Social Policy

Her visit confirmed her longstanding support for existing cooperatives in Ontario, and she encouraged the beleaguered farm movement to promote their expansion once the wider program of the CCF had been rejected. Cooperation emerged as the chief means of achieving greater economic democracy while avoiding excessive nationalization of industry. People organizing for their own economic benefit became the watchword of the United Farmers. "The future is for cooperation, just as the past has been for competition, because cooperation does redistribute back the profits made in proportion to the business done by the individual," Agnes Macphail noted.[5] She was convinced that if the money used to build the country's great industrial concerns had been channelled into cooperatives, people would have created economic structures as strong as themselves. Cooperatives buttressed democracy by allowing all to share in the responsibility for their own affairs. "Democracy will never be strengthened by retaining economic power in the hands of small groups," she maintained. "Without economic power so diffused throughout the whole population, political democracy will not long continue."[6]

Macphail's belief in the power of economic democracy derived from her family background. Her father had invested in the Osprey and Artemesia Cooperative in Flesherton and her brother-in-law, Hugh Bailey, was instrumental in founding the Dundalk Farmer's Cooperative. One of her young supporters from Grey County, R. Alex Sim, helped to organize the Student's Cooperative Residence at the University of Toronto in 1937. Macphail knew from personal experience how difficult it was to launch cooperative enterprises. There were six in her riding, and she sat on the boards of two. When the First

Cooperative Packers at Barrie experienced difficulties, she accepted a position on their board to assist them. Although she also invested in the Durham Farmer's Cooperative, she came to believe that there would be no great expansion in this area without the type of adult education promoted by Maurice Cody and the Antigonish movement through their study groups, the Canadian equivalent of the Danish folk schools. She continued to advocate that the Ontario Agricultural College spearhead such a movement as St. Francis Xavier University did in Nova Scotia but to little avail.[7] When the United Farmers joined with adult educators to create C.B.C. Farm Radio Forum in 1940, one of the most successful and innovative concepts in adult education, Agnes Macphail served on its planning committee.[8]

Anticipating the "think globally, act locally" slogan of a succeeding era concerned with the earth's ecology, Agnes Macphail always aimed at being at the centre while she promoted activities on the periphery. As vice-president of the Cooperative Union of Canada in 1931, she participated in a school held in Woodstock to promote cooperatives among young Ontario farmers. With W. C. Good, she helped plan a reorganization of the United Farmer Cooperative Company that was intended to make it more democratic. She believed that the Coop had become more interested in dividends than in promoting the principles of the movement. The debate over restructuring was especially bitter at the 1932 annual meeting where the opposition to change was led by J. G. Whitmore, a member of the board of directors from Woodbridge, and Gordon Waldron, the company's lawyer. Macphail became indignant at the personal abuse poured on Good and criticized Whitemore from the floor.

> *"Miss Macphail bought five carloads of binder twine," Whitmore flashed back.*
> *"I did not," Agnes retorted.*
> *"Five cars went up to your district," Whitmore continued.*
> *"Well you listen to me and keep your dirty hands and your dirty tongue off my name," Macphail vituperated.*
> *"Coops in southeast Grey bought binder twine."*
> *"I apologize to Miss Macphail," Whitmore finally conceded.*

"It is about time you apologized to somebody," Macphail said as she claimed the last word.[9]

While the reorganization carried, implementation was delayed by the the dire financial conditions created by the Depression. In 1935 H. H. Hannam encouraged Macphail and Good to run for the board of directors in order to champion the ideals he shared with them. When this reform slate was successful and Whitmore lost, Macphail served as a bridge to a new generation of farm leaders. When the time arrived to replace the ailing J. J. Morrison as secretary-treasurer, she and Good proposed Hannam. Macphail also saw that money was devoted to educational initiatives and worked closely with people like Ralph Staples, later president of the Cooperative Union of Canada. In 1941 she sponsored the hiring of Leonard Harman, later prominent in the United Cooperatives of Ontario, for work among rural youth.[10] After serving on the board for a decade, Macphail departed when her brother-in-law was appointed general manager.

While cooperatives allowed ordinary citizens to improve their lot, Macphail advocated greater government support for disadvantaged groups as well as nationalization of sectors such as the insurance industry. She argued that Canada's treatment of the blind, the physically disabled, and seniors was niggardly in comparison to other countries. Greater opportunities for youth needed to be provided by allowing people to retire at the age of sixty with pensions at fifty dollars a month, far above what would be obtained for more than a decade afterwards. She promoted the establishment of county health units, opposed withdrawing pensions from veterans if they secured government employment, and proposed pensions for the wives of veterans who spent their lives giving personal nursing. Macphail continued to insist that priorities were wrong and that money for such programs be found by reducing defence expenditures and imposing higher taxes on wealthy businessmen who had sought shelter with their millions in such havens as the Bahamas and Bermuda. Many agreed with the stand. We "admire you for your fearless attitude," wrote a woman from Manitoba, "your defence of the common people — and for the fact that you are a woman and have the fortitude to speak for us. Behind you I know you have a vast body of Canadian women, who while they make no demonstration of the fact, support you silently, but with sympathy, and a great hope for the future."[11]

With constitutional excuses for government's failure to act Macphail was always impatient: "I cannot believe that we are supposed always to be bound by the fathers of confederation. They had very excellent brains, and they used them in their day and generation; I have no doubt they thought we would do the same. I feel that if they were to come back today they would be thoroughly ashamed of us. I cannot have any respect for anyone who is still relying solely on his grandfather's brains."[12] Still, Macphail was glad when the Liberals extended pensions to the blind in 1937, although it was only twenty dollars a month for those over forty years of age. Canadians, she concluded, "fill the back seat always — a poor conservative people afraid almost of our own shadows, showing great lack of confidence and always afraid of being misunderstood."[13]

Agnes Macphail defended labour unions because she was aware of their importance in improving the health and welfare of workers. When Ontario's Mitch Hepburn's special police roughhandled strikers attempting to organize through the American Congress of Industrial Organizations at Oshawa in 1937, Agnes Macphail retorted that "Labour will organize and a little tinpot like Hepburn will not stop it."[14] The influence of American head offices on Canadian companies concerned her more, especially when they dictated the decisions of food processors like Swift Canadian, but she could not but help see the contradiction in Hepburn's denunciation of American unions while General Motors was itself American-owned. Noting the presence of American multinational corporations, she added, "such is foreign control of industry, but the workers must have no foreign control."[15]

Women and the Industrial Transformation

Macphail came to believe that the transformation of life created by the increased productive capacity of industry required a new social and political outlook, especially for women. Tired adages such as "If a man works not neither shall he eat" needed to be reassessed in the light of women's roles and the supports being developed through relief, old age pensions, mothers' allowances, and worker's compensation. Mackenzie King reacted incredulously when Woodsworth and Macphail argued for the right of all Canadians to basic food, shelter, and clothing. During a momentary fit of pique, the prime minister condemned them as "developing from sincere radicals into clap-trap politicians of the cheapest variety."[16]

Macphail argued that industrialization had altered home life so that there was less for women to do. Most no longer dipped their own candles, made soap, baked bread, created fabrics, or churned butter. The expansion of hospitals increasingly removed the sick from home care while schools had assumed the primary responsibility for formal education. Although she acknowledged that most women felt the urge to motherhood, Macphail also noted that the desire to to serve through work outside the home had increased. Women selecting this option faced major vexations, especially the lack of equal pay for work of equal value, a situation that served to depress general wage levels. She opposed women's minimum wage laws as a barrier to equality and argued that strong unions were a better answer to the problem of low wages. That daughters were still the ones expected to care for aged parents while property was more frequently willed to sons disturbed her. Full freedom would not arrive, Macphail contended, until there was economic independence for everyone and no person possessed property rights over another.

Throughout the 1930s Agnes Macphail strove to assert the significance of work in women's lives and its value to the country as a whole. In contrast to others like Charlotte Whitton, the former director of the Canadian Council on Child Welfare, Macphail did not simply defend the importance of the paid work of the single woman; she considered housewives and farm women to be the hardest workers. Macphail perceived that the lessening of domestic duties would make creative labour outside the home increasingly necessary. She advocated meaningful volunteer involvement that went beyond traditional social functions and earnest resolutions, or a return to the paid workforce when appropriate. Only in this way, Macphail thought, might women return to the central position in life that they had lost during industrialization. "That is why I have always maintained women's right to work — whether single or married," Macphail said in 1939. "To be spiritually happy, women as well as men, must work, must feel their reponsibility."

Like her other thought, Macphail's views on women revealed her as essentially a social democrat or a left-wing liberal. At heart she was always interested in the individual finding personal fulfilment as she had found her own. While she understood the necessity of curbing individual rights in limited instances, Macphail fought to destroy stereotypes that confined women.

Parliament and Women

In Parliament the battle for the acknowledgment of the needs of women was constant. When R. B. Bennett rose to address the "gentlemen" of the House, Macphail quickly interjected, "Not gentlemen only." A young Tommy Douglas fresh from the Saskatchewan CCF raised her ire by speaking only about the economic problems of male youth. "What about the women?" Macphail asked. Douglas responded by altering his remarks, but Macphail remained dissatisfied with this cursory treatment. When it was her turn to speak, she began by saying that "I would like to see Canada composed entirely of young men, and see how they would get on."[17]

The Depression brought various attempts by individuals like Quebec politician Camillien Houde to get women to return to the home in order to release jobs to men. Macphail challenged this assault head on. She argued that there was no economic benefit from such a proposal since one wage-earner simply displaced another at a time when the general level of consumption needed to be increased. "To propose that women be regimented into one groove," she continued, "no matter how widely varied their ambitions and talents, herded back into the home for economic reasons, without a thought of their individual spiritual destinies, betrayed such a superficiality of thought that it simply staggers one."[18] Yet Macphail was always more interested in assisting women than in participating in the war of the sexes. "If both men and women thought clearly," she said during an international radio broadcast in 1937 in which she participated with British M.P. Nancy Astor and U.S. Congresswoman Caroline O'Day, "it would be obvious that the work of the world is neither men's nor women's, but the work of both, each individual performing that part which he or she is best qualified to do."[19]

As a younger woman, Agnes Macphail was reputed to have preferred the company of men, but in mid-life her female friendships were as warm and close as her relations with her extended clan. Together they shared the problem of marital separation, educational upgrading, and re-entry into the workforce that became increasingly common as the century advanced. Through it all Macphail proved the same steadying keel that she had been to the families of her schoolchildren and to her neighbours. "You are like good wine and scarce — and almost certainly of the rare vintage," one of her friends wrote.[20] The depth of affection expressed in such personal correspondence conveys the impression of a deeply compassionate person whom outsiders judged by her flamboyant exterior.

Macphail's stature in public life had reached its pinnacle. Despite her unconventionality, she had become the pre-eminent voice for women's concerns in Canada. Her views still contrasted radically with the accepted norms of her era, but new audiences were always eager to consider her views. Asked to address such established groups as the National Council of Women of Canada in 1936, she acknowledged the thanks of their representative by writing: "I do appreciate your letter. It encourages and helps me to know that a woman like yourself is following what I do and thinks that I have not done too bad a job. I have been, and still am, most anxious to make the way for the women who come after me in public life — and may they come soon and in quantity!"[21]

With the advent of the CCF, more women had stood for election in 1935 than at any previous time, but only Macphail and Louise Black were successful. Macphail had known Black since her arrival in Ottawa in 1922 because her husband had represented the Yukon for the Conservative party. Now that George Black's health was uncertain, his wife ran to keep his seat warm for him even though she did not much like the job that Macphail relished. Nearly seventy years of age, Louise Black belonged to another generation and a different world. In Parliament she commended the cadet training that Macphail had opposed for so many years. She enjoyed being taken to dinner by representatives of the Household Finance Corporation seeking renewal of their charter while Macphail denounced their exorbitant interest charges. "For the life of me," Macphail stated in opposing the legislation, "I cannot understand how people who cannot pay their debts can pay them plus twenty-seven percent per annum." When Macphail advocated credit unions and lamented the unsubtle persuasion of lobbies, Tommy Douglas could not avoid a return swipe. The member for Grey-Bruce, he said, had offered to take him out for a meal. "Very delightful bribery," he told an amused House.[22]

Black and Macphail liked each other personally, but they were separated by more than a gulf in age and political outlook. Macphail felt that the kindly grandmother was not a worthy representative of women because she was insufficiently devoted to her job; Black considered Macphail too unconcerned about her womanly role. Before the Royal Visit in 1939, Black encouraged Macphail to go to Montreal on Saturday to get a new dress. When the weekend arrived and Macphail appeared in the Commons, Louise Black shouted at Agnes across J. S. Woodsworth who sat between them: "Why didn't you go to get your dress?" Macphail replied that the National Defence estimates were to be considered that day, she had a newspaper article to write, and a meeting with her friend, George Graham. "You take yourself too seriously," Black admonished.[23]

The token presence of women in Canadian government stood in marked contrast to the small but significant flood rolling into the positions in the U.S. public service created during Roosevelt's New Deal era.[24] Only four sat in Parliament. In the Senate, Cairine Wilson represented the Liberal party and Iva Fallis the Conservatives, but they joined with Macphail and Black regularly to share their mutual concerns about such problems as social security, laws regulating the family, and Canada's intransigence in regard to European refugees. Macphail concurred with Wilson's views that Canada needed to do more to assist the displaced in Europe, especially Jews forced to flee the anti-semitism of Hitler's Germany, but in other regards they were separated by an unbreachable chasm.

It is tempting to portray Canada's first woman senator as a foil for Agnes Macphail. Cairine Wilson had inherited an immense fortune from her father, a Montreal business tycoon and himself a Liberal senator. Wilson was devoted to the Liberal party and intimately involved with organizing its women at the national level. Early in life she had married a man in the lumber business who was later an M.P. Their marriage had produced eight children, raised by servants in the three houses the family owned. Photographed in formal evening gowns adorned with exquisite jewelry, Cairine Wilson appeared the epitome of high society in dress as well as ideas. She believed that girls wanted to be mothers because that was the role for which they were best suited. Women were superior to men in some ways, Wilson maintained, but inferior in their creative ability. Given to prattling in a monotone, Cairine Wilson also mouthed religious platitudes that found ready acceptance among the aspiring Canadian middle class.[25]

While the differences between the plutocrat's daughter and the offspring of a poor farmer could not have been greater, to set Macphail's originality in bold relief by such an invidious contrast alone would be wrong. Cairine Wilson was modest about her talents and about her appointment as the country's first woman senator when many thought that Alberta Conservative Emily Murphy, who had led the movement to secure women's right of appointment to the upper chamber, would had been a more appropriate choice. She was forthright in admitting that she had languished intellectually following the birth of her children. Macphail and Wilson shared common interests in attempting to liberalize divorce laws, extend health insurance, reduce infant and maternal mortality, improve women's working conditions, and better education. Both were strong supporters of the League of Nations Society in Canada where Macphail served on the executive in 1934, but while the M.P. found the organization too elitist, the senator became its president. Cairine Wilson also condemned the international arms trade as strongly as Macphail. She devoted herself tirelessly to the problem of displaced persons and assisted many individuals through the Canadian National Committee on Refuges but ultimately failed to alter Canadian immigration policies. In contrast to many male politicians, she became increasingly radical towards the end of her political career and criticized morality laws created by a patriarchal society to subject women.[26]

Agnes Macphail's views corresponded more fully with those of Thérèse Casgrain, a woman born into privilege like Cairine Wilson but one who understood life's inequities and devoted herself to achieving women's suffrage in Quebec. Although her husband Pierre was Speaker of the House from 1926 to 1940, Macphail and Thérèse Cagrain were close personal friends who enjoyed each other's company and discussed social problems together. Macphail kept a photograph of Casgrain on her desk and greatly admired her zest for life. "I hope that you will keep that enthusiasm through all the difficulties of life," she counselled the younger woman.[27] At the time of the Royal Visit Macphail joined the Casgrains and Paul Martin and his wife to parade from Parliament to see King George VI and Queen Elizabeth open the new Supreme Court building. Pierre Casgrain marched out in front pompously, as befit the Speaker, with the rest toddling behind as the crowd lining the route taunted, "Poor marching, pick it up there." On the side where Thérèse Casgrain walked, people commented, "Isn't she sweet?" to which Macphail answered admiringly, "She is."[28] After World War Two, Casgrain headed the CCF in Quebec.

Nora Frances Henderson, a youthful and high-spirited city controller in Hamilton, was another of Macphail's friends. Born in England, Henderson was elected as a Hamilton city councillor in 1931, managed municipal relief, headed the board of health for two years, and wrote a column in one of Hamilton's newspapers. Henderson found Macphail a source of inspiration for her own ambitions and those of other women. Their friendship began in 1929, and each summer Henderson spent a week with Macphail in Grey County. The two activists hoped to challenge women into claiming a larger role in public life. Neither subscribed to the conspiracy theory expressed by McClung and Charlotte Whitton that saw men deliberately excluding females from political activity, although Macphail did feel that "Men do not honour women as they say."[29] Like her mentor, Henderson urged women to become more active in political life and lamented the "palpitating deputations of women knocking at the back door of Parliament to plead for measures they should have carried in themselves through the front door."[30] While Henderson and Macphail did not always concur in their views, each felt that

women owed more loyalty to each other. In 1935 Nora
Henderson ran unsuccessfully as a candidate for the Reconstruction Party.

Whether she spoke to a handful of people in a church base-
ment, to interested university women, or to the largest assem-
blies, Agnes Macphail made a lasting impression on her
listeners. To a generation of young women seeking a role
model, she appeared as the exemplar of the possibilities within
themselves. Always uplifting in speaking to women, she also
frequently chided her audiences candidly. "Woman has
courage and faith," she said over C.B.C. in 1939. "She can hold
fast to a vision through a disconcerting period, a fact not un-
connected with the months of waiting for a child. And woman
puts human values first and material things in a secondary
place. To her human beings and their well-being are the chief
things in life. To her, that is life." The nurturing role also led
women, in her view, to fear war and promote peace. Macphail
rejoiced that women were increasingly persons in their own
right and less frequently creatures of sex, though she found it
sad that they had to be "twice as good for half as much pay."[31]
She also feared the repercussions of attempts by Fascists in
Italy and Nazis in Germany to force women from the workplace in order to produce babies. "Fascism spells the doom of
a developing womanhood," she declared. The "traditional activities of women cannot again in the world be centered in the
home to any extent. We shall not, I believe, again make the
family the chief industrial and educational center, and to drive
women back into the home today merely means to sterilize
their creative functions."[32]

At the same time, Macphail criticized her own gender for
accepting too willingly the cult of the lady that had been prev-
alent since early in the nineteenth century. She believed that
too many women killed time in inconsequential activity after
their children were raised. She also thought that women had
accepted too readily their secondary status, especially in political parties, and she felt that they had not yet acquired an
intellectual curiosity as strong as that displayed by men. Too
frequently women failed to extrapolate from concern for their
own children and family to larger social problems. She also
lamented that too few women showed humour at the right
moment and that too many looked suspiciously on the

camaraderie so important to men. While Macphail's criticisms of women were always carefuly couched in comparative rather than absolute terms, it was clear that she wanted more women to be like her.

On the Speaker's Circuit

The tempering of Macphail's views combined with her oratorical abilities to make her a speaker as much in demand in the United States as in Canada. While in the early part of the decade she had spoken largely on the college circuit at universities such as Vassar, from 1933 to 1938 she toured the entire United States. She made her mark first in Dallas when she spoke to the Democratic Women's Club and later at the seventy-fifth anniversary of the University of Louisiana. There she met Huey Long, the state's colourful governor whose populist flare mesmerized many, but not Macphail. Long impressed her with his flattery, but she opposed the methods he had chosen to pursue his peculiar brand of populist reform.

In 1936 Macphail contracted with Harold Peat, a New York booking agent whom she had met through her peace activities and who handled such luminaries as Winston Churchill, André Maurois, and Alfred Adler. She was advertised as "the Lady Astor of Canada," a billing she must have disliked intensely but which kept her speaking schedule full. With Americans she addressed topical issues such as women in politics, currency reform, and Canadian-American relations. What impressed her about the United States were the extent of its agricultural lands, the value placed on adult education, and the immense kindness that Americans unfailingly showed her. Macphail reciprocated. "Unlike many other important people," the president of the International Federation of Business and Professional Women wrote her in 1937, "you lived up to your reputation, even exceeded my expectations."[33]

Earning from one hundred and fifty to two hundred dollars per engagement, Macphail paid off two life insurance policies and purchased a small government annuity which, at maturity in 1947, was to pay her $8.33 monthly. "Like every other fool," she wrote in 1937, "I am trying for security in my old age."[34] Her financial problems remained despite the increased income because she continued to be overly generous and augmented her lifestyle with each increase in pay. Her father's will in 1930 had provided her with only three hundred dollars, which quickly evaporated in the assistance she provided others. Young farm supporters like Alex Sim and Arthur Haas found her home an engaging place for debate and country hospitality as well as a source of financial aid. In discussing an upcoming conference on farm economics at the Ontario Agricultural College, Macphail asked Haas if he were going to attend. When it became apparent that finances prevented it, Macphail paid his way and would not accept a repayment she knew he could not make.[35] Haas later went on to become involved in the Ontario CCF, but as a result of such generosity Macphail found that she had to borrow at the bank to make payment on her annuity when her New York agent was late in remitting funds early in 1938.

Despite her parliamentary responsibilities and her speaking engagements, Macphail spent the summer months at home where her unconventionality was seen in more than her pince-nez spectacles and characteristic cape. When the notion struck her to go into town in the morning to pick up something, she jumped into her car impulsely, clad in housecoat and pyjamas. Her sisters and their three children, now entering their teens, visited her and her mother, but the energy of the children sometimes so taxed them that they were glad when the time came for them to leave. Still, Macphail's nieces loved nothing better than going shopping with their aunt or visiting her in Ottawa for she possessed a vigour that matched their own on such occasions.

On 27 September 1937 Etta MacPhail died in Ceylon. She was interred at the McNeill Cemetery following a service at the Presyterian Church in Priceville. Agnes and her mother had grown closer over the years, and the old antagonisms had receded, but her mother's passing created a new vacuum in Macphail's life. The following year she was informed that her own life expectancy would be shortened if she did not slow down. Her blood pressure was up again, and she was suffering from a stricture and needed another operation. The diagnosis was so serious that Macphail decided she would be sensible and not worry about work until she had fully recuperated. Friends visiting found her so remarkably sweet, happy, and contented that one remarked that she expected her to join the Conservative party.

International Affairs

Macphail's opposition to the party system remained so great that that was unlikely, but once her health was restored she returned to questions concerning foreign affairs. The peace activism that had attracted her in the previous decade was now transformed into a concentration on international problems. Her hopes for lasting peace were shattered by the Japanese invasion of Manchuria in 1931 and the failure of the international disarmament conference in the following year. Macphail felt that Canadians paid insufficient atention to foreign affairs because they were indifferent or felt that they were too complex to understand. While the Liberal government consciously attempted to direct attention away from an international situation it refused to influence, Macphail believed naively that an informed public would serve as a restraint on precipitous military action by the government if war were declared.

Agnes Macphail grew increasingly disillusioned with the League of Nations because she thought that it had become an instrument of the major powers who used it to satisfy their own interests. She abandoned her earlier belief that the roots of all war lay in economics. Like many on the left, the election of Hitler led her to condemn the Treaty of Versailles for having imposed an unjust and vengeful settlement on Germany. "The whole collective system is wrongly based on the defence of immoral boundaries and economic imposssibilities," Macphail declared at a peace meeting in Toronto's Massey Hall that attracted two thousand people in 1935, "or in other words, the Western countries have undertaken to defend the impossible."[36] While she continued to argue that there would be no peace until the world's natural resources were distributed more equitably and while armaments manufacture remained in private hands, the Italian invasion of Ethiopia in 1935 showed Macphail how vainglory stirred men to military conquest. The Spanish Civil War, which erupted in 1936 and to which Canada dispatched the volunteer Mackenzie-Papineau

battalion, also contributed to her growing belief that fascism
would not be contained without a fight.

Even Macphail's involvement with international affairs did
not pass without amusing incidents. When she appeared with
the Duchess of Atholl at a meeting of the communist-backed
League against War and Fascism during the Spanish Civil
War, Macphail looked stunning in a tailored dress and appropriate hat. True to the traditions of British nobility at the time,
the Duchess wore a dowdy feather boa around her neck. The
speeches by both women went well, but later Macphail commented to a friend, "Isn't she wonderful considering the way
she was brought up."[37]

At the time of Ethiopian Emperor Haile Selassie's flight
from his country to plead for intervention by the League of
Nations, Macphail read in Parliament a published list of prominent Liberals. "May I ask my honorable friend," the witty Sam
Jacobs piped up, "is the name of Haile Selassie also attached
to it?" "No," Macphail retorted quick as a flash, "Haile Selassie
has escaped."[38] Jean-François Pouliot, the French-Canadian independent with whom Macphail also liked to joust, knew of
her admiration for royalty and sent her a bottle of perfume
called "Abdication" when Edward VIII left the throne. Such
teasing she loved, but not flattery. When one of her opponents
in the Commons referred to her as having "an earnest, sincere,
sympathetic ..." disposition, she retorted with "Cut out the
cant." The speaker continued, saying, "trusting nature such as
hers, and in view of her interruption, I might add her sweet
femininity."[39] Patriarchal society defines the feminine more
rigidly than the masculine.

International affairs, like all walks of life, needed their touch
of humour, but Macphail found it embarrassing when an invitation from a peace committee she accepted turned out to be
that of the Royal Empire Society in Montreal. "If my colleagues
in Parliament ever found out I spoke to the Royal Empire
Club," she began her speech, "they would never cease to rag
me about it. The Royal Empire Society has never been my long
suit — I cannot fool myself that any empire that goes around
conquering people for that people's good is right."[40] She then
won back her audience with a few fawning comments about
Edward VIII before getting them to think seriously about the
prospect of war. She wisely chose not to proffer any of her

solutions for avoiding Canadian involvement in war. If "we put some of the 'big boys' into the front trenches," Macphail asserted on another occasion, "it won't last very long."[41] Women might be typecast, but the boys divided into the big and the little.

Such matters never restrained her. At celebrations in Niagara Falls in 1937 to mark one hundred and twenty years of peace between Canada and the United States, Agnes Macphail joined a host of other leaders in lauding cooperation and peaceful coexistence between the two countries. She galvanized attention. According to the American press, "the clear-eyed and clear thinking member of the Canadian Parliament … struck the keynote of the meeting and drew applause from the audience" despite her tough words about no declaration of war in Canada without a plebiscite.[42] She also argued that in the unlikely eventuality of war involving the Americas, the pay of enlisted men should be mandated for the entire population for the duration of hostilities.

Addressing the questions of war, federal-provincial relations, and the role of the independent member in 1938, Macphail opened with a disclaimer: "If I were serious and told you what I really think, you wouldn't be happy; if I were serious and didn't say what I think, I wouldn't be happy, so I won't be serious except for two or three points." As part of the CCF campaign that the Canadian Parliament determine the extent of the country's participation in the event of war, Macphail maintained that the "decision to fling us into the next catastophe must come from Ottawa and not Downing Street." She was becoming increasingly anti-British and pro-American in her views, expressing the profound distrust of the British upper classes that some Canadians felt as a result of the World War One. Defending her own position in the House, she said that the "House of Commons respects sincerity in a man more than any other quality. It will always do homage to the sincere member, no matter what his opinions. But the poseur is soon found out and given short shrift." Then offering to answer questions, she brought forward her own.

QUESTION: *What are the powers of the federal government?*
ANSWER: *It does anything the provinces leave undone.*
QUESTION: *Of what does it consist?*

ANSWER: A house and a half of Liberals and a few ob-
servers.
QUESTION: What does it do from year to year?
ANSWER: Supplies money to ungrateful provinces and
thanks God for Roosevelt.[43]

Macphail took her increasingly neutralist and pro-American position to the annual meeting of the United Farmers of Ontario where she appeared with Escott Reid, the national secretary of the Canadian Institute of International Affairs. While Reid spoke dispassionately of the possible avenues for Canadian foreign policy in light of Italy's actions and emphasized the need for democratic control, Macphail denounced the Treaty of Versailles and argued for a resuscitated League of Nations. Adopting an isolationist stance aligned with the United States, she claimed that "Canada had no vital interest in the Continent's [Europe's] hates." Applause greeted her and she went on to affirm that "We will will never have peace until we are a league of people recognizing the right of all people to the raw materials of the earth and the markets of the world."[44] The views of both speakers incurred the wrath of Reid's friend Norman MacKenzie, who believed in collectivism and thought their remarks would make Ontario farmers more isolationist.

The Emergence of the Farm Lobby

The United Farmers of Ontario were increasingly a spent force. The severity of the economic downturn and the increasing political fragmentation in the country led Canadian agriculture to seek a more effective voice through the creation of the Canadian Chamber of Agriculture in 1935. When a new initiative emerged from the West four years later to convert the chamber into a powerful lobby known as the Canadian Federation of Agriculture, Macphail provided leadership in Ontario. Before the Western farm leaders converged on Ottawa early in 1939, John Bracken of Manitoba wired her to assist them with their discussions. She then attended the Eastern Canada Farm Marketing Conference in Montreal where further plans were set. "We are here for improving the lot of the dirt farmer," she said in terms reminiscent of J. J. Morrison, "to find ways and means of lifting him out of the morass which he is in."[45]

After struggling for expression for more than two decades, Canadian agriculture seemed at last to have determined that its interests could best be served through lobbying rather than protest. Macphail was excited by these developments and determined that the insularity of the Ontario farm community not prevent its full involvement in this significant departure. While Herb Hannam was more deeply involved with organizing and later became president of the new federation, Macphail's support was critical. Before the annual meeting of the United Farmers of Ontario she argued that the more than a million farmers in the country required a new organization with the apparatus to ensure that they had the documentation needed to impress governments with the policies they advocated. While 32 per cent of Canadians lived on farms, she said, they drew only 9 per cent of the national income and governments had responded haltingly to their plight. To illustrate her point that rural Canada was disregarded, she recounted a conversation with Graham Towers, the governor of the Bank of Canada whose aristocratic bearing in public was well known. In reaction to her expression of the distress she had seen on the country's farms, Towers had professed disbelief. "Things can't be like that," the pinstriped banker had rejoined. "If they were, great organizations of farmers would send deputations — there would be protests."[46]

Macphail knew only too well how great deputations and protests, sadly divided along regional lines, had failed in the past. Only a more effective agency would allow farmers to formulate policies and see that they were enacted through legislation. But not all in Macphail's audience found her subject enthralling. When she noticed some people dozing, she raised her voice markedly. "I am just speaking more loudly," she yelled, "to waken up the two men in the fifth row." That did it. They awoke with a start. "That is exactly my point," Macphail continued. "Too many of you go to sleep far too easily."[47]

Once again Agnes Macphail had helped to lead the province's organized farm movement in a new direction, but this time the new organization proved much more durable and beneficial than the flirtation with the CCF six years before. In joining the new federation, the United Farmers contributed to the eventual creation of one of Canada's most effective twentieth-century lobbies. While Macphail had detested the influence of such groups when they had represented the business sector, two decades of political experience had taught her the need for them in a liberal democracy.

The Painful Decision

While agriculture and international affairs commanded her attention, Agnes Macphail was finding the isolation of independence in Parliament stultifying. Early in 1938 she began attending the CCF caucus. She agreed to abide by its secrecy rule and contributed financially to the federation, but she reserved her right to dissent. Her admiration for J. S. Woodsworth grew into veneration, especially as he agonized to reconcile his pacifism with the certain eventuality of war. Following one especially momentous debate, she slipped him a note saying "Truly you are a saint." Macphail frequently sat beside the ailing leader, whose sight had been impaired by a hemorrhage, and passed him the cards on which his wife had written notes in letters large enough for him to read. One day when she offered to move back in order to let Angus MacInnis sit beside him, Woodsworth queried reprovingly, "Agnes, don't you love me?"[48]

Agnes Macphail had always been fully committed to civil liberties, but she had generally left their defence in the House of Commons to Woodsworth and others. When Quebec Premier Maurice Duplessis passed his infamous Padlock Law allowing provincial police to close premises propagating communism, Macphail returned to the question. This legislation, passed after the Liberals repealed section 98 of the Criminal Code in 1936, failed to define communism because Duplessis said that it could be felt. Such legislation, Macphail told students at the University of Toronto in 1938, "is only one of many indications of the rising tide against democracy."[49] In the House of Commons her hatred of fascism temporarily eclipsed her reason as she argued for security forces to crack down on Nazi propaganda in Canada.

Neville Chamberlain's settlement with Hitler at Munich led Agnes Macphail to abandon her hopes for Canadian neutrality in the coming war in the same way that it altered the non-involvement policies of Mackenzie King and the Liberals. Hilter's invasion of Austria and Czechoslovakia convinced her that the German dictator's word was worthless and that evil could only be met by force. She recoiled at the timidity of Britain's policy in regard to Germany. "Those who were the great peace advocates are those most upset by the appeasement policy," she said, "and those who were imperialists have become advocates of appeasement, or peace at any price."[50] There was the rub. Macphail was now prepared to pay the price for freedom. "What surprises me more than anything else," she said in Parliament in 1939, "is the fact that the conscience of the world has be seared to such an extent that we can endure the tragedy of China, the betrayal of Czechoslovakia and the unparalleled agony of Spain without doing anything about it."[51]

Macphail did not want anyone to think "that women die less bravely than men. The whole history of the world has shown that women can die bravely."[52] Parting company with Woodsworth, Macphail shuddered at the horror of contemplating a world where "no opposition to Hitler seemed more terrible than even war.... I hate war and the death to liberty that it brings — but then, liberty was dead anyway."[53] Before Parliament was recalled to consider Canada's declaration of war in September of 1939, Macphail was the only nonparty member to participate in the intense meeting of the CCF national council that discussed CCF strategy. So distraught was she and so disturbed at the course of her own thought that she did not utter a single word during the entire, agonizing meeting.[54] In the brief parliamentary session that followed, all eyes centred on J. S. Woodsworth as he gave a stirring defence of his pacificist beliefs that separated him from the majority of his own followers. Macphail voted for war, but she did so reluctantly, the idealistic part of her personality disappointed at the stand she felt compelled to take. Her address to Parliament was anticlimatic and only raised the repercussions of war for Canada's agriculture.

The Election of 1940

By the time war was declared, this Parliament was nearing the end of its term and an election loomed. Mackenzie King assured all parties that another session would be called first, and so, like many others, Macphail felt duped when the government convened the House early in 1940 only to dissolve it within hours. The "master of sophistry," as David Lewis later characterized King, was true to the letter of his declaration but not to its spirit.[55] Macphail was doubly irate because backbenchers had not sat long enough to receive their sessional indemnity. Without a party to rely on, Macphail would encounter problems in meeting her campaign expenses.

Agnes Macphail dreaded a winter campaign and predicted that snow would prevent people from reaching the polls in March. In the main she relied on CCF literature stressing the rights of the Farmer-Labour ticket on which she ran, but as usual she made the positions her own. Her nomination meeting in Hanover set the tone of her campaign. She made an impassioned personal attack on Mackenzie King for the manner in which he had dissolved Parliament, and she decried the loss of civil liberties as a result of the Defence of Canada regulations that had been brought into effect. Then she equated King with Maurice Duplessis, claiming that the regulations were the "Padlock law made national." Believing her past successes to have been an exercise in democratic politics, she said her campaign was an effort "to save democracy at least in this riding."[56]

As incendiary was her campaign literature, which decried police raids in Toronto conducted under the new regulations. "It is useless to fight for democracy abroad," she maintained, "if at the same time we destroy it at home." Macphail advocated that the government allow farmers to participate in planning food policy during the war and condemned conscription outright. "Human life is the most precious thing there is," her flyer quoted her as saying, "and while it may be given in the defence of an ideal, it may not be taken."[57]

With the country at war, the old slogans did not stir as they had in the past, and Macphail's campaign turned sour from the outset. National feeling had superseded democracy in the minds of most voters, including some of her own supporters.

Macphail's bitter personal attacks on the country's wartime prime minister struck an inappropriate note. They seemed arrogant and created disaffection even within her own ranks, but she interpreted any opposition as betrayal. Farquhar Oliver stumped for her as he always had. Her former lieutenant had abandoned the UFO in the 1937 Ontario provincial election to run as a Liberal and had recently received a position in Hepburn's cabinet. Oliver knew that Macphail was committing a grave error, but he owed too much not to help her with some of the thirty meetings she held in her constituency.[58]

The Liberal candiate, Walter Harris, was the youngest opponent Macphail had faced during her nineteen years in politics. A lawyer who had moved to the riding from Toronto nine years before, Harris was an incorrigibly honest man whose reserved personality contrasted sharply with Macphail's explosiveness. He wisely stuck to the Liberal party line that stressed the need for a strong, moderate government to prosecute the war. He did not have to do otherwise; his wife Grace was one of J. J. Morrison's daughters and had been involved with the United Farm Women of Ontario provincially.

When Elmore Philpott visited Agnes Macphail in Ceylon, she confessed that the election was not going well. She knew that the Liberals were posed to sweep the country in an avalanche and worried especially about the Bruce County section of her riding where people were not as familiar with her. The "towns are against us," one of her supporters wrote, "and I suppose always will be. We supply their daily bread etc, and they thank us by biting the hand that feeds them."[59] Macphail clung tenaciously to her independence and castigated both opposition parties as hypocritical tools of big business.

The snow that difted up to ten feet on the back concession roads when the vote was taken prevented some of Macphail supporters from reaching the polls, but the weather effected the outcome of the election less than it influenced the magnitude of her defeat. Macphail finished third, losing to Harris with 6,389 votes against 4,761. Although she had had some inkling of what might happen, Macphail had devoted herself so singlemindedly to her career that she was psychologically unprepared for the result. She interpreted her defeat as a personal rejection, which to a degree it was. Never having been defeated before and lacking the outlets that distracted a person like Nellie McClung when she had lost in Alberta, Macphail became despondent, especially since she had contributed $2,500 personally to her campaign. "I have no idea what I am going to do," she said shortly after the outcome was known. She thought the country would live to regret the sweeping majority given the Liberals. "The entire issue of the election was whether the government can disregard Parliament. After this, we must apparently take it for granted that the government is everything."[60]

The majority of Canadians wanted it that way, and Macphail was as bitter as Mackenzie King had been in the wake of his defeat in 1911. King had blamed his loss on the money the liquor industry had poured into his riding; Macphail found the culprits to be the big party machines and the failure to reform electoral financing. "I told the people the truth at all times," she told a reporter while clearing her Ottawa office, "and they say the truth will make you free. Well it certainly made me free."[61]

Apart from those who emphazied her peace activism, commentators saw Macphail's defeat in larger terms. It was viewed as a setback for all the Canadian women whom she had represented so ably. "Eighteen years ago many disagreed with her feminist and other views," the Toronto *Star* editorialized, "some were openly antagonistic. Today she is generally regarded with pride and affection and has a large following not only among women, but throughout the Dominion."[62] In Ottawa the *Citizen* argued that Macphail's value to the country transcended the locality she had represented. They found her a voice of reason among tempestuous male politicians. "What she said [in the House of Commons] was usually an antidote to the extravagance of mere males who failed to see an issue clearly and see it whole. One of the flaws of the democratic system is that so valuable a representative as Agnes Macphail can be dismissed from public service in such summary fashion."

The letters of affection and admiration that Macphail received were poignant. Cairine Wilson acknowledged that Macphail's defeat had been "a serious setback for the women's cause" and said she was dreadfully disappointed.[63] No letter was more forthright than that of Toronto lawyer Margaret Hyndman: "I think every Canadian woman owes you a debt of gratitude which will never be repaid because you have so conducted yourself as to make it easier for women Members of Parliament who come after you." The standard that Agnes Macphail had set so intimidated Dorise Nielsen, the sole woman successful in the 1940 election, that she professed her trepidation in following in Macphail's footsteps.

To other women, Macphail's fate became a battle cry. "Your defeat emphasizes the present landslide in women's public life everywhere," Toronto civic politician Adelaide Plumptre wrote Macphail. "I never knew a time when, as it seems to me, women were more needed on public bodies, and when there was a more determined stand to oust them."[64] During the election, Toronto Liberal women had revolted by expressing their frustration with the lack of elected female representatives. They noted the contradiction between the official appeals for their service to the war effort and their inferior status within the party and toyed with the idea or resurrecting the Women's party. "Women are not prepared to stand idely by on the sidelines, merely casting their vote," they declared, while men monopolized the patronage plums.[65] Not long afterwards Cairine Wilson admitted the National Federation of Liberal Women had failed to promote women in Canadian politics as it had aspired to do.

All victories find a hundred parents, but every defeat remains an orphan.[66] Unemployed at fifty, Agnes Macphail had reached another plateau as significant as her decision not to marry. While her immediate concern was to support herself, she did not intend to abandon the causes to which she had devoted her life.

PART 3

GREY POWER

Return to the Fold: CCF Member of the Ontario Legislature

If you call the Sabbath a delight and the Lord's Holy day honorable, and if you honor it by not going your own way and not doing as you please or saying idle words, then you will find joy in the Lord.

Isaiah 58:13-14

Though it took her time to adjust to the reversal of 1940 and what she saw as the fickleness of public opinion, Agnes Macphail had no intention of abandoning politics. Within months she tried her luck in a federal by-election, and by 1943 she was sitting in the Ontario legislature as a CCF member. Meanwhile she had to find a source of income.

In striving to become her own person Agnes Macphail had rejected her family's pecuniary values. Accustomed to living better than her parents had, she could not imagine turning back, although her financial resources had been depleted on the 1940 electoral campaign and there were no pensions for members of Parliament. Friends like Hugh Keenleyside in the Department of External Affairs were certain that Mackenzie King would agree with advice that she be appointed to the Senate or the penitentiaries commission, but her attacks on the prime minister during the election had been too severe for her to receive such a reward. Over the course of the 1940s the possibility of such an appointment would be raised many times, but Agnes was more anxious to return to the centre of political life.

Macphail had few resources. She owned her house in Ceylon, but rural property was worth almost as little as her pitiful annuity. She had to work both for her own satisfaction and for the income. The absence of a secretary and stenographer she endured, but Macphail was not prepared to fire her trusted housekeeper. The United Farmers of Ontario seemed to present the best prospect for a job, but when she approached H. H. Hannam and R. J. Scott, they had nothing to offer her. Macphail was deeply resentful even though the Ontario Chamber of Agriculture joined a number of women's groups in supporting her appointment to the Senate. Other friends and admirers made various suggestions about avenues she should try, but they were not always practical. But "my dear sir, what do I eat?" Macphail replied to one suggestion that she freelance for Ontario's numerous weekly newspapers.[1]

Since the immediate prospects for a job appeared dim, Macphail returned to her accustomed roles. Through one of her friends in Ottawa, she helped new M.P. Dorise Nielsen secure an apartment for herself and her three children. Soon she was off to Kansas City on behalf of the coop movement, attending a conference in Saskatoon, and then participating in meetings of the Canadian Civil Liberties Association in Toronto and Montreal. She continued to criticize the Defence of Canada regulations, saying that they should have been passed by Parliament, as in Britain, rather than by executive order. She acknowledged that a country at war was faced with both internal and external enemies, but she lamented the propensity of police to think of the impoverished as traitors. She noted that some seventy people had been arrested in the less than nine months since the declaration of war, among them two seventeen-year old women in Saskatchewan. She observed that they "must have been pretty vicious girls. I don't know which one of the Cabinet ministers was worried."[2] Macphail believed a greater danger to the country emanated from the capricious suppression of fundamental freedoms by those in power. To a considerable extent she was right, especially in regard to Canadians of Japanese ancestry who were forcibly evacuated from British Columbia in 1942 even though neither police nor army saw the need of such drastic action.[3]

Saskatoon By-Election

A by-election in Saskatoon during the late summer of 1940 provided an opportunity for Agnes to return to the political fray. Sitting member Walter G. Brown had represented a local coalition called the United Reform Movement, and Macphail had introduced him to Parliament following his success in a 1939 by-election. When Brown died suddenly after the 1940 election and the government chose not to leave the seat vacant, Agnes Macphail received a telephone call asking her to stand for the nomination. All the advice she received told her not to go except that of Dorise Nielsen, a political neophyte, and women involved in the splinter party in Saskatoon.[4]

The United Reform movement had been created by a charismatic Protestant minister out of a variety of discontented left-wing groups. Although its members were exhausted financially and emotionally as they entered their third campaign in two years, Macphail felt impelled to try to re-enter Parliament. The train ride afforded her the opportunity to read Gregory Vlastos' *Christian Faith and Democracy*. When she arrived in Saskatoon, she found the movement wracked by dissension and lacking in funds. It was ironic that a democratic reform movement had never bothered to elect its own executive. Macphail won the nomination easily, and some 320 people signed up to work for her. This time she more readily acknowledged her support for the war effort and argued that she would rather see "an imperfect democracy than a perfect totalitarian system."[5] She again emphasized the need for collective bargaining and protection of civil liberites. In its desperation to avoid an election, the nominating convention passed a resolution favouring Macphail's acclamation and cabled the prime minister, much to the candidate's embarrassment. Macphail wrote Mackenzie King to dissociate herself from the initiative.

There were six candidates in the by-election, but Conservative lawyer and former city councillor Alfred Bence was recognized as Macphail's chief opponent because the Liberals were badly split. Despite the problems in her own organization, her campaign went well and large crowds turned out to hear her. Her managers stressed that their candidate had inherited Walter Brown's mantle and portrayed her as an independent who would not abase herself before "the order of the Eastern-money dominated Political Machine."[6] Dorise Nielsen campaigned for her. The two women broadcast on the radio and appeared at a rally with the support of a Social Credit M.P. representing Bob Gardiner's old riding. Macphail and Nielsen toured North Battleford, Nielsen's constituency, which made Macphail more anxious to return to Parliament. The poverty she saw seemed the worst she had encountered since visiting Cape Breton. The land had been parched by successive years of drought, people lived in what were little better than hen houses, and a small amount of flour was a prized commodity.

Alfred Bence played his trump card during the election by reading selections of Macphail's speeches on national defence from Hansard. So rattled was the former M.P. that she declared: "I am not a pacifist. I believe sincerely in democracy, and wish to defend it where it is most threatened — which is abroad."[7] Such affirmations did no good. When the polls were tallied, Macphail lost by 745 votes. Harvesting prevented some rural supporters from bothering to go to the polls, but the experience taught Macphail why people like Dorise Nielsen became communists.

Macphail was joined in Saskatoon by Lilla Bell, her former secretary, and the two travelled to the west coast where they visited Elmore Philpott and Nellie McClung. The friendship between the two women, McClung wrote, had "never languished or grown pale."[8] Macphail then made her own way to Macleod in Alberta where Robert Gardiner lay ill. When Gardiner refused to see her, Macphail was totally despondent. She returned to Winnipeg with so little cash that her companion had to pay her return fare. Macphail then travelled to the United States to fulfil a speaking engagement before returning to continue her job hunt.

The prospect of becoming a columnist for the Toronto *Globe and Mail* looked promising, but Macphail preferred the security of a government job since she felt that she would quickly run out of things to say in a newspaper. After approaching Ernest Lapointe, she met with Mackenzie King in Ottawa, but she was unfamiliar with the role of job applicant and could not identify the type of work for which she was best suited. Macphail was greatly relieved when the prime minister assured her of an opening with the Unemployment Commission, but she also met with several other officials and Jimmy Gardiner, the minister of agriculture. Only one interview went well. During another she became so impatient that when she used the telephone she said in a voice loud enough to be overheard that she had "got the run around."[9] She was offered a job as a writer for the Wartime Information Board, but it came too late. The ex-M.P. was already committed to the *Globe*, but before starting her new job, she took a three-thousand-mile journey around the United States.

For the next year Macphail wrote an undistinguished farm affairs column that appeared in the newspaper three times a week. Combining critical commentary on current affairs with personal reflection in a manner that antedated a contemporary journalistic style by decades, Macphail found it difficult to generate new material and the pay was too low. Soon political manipulation was to lead to her departure.

At the beginning of 1942 she stood among two hundred other Ontario notables invited to a glittering luncheon at the posh Royal York Hotel. The invitation had said that a matter of national urgency would be discussed, but the intent of the organizers, James Murdock of Noranda Mines, Simpson's executive C. Burton, and Toronto financier Fred Morrow, was to force the federal govenment to enact conscription for overseas service. Following a speech by Murdock, an advertisement demanding that Canada pursue a policy of total war was read, and the listeners were informed that their names would appear attached to it if they did not object. Macphail was flabbergasted by such tactics. She and W. F. Nickle, the former Ontario attorney-general who had shared her campaign for penal reform, rose to dissociate themselves from the activities of the committee. "It was the rawest thing I have come in contact with for a long time," she informed Mackenzie King.[10] The demands of the Toronto 200 for "Total War Now," which appeared shortly in every daily and weekly newspaper in the province without Macphail's name, served as a prelude to the first and most destructive of the conscription crises that pitted French and English Canadians against each other during the war.

Rightly scenting the hand of *Globe* publisher George McCullagh behind this ruse and feeling his days at the newspaper were numbered, Macphail was furious. McCullagh did leave the paper shortly afterwards, and she was fired. Trying again to obtain government employment from the prime minister, she offered to recruit women for the war effort. "I could put energy and enthusiasm into the task," she told Mackenzie King in March, "but am no dollar a year woman," she emphasized in reaction to the ability of C. D. Howe, minister of munitions and supply, to bring corporate executives into government service with token remuneration.[11] Meanwhile, she kept up her own political contacts. In March of 1942 she met with CCF lawyers Edward Bigelow Joliffe and Andrew Brewin. They convinced her to join the party at the time she left the newspaper.

Family Tragedy

Shortly Macphail moved to Toronto where she rented a large house on St. Clair Avenue. She gave wartime rationing of gasoline and the need to occupy a housekeeper she might not otherwise have been able to afford as the ostensible reasons for settling in the city. But, in fact, in the spring of 1942 a tragedy on the Campbell side of her family forced Macphail to flee Grey County into the greater anonymity afforded by the metropolitan centre.

Robert Campbell, one of her mother's brothers, had farmed on the fourteenth concession of Proton Township — where the MacPhails had originated — for many years. Sixty-eight years old in 1942, he had married a Scots woman, Margaret Haxton, late in life. Three of their four children still lived at home, while the fourth had moved to Toronto. The Campbell farm consisted of two hundred unmortgaged acres, and they owned another hundred acres down the road. Their dwelling, however, provided no clues to their adequate financial condition. The unpainted two-storey frame house stood forlornly on a knoll bereft of any vegetation.

Robert Campbell's health had deteriorated with advancing age. A diabetic, he had suffered a partially debilitating stroke following surgery for mastoids. Slowly he lapsed into depression and mental illness. Increasingly leaving the farm work to his family, he daily perched himself in his kitchen chair cursing and berating those around him. Some nights he would awaken the household and summarily demand that they go to the store to buy tobacco for him. No one could convince Campbell to see a physician. Doctors would steal all his money, he claimed, assuming a stance not uncommon before publicly financed hospitalization and medical care programs.

The Campbell household arose one Saturday morning in April 1942 only to be subjected yet again to Robert's verbal abuse. Following breakfast and a quarrel involving all the family, fourteen-year-old Ruby Campbell left the kitchen and went upstairs. After finding her father's 22-calibre rifle, she returned armed to back up her order that her father leave the house at once. When he refused, she aimed the rifle at his heart and fired one shot. Robert Campbell fell dead at the foot of the wood stove. Ruby then fled upstairs where she discarded the gun, and her sisters ran to the neighbours for help. A doctor summoned from the village of Dundalk took possession of the rifle and then notified the police. They took the young girl into custody in Owen Sound.[12]

When she heard of the murder, Agnes Macphail immediately sought out Joliffe and Brewin. Fortunately, Brewin practised in the same law firm as the acerbic Liberal J. C. McRuer, who had so generously come to Macphail's assistance seven years before. He had considerable stature in the Ontario legal community, and they were able to enlist his support to secure Ruby's release into Macphail's care.

Early in May, McRuer travelled to Owen Sound where Ruby was being held. Appearing before Magistrate E. C. Spereman, the lawyer argued that in view of the girl's age her case should be tried in juvenile court. There it would be easier to secure her release.

McRuer's strategy was successful, and Macphail promptly whisked the Campbell girls away to Toronto where they were removed from the local gossip about the unfortunate killing. To pay her rent on the big house, Agnes was forced to take in boarders, though she hired additional help. She engaged two Japanese Candians as cook and maid at a time when Ontarians sometimes reacted violently to their relocation from British Columbia — including ominous cross burnings in the Niagara peninsula. This large household of family, boarders, and employees interfered with Macphail's public role, but she joined the executive of the Toronto Civil Liberties Union and served on the council of the Canadian Association for Adult Education.

Return to Politics

Macphail's future lay with what she knew best: politics. The United Farmers of Ontario were about to disintegrate. After they folded into the Ontario Federation of Agriculture in 1943, farm leaders joked that the UFO had not failed, but Macphailed because they had spawned the country's foremost woman politician. Macphail valued loyalty highly, but now that her movement had collapsed, she was released. The death of J. S. Woodsworth in March of 1942 had also moved her profoundly. Her association with him had left an imprint on her life more indelible than any other personal encounter. "Some day when political controversy is forgotten and J. S. Woodsworth is gone," Macphail wrote, " he will be recognized as a great man. He has no interests other than improving the conditions of the people. Neither praise nor blame touch him.... He brought an integrity to the Commons and has remained its conscience."[13]

Macphail rejoined the CCF at a very different stage in its fortunes than when she had left it eight years before. As the war economy built up and as programs such as unemployment insurance were enacted in 1941, the CCF's platform struck an increasingly responsive chord among part of the electorate. Support from Ontario agriculturalists had remained pitifully weak during its early years. The chair of its farm committee in its early years, Andrew Brewin later recalled, alternated between "a professor of classics who regularly read a farm magazine and a small manufacturer who knew a farmer — his cousin up Markham way."[14] In an attempt to end this neglect Macphail was hired to organize rural Ontario during the summer of 1942, despite her recent criticism that the party had made a mistake during the previous decade by importing European ideas inappropriate to North America. So called landlordism did not exist in Canada, she had told the press, and far from exploiting others, farmers were themselves the victims of exploitation.

Macphail knew her agricultural constituency well enough to understood the difficulty of the task that lay before her. Since she had the personal contacts, it was hoped that her efforts would at least identify possible candidates for the upcoming election. When she had produced few concrete results by August, CCF General Secretary B. E. Leavens opposed an extension of her contract, adding that her appreciation of CCF principles appeared inadequate. Ted Joliffe, who had become the first Ontario CCF leader, rallied to her support and used his influence to see that she continued as farm organizer until the end of the year.[15] Still, results were few in comparison to the organizing activity among labour.

As the chief party representative for agriculture, Macphail read the report of the farm committee at the 1943 provincial convention. It emphasized the need for public or cooperative ownership of the food-processing industry and the extension of marketing boards in cooperation with the Ontario Federation of Agriculture. Taking to the airwaves, she argued that CCF policies would allow rural Ontario to enter a new period of prosperity. Since fewer than 10 per cent of farms had flush toilets and only one-third enjoyed electricity, Macphail replaced Roosevelt's promise of a chicken in every pot with the goal of a bathroom and electricity in every farmhouse in Ontario. Planning and cooperation were seen as the means to moderate the curves constantly tossed at farmers by the vagaries of weather and fluctuating prices.[16] In that year one of her former young supporters in Wellington county, Art Haas, relieved Macphail of responsibility for agriculture when he was appointed CCF farm secretary on a part-time basis.

CCF national secretary David Lewis pressed Macphail into service to head fund-raising for a foundation to perpetuate Woodsworth's memory, especially through scholarships for young people. She was the wrong person for the task. Despite her achievements, Macphail lacked any close links with wealthy individuals. She hated asking anyone for money even for the worthiest of causes. She accepted reluctantly out of respect for Woodsworth, but it was a mistake. She approached W. C. Good, who was enthusiastic but had no funds. In her meeting with C. B. Sissions, a University of Toronto classicist, he assumed the intellectual's stance that Woodsworth would be remembered whatever the memorials and then added that he thought it was a bad time to raise money. Discouraged, Macphail withdrew, but she agreed to speak with Norman Lambert, who had intimate associations with agriculture and controlled Liberal party finances.[17]

While Agnes Macphail possessed no talent for fund-raising and little patience with administrative details, she continued to be able to arouse controversy. In 1943 she criticized the actions of the Ontario government for appointing a judge rather than a labour board to adjudicate the province's new collective bargaining law. She had never known a progressive judge, she announced, adding that all members of the judiciary were political heelers or they would not not have been appointed to the bench. The war had curtailed civil liberties, and Macphail's comments on the judiciary were raised in Parliament. Minister of Justice Louis St. Laurent agreed only to refer the irritating remarks to the Wartime Information Board.[18]

Her travelling increased again, around the province and nationally for the CCF and the causes she supported. Her belief in the power of youth remained undiminished, but now when she spoke to young people she referred to herself as a grey-head. Showing her capacity for self-deprecation she shared with one rural audience the misfortunes she had encountered prior to her speaking engagement. While she was having her hair done in Toronto, the hairdresser had run out of soap and could not get out all the olive oil. Having her hair washed a second time put Macphail half an hour behind schedule. When she stepped outside, it was raining. To save her coiffure, she put a newspaper over her head but knocked off her glasses, breaking both lenses. She had called Barrie where she was to speak, but could only leave a message. When she finally arrived in the town, there was no one to meet her and rage swelled within her. Eventually she got to the right place and related her misfortunes with amusement.[19]

Back in the fold, Macphail was decidedly more successful in becoming a rallying force for women who hoped that the CCF would bring greater gender and economic equality. As an elder politician, she appeared as a legitimizing force linking one generation to the next. She told the CCF Women's Council in 1942 that the power of women was unlimited. In addition to her insistence on absolute equality, her experience in caring for her young cousins led her to criticize sexist child-rearing that disadvantaged girls. Many women lacked self-confidence, she said, because they had not enjoyed the same privileges as their male counterparts early in life. "If girls are brought up with social feeling and interest in their possibilities of con-

tributing to life," she predicted, "they will spontaneously take
to the task." And, she added, if men shared more equally in
the running of the home, children's attitudes to gender roles
would alter in their adult life.[20] Macphail influenced many
women, but her example had a profound effect on Grace Mac-
Innis, J. S. Woodsworth's daughter. In her early years MacInnis
modelled herself on the older woman and, as a New Democrat,
later found herself in the unenviable position of repeating
Macphail's experience as the only woman member of Parliament.

In the 1943 provincial election Macphail stood as a candidate in York East, an expansive riding with the second highest
party membership in Toronto. It was a large, mixed constituency that comprised Leaside on its western fringe and an extensive rural area. East York was known for its activism.
During the Depression the East York Worker's Association,
which Macphail had addressed in 1933, had been the largest
and most successful of the workers' organizations in Toronto
that attempted to find jobs and protect the living standards of
relief recipients. In reaction to a proposed cut in welfare, they
had organized a strike in 1935 that initially involved twenty-
seven hundred families. Women in the association had argued
for the distribution of birth control supplies with relief allot-
ments, and in 1936 a Parents' Clinic had been established for
this purpose.[21] Elizabeth Morton, a doctrinaire socialist, had
been active in the association, but Macphail had sparred with
her at the CCF provincial council during its breakup.

In an upset showing, the CCF vote soared from 5 per cent
in 1937 to nearly a third of the total in 1943. The party captured
thirty-four seats, only four fewer than the Conservatives, but
it made few inroads into rural Ontario. In a three-way race,
Macphail edged out her Conservative opponent by less than
two thousand votes. She and Rae Luckock became the first
women elected to the Ontario Legislature. Another daughter
of J. J. Morrison, Luckock also represented the CCF, but in
order to assure a double crown for Macphail, she was seated
first when the legislature met. The Liberals under former Premier
Mitchell Hepburn had elected only fifteen M.L.A.s, and Macphail broached with Hepburn the possibility of a collective
accord to prevent George Drew's Conservatives from gaining
power, but he was becoming increasingly erratic. Nothing resulted. A reporter made the mistake of asking Macphail if she

were glad to have been one of only two women elected. "No, I am not thrilled," she replied, "I am not a woman who isn't for women."[22] In contrast, she was unable to constrain her excitement at the prospect of a cabinet position for the brief moment when it was thought that a CCF-Liberal accord might bring the newest party to power. Instead, George Drew became premier at the head of a Conservative administration, and the CCF formed the official Opposition.

Macphail did not make the transition from the Olympian heights of Ottawa to the limited sphere of a provincial legislature easily. Her maiden speech concerned the government takeover of Union Stockyards in Toronto. Warm applause greeted her as she rose from her seat to attack the Drew government for bailing out its business friends while trying to give the appearance that it was helping the farming community. She went on to argue that the Ontario Agricultural College should be returned to the farmers by placing it under an autonomous board of governors, a development that did not occur until two decades later when the University of Guelph was created. Appointed opposition critic for provincial correctional services, Macphail visited the Mercer Reformatory for Girls in 1943 but found its young inmates so intimidated by the staff that they would not discuss anything with her.

Hepburn had downgraded the importance of the Ontario legislature, and it seemed like a small puddle to Macphail. She hated it. Though she felt inconsequential even in caucus, she developed close friendships with Ruth and Ted Joliffe and Margaret and Andrew Brewin. Only her position next to the Leader made the sittings bearable, especially as she sat on the same side of the House as her former protegé, now a Liberal, Farquhar Oliver, and directly faced a new antagonist, Premier George Drew. "I don't like George," she said, "but that shouldn't worry him. He likes himself so much." Her old verve still shone, but it found few outlets during a short legislative session. Reporters asked the same old questions about the role of women in politics. "Most women think politics are not lady-like. I'm no lady. I'm a human being," Macphail replied to a perennial. "Anybody who has known me for a long time would not think of calling me a lady or gentlewoman. They just call me Agnes. There are those who behind my back label me Aggie, but they are not brave enough to say it to my face.

As for my enemies ... well ... what they call me is simply not fit to print." When she was asked if she would wear a hat into the legislature, Macphail replied by saying that "I'd like to wear this hat with the big plumes and have Mr. Drew sit behind me." The old wit sparkled during sittings as well, as in one debate when Macphail referred to Drew as a perfectionist who thought he could do no wrong.

> "The Premier gets so wrapped in the flag that one can hardly see him," Macphail asserted.
> "Don't you like the Union Jack?" a Cabinet minister interjected.
> "Not with the Prime Minister in it," Macphail retorted even to Drew's amusement.
> "I assume that the honorable member," Drew remarked. "will never have me in or out of it."
> "That's a great relief," Macphail sighed.[23]

Counterattacks on the CCF by the Conservatives were often more scurrilous. None concerned Macphail more than the contention that a CCF government would confiscate farms to achieve the public ownership of property. At convention in 1944, when Macphail was again elected to provincial council, a new policy attempted to destroy the old bogey by asserting that the "CCF believes in the family farm as the basis of Canadian agriculture. It believes that Canadian farms should be owned by the farmers themselves." Their elaborate statements did little good, and the Ontario CCF remained primarily an urban and northern party. Agnes Macphail was no more successful in carrying the farm vote into the CCF in this decade than she had been previously, but no one else could have either. She continued to chair the CCF committee on agriculture, but her attention turned increasingly to other issues. Canada was now an urban society in which agriculture had to agitate behind the scenes to make its influence felt.

In her middle fifties, Agnes Macphail had passed her prime but not her usefulness. Early in 1945 she suffered a celebral thrombosis, but she remained as committed and fiesty as ever. Her doctor counselled rest, but at first she did not agree. "So, I don't live long," she said, "I'll live what's left doing what I want to do."[24] In the provincial election later that year the slide tilted downwards in a disastrous reversal for the CCF. The Conservatives adopted the same despicable tactics that they had employed against the communists before, but with greater intensity because they had more to lose. Anti-semitic slurs were voiced publicly, and George Drew misled the electorate by equating Ontario socialism with fascist Germany's National Socialism. "The decision rests between freedom and fascism right here at home," the premier announced. Then, quoting from the Communist Manifesto to show its similarity with CCF policies, he concluded that it "is time to stop talking about fascism having been destroyed. This is fascism."[25]

The CCF was buffeted by both left and right. In a repetition of events following World War One when the Canadian Manufacturers' Association had collected huge sums to defeat free trade as proposed by the Progressive movement, business gave freely to arrest the advance of the CCF. In 1944 and 1945 some three million copies of an abusive propaganda pamphlet entitled *Social Suicide* were distributed around the country with the assistance of businesses such as the Robert Simpson retail chain.[26] Following the entry of the Soviet Union into the war on the Allied side, the communists had changed their tactics and reversed their former ideas about forming popular fronts with democratic socialists. A new ideological line direct from Moscow dictated that capitalism would be more readily defeated by the triumph of traditional bourgeois parties. Knowing that Hepburn's Liberals could not win, the Labour Progressive party backed the Conservatives in the election by contesting the CCF in twenty-seven of the thirty-seven seats in which they mounted candidates.

The most dramatic and shameful episode in the 1945 election involved Agnes Macphail directly when one of her former Grey County constituents who was a member of the provincial police learned of Drew's illegal use of the force to spy on CCF activities. He approached his ex-member, and she quickly transmitted the intelligence to Ted Joliffe. Unfortunately, the CCF leader denounced the Ontario "Gestapo affair" during an eleventh hour radio broadcast. In responding to the charges, the premier lied unconscionably, but his deceit was not uncovered until years after his election victory.[27]

Women and Politics

These sensational political developments combined to ensure massive defeat for the CCF federally and provincially in 1945. Macphail stood among the victims. When the house she rented was sold, she was forced to move, but not without a successful fight to have her lease extended. With the some seven thousand dollars she inherited from the estate of Bob Gardiner she was now able to live without financial worry, and she retired to Ceylon. She travelled to Mexico with Lila Tinker, an old friend who had rented her a room in Ottawa many years before, and the pleasure of their holiday was increased by the hospitality of Canadian ambassador Hugh Keenleyside. Home again, she began to write her memoirs but found that she could not get beyond her first election. Hearing that R. B. Bennett was also ill, she wrote him recalling the glories of the past. Bennett was, Macphail said, "the most human and picturesque figure in Canada, coming within my experience." She explained that she had suffered an attack "and have been a lame duck ever since. I feel well but my activities are limited and that does not go well with my impatient disposition."[28]

Her own defeat and Rae Luckock's failure to secure nomination in the 1945 election because of her communist affiliations removed the last women in provincial legislatures east of Saskatchewan. During the 1920s women's suffrage in Canada had achieved little, and now Conservative Charlotte Whitton claimed that Canadian women had been a flop in politics and said their level of political involvement was the worst in the Western world. Leftist writer Dorothy Livesay joined the chorus by noting the large numbers of women involved politically in England and France as the well as the effectiveness in the United States of such lobbies as the League of Women Voters and the Women's Trade Union League.[29] The contrast between the Canadian experience and that in other Western countries was becoming too great to continue to lay the blame only at the feet of men as Nellie McClung had during the 1920s. Few considered the effects of the late arrival of suffrage in Quebec and the intricacies of the country's regional politics even as part of the explanation. More often, the unwillingness of women to enter the political fray and their lack of economic independence — rather than restrictions imposed by maternity — were criticized. Women, it seemed, exemplified Macphail's characterization of Canadians as timid.

Macphail herself was not so negative, despite Whitton's kindness in evaluating her own contribution to politics. Macphail encouraged Whitton to run in the 1945 federal election because, despite their differences in outlook, she admired Whitton's spunk and ability. "Women have fallen below the standard of citizenship which those who fought for the suffrage set for them," Macphail thought. "Women in politics have not flopped, because women politicians have on average exceeded their male counterparts, but there have been too few of them." Macphail believed that women lacked the training to see the connections between their homes and government and that despite the war, they had not earned enough money to secure financial independence. "My interest in politics is so deep and abiding," she affirmed, "that it is hard for me to see why other women do not work at the job." At the same time she acknowledged that she had not received the same breaks in life as men, but she was not bitter. "These things take time," Macphail concluded.[30]

While the desire to triumph at the polls with a plurality of seats is often derided in left intellectual circles as "electoralism," Macphail had struggled too long in the committee rooms and on the political rubber chicken circuit not to hope for a CCF victory. She knew only too well that the main point of the political exercise was to get elected so that the party could begin the types of reforms seen in Saskatchewan after Tommy Douglas became premier in 1944. Only minor parties lose sight of this goal in the way that the Ontario CCF Women's Committee did in 1947 and 1948. At issue stood the alleged infiltration by the Labour Progressive party of the Housewives Consumers' Association associated with ex-M.L.A. Rae Luckock and the degree of involvement appropiate for political women in its rival, the Canadian Association of Consumers. Party adherents were divided three ways in an interminable but inconsequential dispute. Macphail assumed a singular position that placed her in a minority of one. She argued that there was no halfway house needed to introduce women to political action and that consumer organizations, whatever their other benefits, detracted from the CCF's primary objective, winning at the polls.[31]

Last Electoral Success

In the provincial election of 1948 Agnes Macphail was asked to run again in York East, and this time she won. David Lewis was scheduled to assist her, but he could not because his wife fell ill. "You won without me," Lewis wrote, "and there is at least a possibility you might have lost if I had stuck my face in the campaign."[32] Once again she was the sole successful female candidate. Her plurality was not large — less than a thousand votes — but she triumphed over the Progressive Conservative whom she had beaten in 1943 and who had trounced her in the 1945 election. Her riding was so big that the number of votes she won was the largest in the history of the province.[33] An increase in the rural vote was not translated into seats for the CCF, but the lack of women in Ontario politics was the source of greater indignation. "It is a damning comment on our society," the *Canadian Forum* editorialized, "that there is only one woman in the federal House of Commons, and that Miss Macphail should herself be the only woman in the Ontario House."[34]

Despite the frustration felt by some members of the CCF Women's Committee who thought that inadequate attention was paid to their concerns, the party promoted women more than the other two and ensured them greater centrality. Between 1937 and 1951 more than half of the female candidates fielded in the province belonged to the CCF, but often they stood as little chance of being elected as those representing the other parties.[35] While a quarter century had changed little in terms of women's success at the polls, the CCF won twenty-one seats in 1948 and regained its status as the official Opposition. During the next three years the CCF would use its position to foster genuine pay equity for women, but the difference between majority will and minority concern soon became apparent in the last important political battle in Agnes Macphail's public career.

10

Feminism and Pay Equity: The Last Campaign and the Later Years

"So I said that I would pour out my wrath and spend my anger against them in the desert."

Ezekiel 20:21

Be strong, fear not, your God will come; he will come with a vengeance.

Isaiah 35:4

Agnes Macphail returned to Queen's Park reinvigorated in 1948. Her medical condition had moderated her tendency to fuss needlessly over inconsequentials without dampening her reform spirit. "If anything," she admitted, "I have become more radical."[1] Returning to her role as critic for correctional services, Macphail discovered a more open atmosphere in penal facilities she visited as a result of personnel changes under the Conservative government. The extension of parole services she continued to insist upon because Ontario lagged behind other jurisdictions, but Macphail also showed how women's institutions got shortchanged in comparison to those for men. As part of a program to improve correctional services, Minister of Reform Institutions William C. Hamilton paid for her to visit a correctional centre for women in West Virginia that was reputed to be the best in the United States.

After returning to Toronto, Macphail spoke to a Unitarian church women's group in 1951 about the lessons to be drawn from American experience. She advocated a system of volunteers to assist inmates in the transition to civilian life upon their release. A branch of the Elizabeth Fry Society had begun in Vancouver a dozen years before, and Macphail's suggestion struck a responsive chord. A section of the society was incorporated in Toronto, and Macphail became its honorary president.

As she reached the status of senior citizen, Macphail worried incessantly about the inadequacy of her sessional indemnity. She conveyed the impression that her riding consumed every penny of the three thousand dollars she received from the government, but in reality she was not poor, only as unwilling as ever to live within her means. She fiercely promoted programs for the disadvantaged as she had in Ottawa, but she zeroed in especially on the failure to provide adequate assistance to the aged. While there was a boom, rather than a slump following World War Two, rampant inflation as high as 14 per cent in 1949 hurt pensioners and others on fixed incomes. "If, as some philosphers believe, a country's mark of civilization is its care of the aged," the exemplar of grey power thought, "Canada doesn't look too civilized."[2] Macphail was unequivocal in arguing for an end to the means test for government pensions and in calling for a provincial supplement to the federal old age pension. "All right," she challenged the legislature, "it costs $700,000 a month and I can sleep better at night and enjoy my meals more, and so will you. Any honorable member who can say 'It does not make any difference to me' — let them stand up and be counted."[3] At a nomination meeting for Eugene Forsey, research director for the Canadian Congress of Labour, Macphail conveyed her message by challenging George Drew. "What freedom does he think old age pensioners have on $30 a month? What freedom would Mr. Drew have on $30 a month? What freedom have mothers and children on children's allowances? Groups like these, living in an economic straitjacket, have no freedom."[4]

The positions that Agnes Macphail assumed closely mirrored the Ontario CCF program. She argued for better programs for seniors in provincial institutions, subsidized housing, better care for the blind, larger pensions for teachers, and government hospitalization insurance, which the CCF had implemented in Saskatchewan in 1947 and which would not become nationwide for another ten years. Several trips to the Ontario north aroused in her a deep suspicion about the extent of American control of Canadian resources. In 1951 she said she was savage on the issue — many years before the Gordon inquiry into Canada's economic prospects and the debate over foreign control during the succeeding decade. Nor had her interest in foreign affairs abated. She watched with pride as Canada finally assumed responsibility as an activist middle power in postwar affairs, principally through the United Nations and in the creation of the Atlantic alliance. Before turning to her principal concerns before a southwestern Ontario audience in 1949, she berated her listeners in typical fashion because a smaller number had turned out to hear Lester Pearson, the diplomat who later won the Nobel peace prize.[5]

Agnes Macphail took great comfort in seeing the realization of social security programs she had advocated since early in her career. She enjoyed no less trying to loosen the niggardly purse strings of "the big boys," the description she had come increasingly to favour to describe her ministerial opponents. With the two communists represented in the legislature by the Labour Progressive party she could be even more devastating. When Joe Salsberg complained about inadequate office facilities for himself and his colleague, objecting that "we have no window," Macphail retorted, "They're afraid to let any light in. It might dissolve the party."[6] Beaten, the veteran debater threw up his hands and admitted defeat.

For Premier Leslie Frost, Drew's successor, Macphail had the highest regard. Old Man Ontario worked his incomparable charm on her. "You're the smoothest politican I've ever heard," she flattered the premier.[7] Despite the warmth of their relationship, Macphail did not forget they represented very different political persuasions. "He looks so nice," Macphail commented, "and as if he would not say a nasty or mean thing, and it always surprises and disappoints me that at the core of him he is a Tory."[8] In 1951, when the Speaker of the House temporarily vacated his chair to afford her the honour of occupying it during a session, Frost led the applause as she was escorted to the dais. Macphail then promptly asserted the Speaker's authority by squelching the premier's attempt to interrupt debate — and Frost applauded again.

In Canada, the spur to union organization provided in her southern neighbour by the Wagner Act of 1935 was not duplicated by the federal government until the issuing of order in council P.C. 1003 in 1944. Accordingly, membership rose dramatically in the postwar years. Agnes Macphail embraced and promoted these activities. In 1949, when union membership in the country surpassed the one million mark, she spoke to the first seminar sponsored by Local 1000 of the Retail Wholesale Department Store Union, which was attempting to organize employees at Eaton's in Toronto. While her wit delighted her audience, her message stressed the importance of union activity in fostering public awareness of how government might be used to better individual lives. Capitalism, she said, reminded her of the elephant who cried "every man for himself" as he danced among the chickens.[9]

Agnes Macphail did not welcome all the trends that surfaced in the postwar wars. She criticized the contraction of the daycare facilities that had expanded as women had assumed male jobs during the war. With changes in income tax deductions designed to make it less profitable for wives to participate in the paid workforce and with the barrage of advice to women to leave their jobs for a return to domestic duties, the proportion of married women working in 1951 was no higher than it had been ten years before. Macphail became especially critical of sexist child-rearing because she knew it gave boys an unequal advantage. Women hid their intelligence, she felt, since men "don't like smart girls at any age."[10] As a result women had little self-confidence, which made it possible for men to assume control of anything important that women had created. Macphail was dismayed that women still encountered formidable barriers in their careers and that few got a chance even to become school principals.

Macphail's belief in woman's unique role and character remained unaltered. Asked if she would rather have been born a man, she replied without hesitation, "No, I'd rather be a woman — if the world would treat me as it treats a man." She felt that she had "sought to do my work in a way that will reflect credit on all women who are working to build a finer and better life. I have always wanted to be womanly because I think that it is only when we look deep within our own nature and express our womanly quality that we can do our full share in this great task of building a better life."

While Macphail's political outlook during the 1940s reflected the party she represented, feminism triumphed over partisanship when she expressed her concern for a country that continued to be "governed by half the human family." She tried to convince more women to enter public life and advocated that they stand together as men did. Her inveterate individualism remained unsuppressed. "What I stand for, I stand for," she said. "Without oil, without vanity and without bombast, I stand for it without equivocation. It's not particularly female. Its a matter of personality. Some men are the same." Looking back over her own career, she felt that she had survived because her flammable temper had been mitigated by a sense of humour. "But most importantly," she concluded, "I tried to be natural, to say what I thought sincerely, and to abide by my own standards. That sums up the most important advice I can pass on to women today." But she was willing to change her views as circumstances dictated.

The Political Difference: Equal Pay Versus Pay Equity

Legislation creating equal pay for equal work became the most important achievement affecting women after World War Two. In a significant reversal of her previous stand that affirmative action was special privilege, Agnes Macphail made the issue her own. Organized labour in Canada had advocated equal pay as early as 1914 — because they viewed it as a means to stop women's wages undercutting those of men. Various women's groups had adopted the measure in their platforms for many years before the policy of equal pay for work of equal value was implemented during World War Two in order to encourage women to take paid employment. A royal commission in Britain examined the issue between 1944 and 1946 with a view to understanding its repercussions during peace.

Margaret Hyndman, the president of the Canadian Federation of Business and Professional Women's Clubs, submitted a brief to Ontario's Conservative government arguing for the continuation of equal pay provisions in government contracts, but without effect. The adoption of the Universal Declaration of Human Rights — the first draft of which was written by McGill University professor John Humphrey — by the United Nations in 1948 added weight to their case in the same way that the international body would later shame the country into amending its discriminatory laws constraining Indian women. The declaration included a statement that everyone "has the

right to equal pay for equal work." This simple assertion produced major differences of interpretation that immediately
established battle lines between those like Macphail who
believed in genuine pay equity and those who propounded
much more ineffectual laws.

As gender equity had long been a goal of European socialist
groups, the CCF in Regina in 1933 had affirmed the need for
a national labour code that would enshrine equal pay and
nondiscrimatory labour practices. Following the implementation of new legislation in several American states, CCF women
collected information on female working conditions. Women's
labour was badly documented, and the CCFers wanted a
sound basis from which to pursue their case. In 1948 Barbara
Cass-Beggs, vice-president of the Ontario CCF Women's Committee, and Toronto CCF Women's Council member Edith
Fowke compiled a report that lawyer Andrew Brewin used to
prepare the first pay equity legislation introduced in Canada.
The bill aimed consciously at closing loopholes and asserted
equality between men and women in "work of comparable
character or work on comparable operations, or where comparable skills are involved."[11]

Many thought the bill utopian, and others dismissed the
principle of pay equity as one that would drive women out of
the workforce when employers hired men instead. Agnes Macphail did not think that would be the case when she rose in
the legislature in 1949 to second the CCF bill. She argued that
it would have an opposite effect, protecting men from being
displaced by employers seeking women as cheap labour.
While she had herself first proposed such a law in the late
1930s, she liked to say that there "is nothing so powerful as an
idea whose day has arrived."[12] Certain that gender discrimination in the workplace must end, Macphail dug into the history
of the struggle for women's rights and concluded that this
measure was straightforward justice for half of the population.
She also sought deeper for the reasons for male unwillingness
to treat women equally:

> I think it is a disgrace to men that they are not willing that
> women should get the same pay for doing the same work. Why
> should they not? Is it because women, in their homes, do a lot
> of work — well, I would not like to say "without pay," but

certainly not for a stated sum? It has become a habit of mind, that may be it; some explanation must be found to let the boys down, Mr. Speaker, so I will advance that it is simply that they are used to women doing a lot work for nothing, so they do not see why, in factories and other places of employment, they should not do the same.[13]

Although the legislation failed, Macphail believed so fully in pay equity that she was unwilling to tolerate even close friends who opposed the measure. While they were dining together in a restaurant, Macphail's companion Lila Tinker made the mistake of pulling out the old chestnut that men needed to earn more to support a home and family — the "family wage" that had become deeply embedded in the collective psyche in the late nineteenth century. Agnes immediately flew into a rage, stood up, and was on her way out of the restaurant when she was retrieved by Tinker's son.

Attributing the injustices experienced by women to male tribalism, Macphail concluded that men "are spoiled from the time they are born, first by their mothers, and then by their wives and daughters."[14] In a world dominated by men, women had to defend themselves against male aggressiveness. She saw women's battle with men at home and on the job as relentless. "A woman in a man's world has to cope at every moment with the danger of wounding the male ego. All men are too pompous," Macphail wrote. "Their egos are a bother. They're like the big balloons used over London during the war." While she paled before the sight of women wrestlers, Macphail advised women to reject commercial values portraying their gender only as colourful but ineffectual appendages to men. Acknowledging that there "are civilized men, men with a sense of responsiblity, with wisdom and tolerance ... who think a woman should get a fair break," Macphail advised women to strive for equality in all walks of life.

The pay equity issue did not die. After the federal Conservatives introduced an equal pay plank into their platform in 1949 and the Frost government forecast a new Fair Employment Practices Act in 1951, Margaret Hyndman met with the premier to persuade him to include gender along with nationality, race, and creed as invalid grounds for discrimination. When he proved reluctant, Hyndman prepared a brief and a proposed bill which the Business and Professional Women lobbied for intensively. The Conservative government responded with a Female Employees Fair Renumeration Act, which it introduced hurriedly later that year in anticipation of an election. By referring only to the "same work" in its operative clause rather than to comparable work as Brewin had originally formulated, the Conservative bill severely limited the number of women it would affect. Macphail was disappointed, but she naturally failed when she tried to have the legislation amended to broaden its applicability and remedy other deficiencies. She thought that Leslie Frost would have difficulty explaining the law's shortcomings to Ontario women. "Pious and pretty sentiment in print," she judged Canada's first equal pay law before it came into effect in 1952. "Nothing else. It has no meaning in the world."[15] She was equally condemnatory of the Conservatives' failure to include sexual discrimination in its Fair Employment Practices legislation.

Defeat and Retirement

Macphail's home life was considerably more settled than events in the turbulent political arena. She bought a duplex in Toronto's Leaside district, rented the lower storey, and lived upstairs with Ruby Campbell. Margaret Campbell, Ruby's mother, frequently came to stay with them. Although the younger Campbell served as Macphail's foremost adviser in critiquing her speeches, she idolized the older woman both for her achievements and for her modesty despite her fame. Agnes asked her more prudent charge to prepare a budget so that she could manage her financial affairs better. Ruby wrote the budget, but Macphail rejected it by writing at the bottom, "Nothing left for Agnes." Encouraged by Macphail to enter the teaching professon, Campbell first experimented with the prospect by instructing on a temporary permit in Muskoka in 1949 and then returning to the capital the next year. She graduated from the Toronto Teacher's College in 1951 and later became a lawyer articling with Andrew Brewin's firm.

The young people around Agnes Macphail interpreted her customary flamboyance and single-minded determination as the eccentricity of a senior. Arriving at Queen's Park with her nieces one day, a guard stopped her car. She could not park there, he informed Macphail, because the space was reserved for members only. "That's a good idea," she replied and then, without further comment, proceeded to park in her usual spot much to the girls' delight. Another time while driving to work she rammed her little English car into an abutment, but so concerned was Macphail to arrive at the legislature that she did not bother to call a garage. She flagged down an approaching motorist, made it to work, and did not give her abandoned vehicle another thought until the end of the day.

Macphail forecast difficulties for the Conservatives in the provincial election of 1951, and she seemed unaware that the CCF was to come close to drowning as it swam against the currents of a reactionary postwar atmosphere permeated with cold war animosities. In her last electoral campaign Macphail was joined by Grace Woodsworth MacInnis, and as in her first, there was a mishap when their car got stuck in a snowdrift in a rural part of East York. Her health weakening further, Agnes had to curtail her speaking engagements, but she was as impetuous as ever. She still had trouble sitting still when others commanded the floor. At one meeting where she sat muttering and squirming in her seat while Grace spoke, MacInnis turned around to look at her. "All right, Grace," Macphail replied, "I'll be good."[16] On polling day the CCF was massively rejected by the voters, and retained only two seats in the legislature. Macphail went down to resounding defeat along with Ted Joliffe, who lost in the party stronghold of York South. Macphail's opponent bested her by nearly eight thousand votes. Though her interests and spirits remained high, Macphail knew that this time her retirement from active politics was final.

Declining Years

The next year, while she was visiting Windsor, Macphail suffered a celebral hemorrhage. "It's Lilly," she murmured as she opened her eyes in a local hospital to see that her sister had arrived.[17] Her visitor thought her delirious, but as she returned to life, she planned a new adventure. "Lilly," she blurted, "I'm going to Scotland." She was transferred to a hospital in Toronto and she spent three more months recovering. Afterwards, she sailed for the land of her forbears accompanied by her old friends from East Gwillembury days, Clara and Bill Wilmot, who had remained active in agrarian organizations. Her hands swollen with arthritis and needing a cane to walk, the sixty-two-year-old Macphail resisted the restrictions of declining health as she had other adversities and refused to let infirmities interfere with her pleasures. The splendour of the Scottish countryside in Kilmartin, a hamlet several kilometres north of Oban from which the MacPhails had emigrated, contrasted in her mind with the depth of the economic deprivation that had forced her family to leave for Canada.

As she stood in the doorway of the Kilmartin church, her spiritual beliefs surfaced. How "like the church is family tradition," she thought. "No one generation built the church or gave all that stained glass or put up those plaques, but each had its part in something which by its very age and continuity became more than the sum of all of them." Watching the ship plough through rough waters on her return to Canada from Scotland, Macphail remarked to Clara Wilmot: "Yes, one must readily realize the Navy must believe in God. You know, Clara, we don't have to be in church to pray. Many a time I stood in the House of Commons and prayed for direction on how to vote."[18] To this faith was attached an abiding belief that churches must help the disadvantaged economically. In the past her public references to Christianity had emphasized its cooperative practical aspects.

Even defending the Farmers' platform on prohibition in the face of Howard Ferguson's decision to introduce new liquor control laws in 1926, Macphail had evoked the dangers of drinking and driving in the era of the automobile rather than speaking in moralistic terms. But now in Leaside she attended Don Mills United Church and taught Sunday School. She believed that to "be happy we all need to lose our little spirits in the Great Spirit which is called God. A person who has no idea bigger than himself is almost certain to be a deeply unhappy person."

Friends and admirers did not readily accept her retirement despite her illnesses, and they launched another attempt to secure a senate seat for Macphail. *Saturday Night* magazine called her "a sort of Beatrice Webb of Canadian socialism" and joined other publications in recommending her appointment.[19] A Gallup poll conducted in 1952 showed that 55 per cent of those asked knew her name, surely the highest recognition achieved by a woman in Canadian public life until that time. Agnes relished the prospect of returning to Ottawa, principally because it would augment the meagre retirement income that she felt restricted her access to pleasures like live drama, especially that employing Canadian talent in venues such as the Crest Theatre. When she went, she always ordered the best seats, but to her young acting friends she bemoaned her limited financial resources. On a visit to Ottawa she even picked out the place where she wanted to live and told a friend, "I hope I get into the Senate, just long enough to make a motion to abolish it."[20]

During these last years, Macphail kept up with her legion of acquaintances, but genuine friendships with other women were her major emotional support. Macphail's personal life in her declining years remained richly embroidered within the context of companionships stretching back to high school days and associations in Grey County. She was neither bored nor lonely; her only expressed regret stemmed from feeling no longer as much use to other people as she had once been. Violet McNaughton visited her from Saskatchewan and encouraged her to complete the autobiography she had begun following her defeat in 1945, but her hands were no longer capable of typing and she could not afford to hire a secretary. Resisting her infirmities, she travelled to Grey County to throw her support behind Dr. R. L. Carefoot, an old friend running as a Conservative candidate, but denting a gas pump with her car showed what a menace she had become on the roads.

In Toronto she willingly made herself available to CCF workers Doris French and Margaret Stewart as they prepared a tribute to her accomplishments, but she controlled the information related to them as carefully as she had learned to manage the press corps. Looking back on her career, the politican in her surfaced. "I didn't represent women," she told her interviewers. "I represented all my constituents — and most of all the children, because it takes so long to get things done."[21] And she was not forgotten as an advocate of penal reform. The Elizabeth Fry Society used her as a fund-raising mascot and suggested that her portrait be painted as a way to raise money, but she paled at the expense. At the same time the American

Congress of Correction meeting in Toronto in 1953 acknowledged her formative role.

Macphail also remained interested in the fortunes of the CCF. Her populism resurfaced in a concern that the CCF's popularity had been affected adversely by a surfeit of intellectuals. She was close friends with both Miller, whom she dubbed the godfather of the party in southwestern Ontario, and Margaret Stewart. Following the resignation of E. B. Joliffe as Ontario leader, Macphail encouraged Stewart to run. "We have been depending too much on brains in the CCF; we need a change," she said. "Miller, why don't you run for leader?" she asked oblivious to the unintended insult. Macphail gave this message to the convention that elected Donald C. MacDonald as new leader in November of 1953. With eyes darting from behind spectacles held in place by a thick black cord, Macphail had her audience in stitches of laughter with her rapier-like descriptions of intellectuals. Federal leader M. J. Coldwell thought her speech one of the most brilliant he had ever heard.

Although Macphail talked of settling into a quiet retirement, she could not. Early in February two men appeared at her home asking for assistance. Although one had a criminal record, they were not turned away empty-handed. The following Sunday she was visited by two old friends, one of whom she had remained close to since high school. She continued working on a report about the status and welfare of women in Ontario, but several days later she suffered a heart attack and was rushed to Wellesley Hospital. She carried with her an inquiry from the *Canadian Encyclopedia* requesting information on her life. Under the section asking about acclaim, Macphail wrote, "No special honours except the love of the people which I value more than any other" before she suffered a relapse, fell into unconsciousness, and died on 13 February 1954 at the age of sixty-three.[22]

At the funeral held three days later at her church the minister noted how her "life could have been much easier. But this was the path she chose — the craggy course."[23] Two memorial services and interment in Grey County followed. As her body was lowered into the ground at McNeill cemetery near Priceville where her parents were buried, the wind whipped the snow around in whirls that reminded many of the day of her electoral defeat in 1940. Innumerable stories of her past triumphs were repeated among those attending.

Prime Minister Louis St. Laurent had said that he intended to appoint her to the Senate, but by the time the list reached his desk, Agnes Macphail was dead. The inmates at Kingston penitentiary remembered her courage. "Imprisonment at its best is distasteful and degrading," their newspaper read, "yet conditions today in Canadian penitentiaries are far better then they were in the 1930s when Agnes Macphail set forth within the old North Gate. The changes wrought within these cold gray walls were her handiwork, to her must go our tribute."[24] Macphail's estate amounted to little. In her will she left bequests to the CCF, the Elizabeth Fry Society, and East York Neighbourhood Workers' Association as well as to relatives and to Ruth Joliffe and Margaret Brewin.

The chorus in praise of Macphail's accomplishments was universally nonpartisan, just as she had devilishly predicted to her nieces it would be once she was dead. One Toronto paper eulogized that "Agnes Campbell Macphail will have a secure place in the history of the country.... She will be remembered long as a representative of Canadian women, a pioneer in a new field of activity, and as a great soul."[25] Now that she was no longer a political contender, Senator Cairine Wilson added Macphail's name to the list of women worthies she liked to recite in her speeches. In Montreal's *Le Devoir*, Germaine Bernier concluded her editorial by saying that if "Canada had more men and women politicians of the stamp of Agnes Macphail, we would have a genuinely Canadian public policy favouring the interests of the country while ridding ourselves of followers and imitators who infest democracy."[26]

Ellen Fairclough, a Conservative from Hamilton who was appointed three years later as the first woman to hold a federal cabinet position, headed a committee to commemorate Macphail. They obtained the bust created by Austrian-born sculptor Felix Weihs de Weldon and presented to Macphail by the Canadian section of the Women's International League for Peace and Freedom in the early 1940s. At the unveiling in Parliament in 1955, the man whom Macphail had once tried to skirt in its corridors when he was in his cups came closest to identifying the politician's larger significance. The fact that

Agnes Macphail was the first woman member of Parliament, Chubby Power said, "alone does not explain the respect she won and the influence she played on Canada's national life. Personal qualities of intelligence, courage and unselfish industry were the real factors in her rise to prominence." In the "hearts and minds of those who knew her and had the privilege of serving with her," the dean of the Commons concluded, "there is a memorial also of a kindly, considerate, sincere woman who will long be remembered by those who were fortunate enough to have been her colleagues."[27]

Conclusion

Openness to new ideas, strength of conviction, willingness to overcome the limitations of her background, unbounded faith in humanity and in democratic values, humour, and idealism tempered by experience were the indelible marks of Agnes Macphail. As determined an individual as any who influenced national life and reached the international stage, Macphail understood that competitiveness needed to be balanced by cooperation. She emerged in Canadian federal politics at a critical juncture when the party system was assaulted seriously for the first time. Never truly an independent, Agnes Macphail was always a populist whose radical and social democratic values ensured that she would remain an opposition politician. She emerged first in the United Farmers of Ontario, an organization whose democratic structures contrasted with those of the two old parties, but when substantial reform of the party system appeared no longer likely and the UFO collapsed, Macphail joined the CCF as the party that came closest to her beliefs.

Through her consistent advocacy of women's rights during three decades, Agnes Macphail carved a special place for herself in the development of gender relations. Her career spans the transition period between two very different forms of feminist expression: that of the suffragists early in the twentieth century, who had often invoked a maternal feminism to justify their argument for extending the franchise, and the more recent women's movement that emerged during the 1960s. Expanding research on the first half of this century convincingly demonstrates that contemporary feminism is not a second but a third wave.[28] The activities of women like Macphail provided the transition during the first part of the century when social values were much more hostile to their aspirations than they are now.

Agnes Macphail did not originate the argument for women's equality based on fundamental human rights. Those ideas had first found full expression during the European Enlightenment two centuries before. Nor was she their first exponent in Canada, although their airing had been extremely limited before World War One. Macphail's importance lies in associating feminism, equality, and social justice more completely than any other Canadian and in finding legislative expression for those beliefs. Only by working for genuine social and economic democracy, she believed, might greater gender equity be achieved. Those beliefs she imparted to women like Thérèse Casgrain, the first woman to head one of the three mainline political parties in Canada, and Grace MacInnis. The binding of feminism with equality and social justice remains Macphail's essential legacy today.

In democratic politics many more are called than chosen, but women legislators of whatever political persuasion make a difference in public policy formation. Canadian women politicians, whether feminists or not, have brought a gender-based perspective to contemporary problems.[29] While the work of political scientists reveals lucidly the barriers restricting full female participation at all levels of public life, the marvellous elixir creating success or longevity in politics remains forever a mystery.[30] Despite the odds, active participation in the political process remains democracy's principal bulwark and the only sure route to greater gender equality.

Contemporary feminists have demonstrated the gender-based structural inequities that inhibit women from enjoying the same benefits as men in both private and public spheres. The strength of this most recent feminist wave stemmed initially from its voluntarist grassroots approach, which, along with a homogeneity inherent in such groups, developed into a weakness over the longer course.[31] Institutionalization arrived slowly and unevenly, but much of it has rested on government funding at the federal and provincial levels. The campaign of women for equality provisions in the Canadian Charter of Rights and Freedoms, the extension of equal pay for work of equal value into genuine pay equity, the provision of daycare, and the controversy over abortion and access to medical facilities have further asserted the primacy of politics in the lives of women.

In other ways women have not impressed their strength upon the national will. As the share of Canada's wealth controlled by those with the most money increased during the 1980s and that supporting the lowest income earners slid downward, studies showed that poverty in Canada risks being feminized more than ever. In contrast, the country has proportionally five times the number of billionaires as the United States, and according to the Ontario Securities Commission, four-fifths of the companies on the Toronto Stock Exchange's 300 Index were controlled by just seven families in 1984.[32] As long as poverty in Canada remains widespread and wealth more highly concentrated than in the United States, the importance of the political agenda linking feminism, equality, and social justice remains clear.

In the same way the reform of the party system that Macphail fought for remains incomplete despite advances in recent decades. Corporate influence in the federal Conservative and Liberal parties continues to be so strong that in 1988 it amounted to 37.7 million dollars representing 60 per cent of the contributions they received.[33] Are political parties truly democratic when they derive most of their financial support from business rather than individuals? Are polls conducted during elections beneficial to the political process, or should they be regulated as in some European countries? Is Canada's "winner takes all" electoral system the best expression of democracy, or should alternatives such as proportional representation that have been adopted in other parts of the world be tried?

While Agnes Macphail believed in extending democracy in new directions, she enjoyed no small measure of luck in her life, but she also incurred significant setbacks. She worked hard for the opportunities she helped to create for herself and others. Associating her own determination to defy gender restrictions with the larger struggles of the disadvantaged and minority groups striving for dignity and better lives, her commitment to social amelioration and her enjoyment of public life forced her to make painful decisions as a woman. In choosing a career rather than motherhood, she made a decision that she understood to be less clearcut for most others. Finding public and employment policies that fully comprehend the differing life courses of women and men remains as part of an uncompleted agenda.

Constantly challenging outmoded ideas, Macphail's root convictions remained intact throughout her life, even though some underwent significant modification. While early in her life Macphail had inveighed against the expansion of government activities and denounced what she termed as special privilege for women, her adoption of pay equity as a pressing issue late in her life revealed a new understanding of the ways in which politics might be used to ensure equality through difference — the central dilemma in gender relations today. Never lured by the trappings of power, throughout her life Macphail remained optimistic that injustice might be righted. In an affirmation that turned Karl Marx on his head by asserting that consciousness precedes being, Macphail believed that when the number of women in politics equalled that of men, a more just and humane society would be achieved. In forging the politics of equality, Agnes Macphail imparted her greatest challenge to succeeding generations.

Endnotes

Glossary of Acronyms

AMP Agnes Macphail Papers
CCF Cooperative Commonwealth Federation
HCD Canada, House of Commons, *Debates*
MTPL Metropolitan Toronto Public Library
NAC National Archives of Canada
OA Archives of Ontario
ODLA Ontario, Legislative Assembly, *Debates*
SFP Stewart-French Papers
SAB Saskatchewan Archives Board
UCO United Cooperatives of Ontario Archives
UFO United Farmers of Ontario
UFWO United Farm Women of Ontario

Chapter 1

1. Quoted in John Kenneth Galbraith, *The Scotch* (Toronto, 1964), p. 130.
2. Alice Munro, *Lives of Girls and Women* (New York, 1974), pp. 27-28.
3. Agnes Macphail recounted her family's history in a variety of published and unpublished forms over the course of more than three decades with remarkable consistency. The first account appeared in her column, "Women Pioneers," *The Farmers' Sun*, 21 November 1920. See also her "Farm Betterment" column, Toronto *Globe and Mail*, 2 October 1941 and "My Ain Folk," Ontario Archives, Stewart-French Papers (SFP), MU 7117, ser. I, file 2.

    All of Macphail's farm betterment columns from the 1940s were collected by S. B. McCready. They can be found in the University of Toronto Archives, Fisher Rare Book Library, Woodsworth Collection: S. H. Taylor Papers, manuscript #35, box 47 and in the United Cooperatives of Ontario archives (Mississauga), file 510.
4. Toronto *Star*, 7 October 1921.
5. Toronto *Evening Telegram*, 14 March 1922, p. 10.

6. AMP, obituary, Dougald MacPhail, Flesherton *Advance*, January 1930.

7. Saskatchewan Archives Board (Saskatoon), United Farmers of Canada (Saskatchewan Section) papers, G 310.15, Agnes Macphail, address to the United Farm Women of Ontario [n.d., 1922 or 1923].

8. AMP, vol. 7, file 4 (ca. 1930).

9. SFP, 7116, series F, C.B.C., "Agnes Macphail, Portrait in Memory," 1957; Gertha Reany to Doris French, 21 September 1957.

10. Gertrude E. S. Pringle, "The Only M.P. Who Can—Bake, Churn, Cook, Milk, Sew, Hitch, Teach, Talk—and Do 'em All Well," *Maclean's*, 15 June 1922, pp. 22-24.

11. SFP, 7116, Agnes Macphail interview notebooks.

12. David Gagan, *Hopeful Travellers: Families, Land, and Social Change in Mid-Victorian Peel County, Canada West* (Toronto, 1981), p. 100, found that 20 per cent of rural families showed no signs of improvement between 1851 and 1861 in terms of property ownership, upgraded housing, increasing complexity of the household, or employment of hired hands—the same proportion of people living in poverty as a century later.

   Examples of such poverty a half-century later can be found in Canada, Commission of Conservation, Charles Hodgetts, *Unsanitary Housing* (n.p., 1911), p. 48ff.

13. Canada, Parliament, House of Commons, *Debates* (HCD), 23 May 1922.

14. SFP, 7116, series F, C.B.C. "Portrait in Memory," 1957.

15. Quoted in Toronto *Star Weekly*, 14 November 1925.

16. Genevieve Lipsett-Skinner, "The Little Farmer's Daughter Who Became World Famous," *Canadian Magazine*, September 1926.

17. Susan M. Trofimenkoff, "Thérèse Casgrain and the CCF in Quebec," in Linda Kealey and Joan Sangster, eds., *Beyond the Vote: Canadian Women and Politics* (Toronto, 1989), p. 141.

18. SFP, 7116, Agnes Macphail autobiographical notes, p. 20. Lipsett-Skinner, "The Little Farmer's Daughter."

19. SFP, 7116, file 20, Lilly Bailey to Doris French, 20 February 1959. The only emendation by Macphail to the article by Lipsett-Skinner concerned her mother in relation to the question of her going to high school. See the copy in the AMP, vol. 4, file 14.

   Agnes Macphail was as reticent about her family life as she was of her sexual life, but see R.T.L.(Charles Vining), "Miss Macphail,"*Maclean's*, 15 June 1933. This article was reproduced in R.T.L. (Charles Vining), *Bigwigs: Canadians Wise and Otherwise* (Toronto, 1935), pp. 102-5.

20. Ellen E. Mackie. "The Biggest Moment of My Life!" *Chatelaine*, September 1933, p. 44.
21. *Farmers' Magazine*, 22 December 1921.
22. Lipsett-Skinner, "The Little Farmer's Daughter."
23. HCD, 11 April 1924.

Chapter 2

1. Toronto *Star*, 7 October 1921.
2. SFP, ser. I, file 2, Agnes Macphail autobiographical notes. All unidentified quotations in this chapter derive from this source.
3. Ramsay Cook, "Tillers and Toilers: The Rise and Fall of Populism in Canada in the 1890s," *Historical Papers 1984/Communications historiques 1984*, pp. 1-20.
4. In addition to her autobiographical notes, this incident is also recounted in AMP, vol. 7, file 6 (ca. 1930).
5. Toronto *Star Weekly*, 31 December 1932.
6. The only evidence bearing on this matter is indirect. Twice in her Bible Macphail underlined the prohibitions against divorce on grounds other than marital unfaithfulness in Matthew's gospel (5:32, 19:9). The writing in this Bible suggests a younger hand before Macphail's writing style broadened distinctively. AMP, Macphail Bible.
7. See the UFO pamphlets in SAB, UFC(SS), E81, "Proportional Representation," "Proportional Representation and the Transferable Vote in Single Member Constituencies," "Direct Legislation by the Initiative, Referendum and Recall," and W. C. Good, *Farmer Citizen: My Fifty Years in the Canadian Farmers' Movement* (Toronto, 1955), pp. 138-40. These measures were adopted by the board of directors of the United Farmers in 1921. UCO, UFO minutebook, 15 March 1921, pp. 20-26.

    J. A. Corry, *Democratic Government and Politics*, 2d. ed. (Toronto, 1952), p. 274, provides an explanation of the transferable vote, while David Laycock, *Populism and Democratic Thought in the Canadian Prairies, 1910-1945* (Toronto, 1990), examines many of the political concerns central to Macphail's career within the context of the prairies.
8. Martin Robin, *Radical Politics and Canadian Labour, 1880-1930* (Kingston, 1968), chs. 9 and 10. James Naylor, "Ontario Workers and the Decline of Labourism," in Roger Hall, William Westfall, and Laurel Sefton MacDowell, eds., *Patterns of the Past: Interpreting Ontario's History* (Toronto, 1988), pp. 278-300.

9. NAC, J. J. Morrison memoirs, p. 52. Melville H. Staples, *The Challenge of Agriculture* (Toronto, 1921), pp. 139-47. The remonstrance is printed on pp. 193-96. See also W. R. Young, "Conscription, Rural Depopulation and the Farmers of Ontario 1917-1919," *Canadian Historical Review* 53 (September 1972).

10. Barbara Roberts, "Women's Peace Activism in Canada," in Kealey and Sangster, *Beyond the Vote*, p. 281.

11. *Grain Grower's Guide*, 16 October and 11 December 1918; McNaughton Papers, Women's Party file also contains the unity program. See also Carol Lee Bacchi, *Liberation Deferred? The Ideas of the English Canadian Suffragists, 1877-1918* (Toronto, 1983), pp. 129-31.

12. Staples, *Challenge of Agriculture*, pp. 115-32; Terry Crowley, "The Origins of Continuing Education for Women: The Ontario Women's Institutes," *Canadian Woman Studies* 7, 3 (Fall 1986): 78-81; Margaret Kechnie, "The United Farm Women of Ontario: Developing a Political Consciousness, " *Ontario History* 77(1985): 267-80.

13. See Michael Bliss, *A Canadian Millionaire: The Life and Times of Sir Joseph Flavelle, Bart. 1858-1939* (Toronto, 1978), pp. 329-62, and Desmond Morton with Terry Copp, *Working People: An Illustrated History of Canadian Labour* (Ottawa, 1980), p. 105.

14. "An Appeal to the Organized Farmers of Canada," *Canadian Farm*, 28 November 1917.

15. Macphail, "Men Want to Hog Everything."

16. Toronto *Star*, 20 December 1921; Toronto *Star Weekly*, 31 December 1922.

17. Charles M. Johnston, *E. C. Drury: Agrarian Idealist* (Toronto, 1986), provides the best account of the rise of the United Farmers of Ontario and the surest guide to the historical literature.

18. *Farmers' Sun*, 24 November 1920.

19. SFP, 7116, Clara Wilmot to Margaret Stewart, 19 February 1958.

20. Underlinings in Macphail's Bible appear to date from this period in her life. Many, especially those from the Old Testament, dealt with taxes, deliverance, and the need for strength in the midst of the fray. Their relevance to political struggle was apparent.

21. *Farmers' Sun*, 4 December 1920.

22. Ibid., 8 and 20 January, 2 and 23 February 1921.

Chapter 3

1. Sixth Census of Canada, 1921, 1:63, 293, 678-79; 5:150, 226, 711, 749.
2. Interview with Ruby Mercer Macleod, 6 June 1989.
3. W. C. Good, *Production and Taxation in Canada* (Toronto, 1919), pp. 6-7.
4. *Farmer's Sun*, 29 October 1921. HCD, 1 June 1922, p. 2385.
5. SABS, McNaughton Papers, Macphail to Violet McNaughton, 20 May 1921. UCO, United Farm Women of Ontario, minutebook 1918-43, 16 March 1921. The book by Good was *Production and Taxation in Canada*.
6. SFP, Agnes Macphail, autobiographical notes.
7. Hanover *Post*, 29 September 1921.
8. Macphail, "Men Want to Hog Everything," SFP, ser. I, file 2, Agnes Macphail autobiographical notes.
9. W. L. Morton, *The Progressive Party in Canada* (Toronto, 1950), pp. 62, 302-5.
10. Johnson, *Drury*, pp. 136, 150-54. E. C. Drury, *Farmer Premier: The Memoirs of E.C. Drury* (Toronto, 1966), p. 108.
11. Floyd S. Chalmers, *A Gentleman of the Press* (Toronto, 1969), p. 227. J. B. Maclean, publisher of the paper, was a friend of E. C. Drury.
12. Queen's University Archives, Thomas Crerar Papers, vol. 139, UFO file. UFO minutebook, convention resolutions, 15-17 December 1920.
13. *Farmers' Sun*, 18 December 1921. See also W. R. Rolph, *Henry Wise Wood of Alberta* (Toronto, 1950), C. B. Macpherson, *Democracy in Alberta* (Toronto, 1953), ch. 1, and Anthony Mardiros, *William Irvine: The Life of a Prairie Radical* (Toronto, 1979), pp. 265-69.
14. Metropolitan Toronto Public Library, biographical scrapbooks, vol. 15, 1922. Toronto *Telegram*, 23 March 1922, p. 12.
15. Veronica Strong-Boag, *The Parliament of Women: The National Council of Women of Canada, 1893-1929* (Ottawa, 1976), pp. 438-39, reproduces the entire platform, but a detailed summary of the federal portion was produced in *The Canadian Annual Review of Public Affairs for 1921*, p. 503.
16. MTPL, biographical scrapbooks, vol. 15, 1921 (and the following unattributed quotations). "Tariff's Toll of Children," *Farmers' Sun*, 10 November and 5 October 1921.
17. Toronto *Star*, 7 October 1921.
18. NAC, Macphail Papers, vol. 7, file 6.
19. Reported in Dundalk *Herald*, 21 November 1921.
20. Pringle, "The Only M.P."
21. Ottawa *Journal*, 14 March 1922.

22. Quoted in NAC, Macphail Papers, Macphail to Virginia Roderick, 5 May 1922.
23. Toronto *Star Weekly*, 17 December 1921.
24. Hanover *Post*, 17 November 1921, 6 April 1922.
25. Ibid., 1 December 1921.
26. Toronto *Mail*, 19 October 1921.
27. Dundalk *Herald*, 24 November 1921.
28. SFP, Macphail autobiographical notes.
29. The other candidates were Rose Henderson who ran as a Radical-Socialist in Montreal; Mrs. John Dick, as a Socialist in Winnipeg; and Mrs. Hector Prenter, as a Socialist and Labour candidate in Toronto West.
30. Flesherton *Advance*, 8 December 1921; Hanover *Post*, 15 December 1921.
31. *The Best of Bob Edwards*, ed. Hugh Dempsey (Edmonton, 1975), pp. 41-42.
32. Toronto *Globe*, 12 December 1921. In 1949, Macphail used the word "freak" to describe how she was regarded in 1921.
33. Toronto *Star*, 7 October 1921.
34. Flesherton *Advance*, 8 December 1921.
35. Toronto *Globe*, 12 December 1921.
36. See Morton, *The Progressive Party*, ch. 4.
37. Crerar Papers, box 78, J. J. Morrison to Crerar, 4 December 1921. Morrison attributed the small number elected to the failings of the Drury government.
38. UFO minutebook, convention, 14 December 1921.
39. *Farmer's Sun*, 17 December 1921. C. B. Sissons, *Nil alienum: The Memoirs of C. B. Sissons* (Toronto, 1964), p. 204. UFO President R. W. Burnaby expressed the view that the Farmers stood "in the fortunate position of not having the actual responsibilities of government." UFO minutebook, convention, 15 December 1921.
40. *CAR 1921*, p. 521. Crerar Papers, box 78, J. J. Morrison to Crerar, 4 December 1921.
41. Crerar Papers, box 79, ser. 2, Crerar to J. B. Musselman, 5 January 1922. NAC, William Lyon Mackenzie King Papers, reel C2311: 139961, Macphail to King, 4 October 1929.
42. Crerar Papers, box 79, ser. 2, Crerar to A. B. Mitchell, 10 June 1922.
43. UCO, UFWO minutebook.
44. Toronto *Globe*, 20 January 1922. Macphail Papers, vol. 6, press clippings, 1921-26.

Chapter 4

1. Agnes Macphail, "Impressions of the Big House on the Hill," *Farmer's Advocate*, 14 December 1922, p. 1654. Mardiros, *Irvine*, p. 115.
2. B. F. Bolton, "When Agnes Comes to Ottawa," 1922 (v. l). Clipping from a Brockville newspaper in UCO, file 510 (Agnes Macphail), 29 January 1922.
3. SFP, ser. F, C.B.C. "Portrait in Memory" (1957); Milton Campbell to Doris French, 18 September 1957.
4. Boston *Herald*, 4 April 1928. Compare Nellie McClung on chivalry, *In Times Like These* (Toronto, 1915), p. 54.
5. *Evening Telegram*, 13 March 1922. Macphail was also visited by a journalist from the Ottawa *Journal*, but its accounts were written with less invective. See its issues of 10, 13 and 14 March 1922 for very different renderings of the same events.
6. Ibid., 14 and 29 March 1922.
7. AMP, vol. 4, biographical file.
8. Christopher Sykes, *Nancy: The Life of Lady Astor* (London, 1972), pp. 216, 227-28, 230.
9. SFP, George Coote to Doris French, 24 August 1957.
10. HCD, 27 March 1922.
11. Macphail, "Men" (1949).
12. Ibid.
13. HCD, 29 March 1922.
14. See Don Macgillivray, "Military Aid to the Civil Power: The Cape Breton Experience in the 1920s," in Don Macgillivray and Brian Tennyson, eds., *Cape Breton Historical Essays* (Sydney, 1980), pp. 95-109.
15. HCD, 30 March 1922.
16. AMP, vol. 1, file 1, Macphail to J. M. Murray, 4 May 1922.
17. Montreal *Star*, 22 May 1922.
18. Margaret Stewart and Doris French, *Ask No Quarter: A Biography of Agnes Macphail* (Toronto, 1959), pp. 71-72.
19. HCD, 11 April 1927, p. 2260.
20. NAC, Edith Holtom Papers, vol. 1, Macphail to Holtom, 2 May 1940.
21. UFO minutebooks, 15-17 December 1920, 6 September and 15 December 1921, 14 December 1922, 15 July 1923. For other women's peace activities, see McClung, *In Times Like These*, p. 15; Veronica Strong-Boag, "Peace-Making Women in Canada, 1919-1939,"in Ruth Roach Pierson, ed., *Women and Peace: Theoretical, Historical and Practical Perspectives* (London, 1987), p. 181; Roberts, "Women's Peace Activism," p. 281; Thomas Socknat, *Witness against War: Pacifism in Canada, 1900-1945* (Toronto, 1987), pp. 92-94.
22. HCD, 9 April 1927, p. 2205.

23. Violet McNaughton Papers, no. 483, Laura Jamieson to Violet McNaughton, 27 March 1929.
24. Quoted in Stewart and French, *Ask No Quarter*, p. 141.
25. SFP, Grace McInnis to Doris French, 23 March 1957.
26. Socknat, *Witness*, pp. 107-8. Gertrude Bussey and Margaret Tims, *The Women's International League for Peace and Freedom, 1915-1965* (London, 1965), pp. 45-50.
27. UFWO minutebook, 1924. AMP, vol. 6, press clippings, 1921-26.
28. HCD, 18 July 1924, p. 4796-97; 24 June 1925, p. 4845; 9 April 1927, p. 2201. Agnes Macphail, *Education for the New Social Order* (address to the United Farmers of Alberta, 20 January 1927).
29. AMP, vol. 1, A. Collins to Agnes Macphail, 8 May 1924. Toronto *Globe*, 22 November and 18 December 1924.
30. Toronto *Globe*, 18 December 1924. Macphail shared her views with her colleague W. C. Good, who concluded that "Farmers would not be such political non-entities if they got away from party and discussed political questions on their own merits." NAC, Good Family Papers, vol. 18, W. C. Good, "Farmers' Organizations and Politics" (ca. 1925).
31. Crerar Papers, vol. 105, Crerar to E. C. Drury, 26 June 1923; vol. 79, Crerar to H. B. Mitchell, 10 June 1922.
32. AMP, vol. 1, file 1, Macphail to J. M. Murray, 4 May 1922. Crerar Papers, box 105, Ser. 3, Crerar to Manning Doherty, 20 January 1923. Winnipeg *Free Press*, 15 December 1922. These events are discussed in more detail in Morton, *Progressive Party*, pp. 159-64, and Johnston, *Drury*, pp. 185-87.
33. Crerar Papers, vol. 117, J. Fred Johnston to Crerar, 22 August 1922, 28 February 1923. A meeting of Progressives on 21 August 1922 agreed that a two-thirds majority of its members was needed to cement an alliance with the Liberals.
34. Ibid., J. Fred Johnston to Crerar, 28 February 1923. UFO minutebook, 2:238, convention, 10 December 1923.
35. NAC, Good Family Papers, vol. 8, "The Death of the Progressive Party," November 1925.
36. See Conor Cruise O'Brien, "The Decline and Fall of the French Revolution," *New York Review of Books*, 15 February 1990, pp. 46-51, and Laycock, *Populism and Democratic Thought*, especially pp. 14-19.
37. Macphail's views on electoral reform were expressed most fully in the Montreal *Star*, 22 May 1922, New York *Times*, "Canada's Woman M.P. Wants Group Rule," 7 June 1925, sec. 9, p. 5, and Boston *Herald*, 4 April 1928, and during the next decade in her weekly newsletters, AMP, vol. 6, 18 February and 6 November 1933, and at the Couchiching confer-

ence, Toronto *Globe and Mail*, 19 August 1939. For the congruence of her views with those of J. S. Woodsworth, see Kenneth McNaught, *A Prophet in Politics: A Biography of J. S. Woodsworth* (Toronto, 1959).

38. AMP, vol. 6, press clippings, 1921-26. NAC, Good Family Papers, vol. 23, minutes of the Canadian Labour Party convention, 22 March 1924. See also Richard Van Loon, "The Political Thought of the United Farmers of Ontario" (M.A. thesis, Carleton University, 1965).

39. AMP, weekly newsletter, 22 March 1935. HCD, 1 June 1922, p. 2385; 15 March 1923; 13 April 1923, p. 1844; 19 April 1923, p. 2022.

40. University of Guelph, Frank Harding Collection, Durham *Review*, 24 April 1924; Durham *Chronicle*, 24 April 1924. SFP, George Coote to Doris French, 24 August 1957.

41. SFP, Macphail interview notebooks.

42. New York *Times*, 7 June 1925.

43. HCD, 11 April 1924, p. 1290.

44. Ibid., 18 June 1923, p. 4048.

45. NAC, William Lyon Mackenzie King Papers, reel C2285: 108345, Fraser Alysworth to King, 19 January 1926. Toronto *Star Weekly*, 14 November 1925.

46. Crerar Papers, vol. 79, Crerar to J. B. Musselman, 5 January 1922.

47. McNaught, *Prophet in Politics*, p. 211.

48. Ibid., pp. 207-14; Mardiros, *Irvine*, pp. 133-40; Morton, *Progressive Party*, pp. 190-200; H. Blair Neatby, *William Lyon Mackenzie King: The Lonely Heights 1924-1932* (Toronto, 1963), pp. 12-22; Norman F. Priestly and Edward B. Swindlehurst, *Furrows, Faith and Fellowship* (Edmonton, 1967), pp. 90-95.

49. UFO minutebook, 3: 155, 7 December 1925. *Farmers' Sun*, 10 December 1925. UFO presidents R. W. Burnaby and W. A. Amos expressed similar viewpoints.

50. See Modris Eksteins, *Rites of Spring: The Great War and the Birth of the Modern Age* (Toronto, 1989), and Doug Owram, *The Government Generation: Canadian Intellectuals and the State, 1900-1945* (Toronto, 1986).

Chapter 5

1. N. D. Farrow, "Political Aspects of the United Farmers of Ontario" (M.A. thesis, University of Western Ontario, 1938), pp. 372-73.

2. UFWO minutebook, 4 December 1928.

3. Toronto *Star Weekly*, 14 November 1925.

4. See John Mellor, *The Company Store: James Bryson McLachlan and the Cape Breton Coal Miners, 1900-1925* (Toronto, 1983).
5. SFP, C.B.C., "Portrait in Memory" (1957).
6. HCD, 30 March 1925, pp. 1726-35.
7. AMP, vol. 6.
8. Dundalk *Herald*, 29 October 1925. Toronto *Star*, 30 October 1925.
9. Quoted in Toronto *Star Weekly*, 14 November 1925.
10. King Papers, C-2285: 108345, Fraser Aylesworth to King, 19 January 1926. HCD, 29 June 1926, p. 5148. Neatby, *King*, p. 116.
11. *Farmers' Sun*, 29 April 1926. The beneficial impact of these tariff changes is discussed in Ian Drummond, *Progress without Planning: The Economic History of Ontario from Confederation to the Second World War* (Toronto, 1987), pp. 214-19.
12. NAC, Mackenzie King diary, 6 June 1926.
13. Eugene Forsey, *The Royal Power of Dissolution in the British Commonwealth* (Toronto, 1943), not only concluded that Baron Byng had been right in the exercise of the royal prerogative but also that he had a duty to refuse King's request. Roger Graham ed., *The King-Byng Affair, 1926: A Question of Responsible Government* (Toronto, 1967) introduces the controversy and serves as a guide to the literature.
14. King diary, 1 July 1926. This belies the innumerable stories told about this event.
15. *Farmers' Sun*, 8 July and 19 August 1926.
16. Toronto *Telegram*, 3 September 1926.
17. King Papers, C2291: 114671, Macphail to King, 21 September 1926.
18. British Columbia Archives and Record Service, Nellie McClung Papers, vol. 7, file 30, "Women and Politics"; vol. 3, file 26, "How It Feels to Be a Defeated Candidate."
19. King diary, 6 January 1926. NAC, Cairine Wilson Papers, vol. 12, file 16, Ottawa *Citizen*, 2 August 1923. Arthur R. Ford, *The World Wags On* (Toronto, 1950), p. 155, provides an amusing anecdote about Ferguson's woman candidate. See also Sylvia B. Bashevkin, *Toeing the Lines: Women and Party Politics in English Canada* (Toronto, 1985), pp. 100-108.
20. Toronto *Star*, 22 March 1928.
21. Macphail, "Men Want to Hog Everything." On Bourassa, see Susan Mann Trofimenkoff, "Henri Bourassa and 'The Woman Question,'" *Journal of Canadian Studies* 10 (1975): 3-11.
22. R. E. Knowles from the Toronto *Star*, AMP, vol. 6, press clippings, 1921-26. New York *Times*, 7 June 1925, sec. 9, p. 5.
23. See Deborah Gorham, "Flora MacDonald Denison: Canadian Feminist," in Linda Kealey, ed., *A Not Unreasonable Claim:*

Women and Reform in Canada, 1880s-1920s (Toronto, 1979), pp. 47-70, and Susan Walsh, "The Peacock and the Guinea Hen: Political Profiles of Dorothy Gretchen Steeves and Grace MacInnis," in Alison Prentice and Susan M. Trofimenkoff, eds., *The Neglected Majority*, vol. 2 (Toronto, 1985).

24. See Veronica Strong-Boag, *The New Day Recalled: Lives of Girls and Women in English Canada, 1919-1939* (Toronto, 1988), p. 62, and Ruth Roach Pierson, *"They're Still Women After All": The Second World War and Canadian Womanhood* (Toronto, 1986), ch. 2.

25. Bryan Palmer, *Working-Class Experience: The Rise and Reconstitution of Canadian Labour, 1800-1980* (Toronto, 1983), pp. 192-93.

26. *Farmers' Sun*, 20 January 1927. Toronto *Mail*, 16 January 1931.

27. New York *Times*, 7 June 1925. HCD, 29 June 1926, p. 5148. Toronto *Star Weekly*, 28 January 1928. For the similarity of these views with those of American feminist pacifists, see Roberts, "Women's Peace Activism."

28. Helen G. McGill, *Laws for Women and Children in British Columbia* (B.C. Women's Institutes and Local Councils, 1939), p. 17, quoted in Sandra Burt, "Legislators, Women and Public Policy," in Sandra Burt, Lorraine Code and Lindsay Dorney, eds., *Changing Patterns: Women in Canada* (Toronto, 1988), p. 147. Burt is one of few to take this contention seriously.

29. Ottawa *Citizen*, 29 February 1928.

30. Toronto *Globe*, 24 January 1929. Boston *Herald*, 4 April 1928.

31. Helen Beattie, "Old Warrior," *Canadian Home Journal*, February 1949.

32. SFP, file 16, interview with J. C. McRuer, 3 September 1957.

33. *Queen's University Journal*, 8 March 1927. *McGill University Daily*, 14 February 1928.

34. HCD, 26 February 1925, p. 570.

35. Ibid., 4 June 1925, p. 3864.

36. Ibid., 9 May 1930, p. 1950; 15 April 1929. p. 1605. McNaught, *Prophet*, pp. 237-41, discusses Woodsworth's skilful manoeuvring in Parliament to secure the Ontario divorce court.

37. Calgary *Albertan*, 24 January 1927.

38. See Jonathan Spence, *The Gate of Heavenly Peace: The Chinese and Their Revolution, 1895-1980* (New York, 1981), pp. 221-31. The sources for the following are Toronto *Mail*, 9 April 1927; Toronto *Globe*, 8 and 9 April; SFP, interview notebooks and C.B.C., "Portrait in Memory." The textbook in question was *A History of Europe* by James H. Robinson and Charles Beard.

39. Boston *Herald*, 4 April 1928. HCD, 7 June 1928, p. 3885. Montreal *Gazette*, 13 February 1928.
40. HCD, 26 March 1931, pp. 326-27.
41. Ibid., 8 May 1929. See Lita-Rose Betcherman, *The Little Band: The Clashes between the Communists and the Political and Legal Establishment in Canada, 1928-1932* (Ottawa, n.d.), and Leo Heaps, *Rebel in the House: The Life and Times of A. A. Heaps* (London, 1970), pp. 97-99.
42. HCD, 19 March 1929, p. 1090. Ottawa *Journal*, reprinted in the Hanover *Post*, 15 March 1928. Boston *Herald*, 4 April 1928.
43. Toronto *Star Weekly*, 1928; Macphail, "Men Want to Hog Everything."
44. Dundalk *Herald*, 8 March 1928. SFP, interview with Lilla Bell, 13 August 1957.
45. King Papers, C2304: 131563-66, Macphail to King and King to Macphail, 3 October and 13 November 1928. Violet McNaughton Papers, Macphail to McNaughton, 22 March 1930.
46. Violet McNaughton Papers, Laura Jamieson to McNaughton, 20 February and 27 March 1929; Macphail to McNaughton, 1 and 19 March 1929; Laura Jamieson to Vancouver branch, WILPF, 7 September 1929; McNaughton to Madeleine Doty, 3 December 1929. See also the *Western Producer*, 29 August, 19 September, and 10 October 1929.
47. *The New Outlook*, 9 October 1929.
48. Toronto *Mail*, 16 January 1931. *Memoirs of Hugh L. Keenleyside*, vol. 1, *Hammer the Golden Day* (Toronto, 1981), pp. 254, 429.
49. Canada, House of Commons Standing Committee on Industrial and International Relations, *Report* (Ottawa, 1930).
50. Violet McNaughton Papers, Macphail to McNaughton, 22 March 1930. New York *Times*, 9 February 1930, p. 12.
51. SFP, Laura Jamieson to Doris French, 15 March 1958. Violet McNaughton Papers, Macphail to McNaughton, McNaughton to Macphail, 29 October and 4 November 1930; McNaughton to Lucy Woodsworth, 17 November 1930. New York *Times*, 9 February 1930, p. 12.
52. AMP, vol. 7, file 6, press clippings.

Chapter 6

1. SAB, Violet McNaughton to Katherine Blake, 14 November 1930.
2. *Western Producer*, 21 November 1931.
3. AMP, vol. 8, file 1, speech to Dairymen's Association, 1937. Nellie McClung went further, believing that "women's in-

tuitions are truer than a man's reasoning" (McClung Papers, vol. 7, file 30, "Women and Politics").

4. Toronto *Mail*, 16 January 1931.
5. Winnipeg *Tribune*, 3 July 1940.
6. See Drummond, *Progress without Planning*, pp. 39-40, and Neil McKenty, *Mitch Hepburn* (Toronto, 1967), p. 41. In 1932 the UFO maintained that farm purchasing power had decreased by half since 1913.
7. Wilfred Eggleston, "Farmers' Income from Field Crops down 60 Percent," *Weekly Sun*, 16 March 1933.
8. John H. Thompson and Allen Seager, *Canada 1922-1939* (Toronto, 1985), p. 225
9. HCD, 24 February 1936, p. 461. AMP, vol. 1, notes for a speech in Texas, 1935.
10. Agnes Macphail, "Out of My Experience," *Addresses Delivered before the Canadian Club of Toronto*, vol. 32 (1934-45), pp. 245-46.
11. SFP, interview with Harold McKechnie, August 1957. Macphail not only secured a pension for this veteran, but gave the family ten dollars for clothes. The millionaire R. B. Bennett, in contrast, typically sent one dollar to such cases when they affirmed some form of political loyalty. See the letters in Linda Grayson and Michael Bliss, eds., *The Wretched of Canada* (Toronto, 1972).
12. AMP, vol. 1, Margery Noble to Macphail, 2 May 1936.
13. HCD, 11 March 1932.
14. Ibid., 20 June 1936, p. 4024.
15. Toronto *Star Weekly*, 31 December 1932.
16. SFP, Milton Campbell to Doris French, 18 September 1957; Grace MacInnis to French, 1957; interview with Muriel Kerr.
17. AMP, vol. 1, [Illegible] to Macphail, 10 November 1936; weekly newsletter, 10 February 1934; vol. 2, Una to Macphail, 17 May 1938. SFP, Macphail interview notebooks. UCO, file 510, newspaper clipping.
18. SFP, Macphail, autobiographical notes. Toronto *Globe*, 30 April 1933.
19. AMP, vol. 6, weekly newsletter, 23 June 1934.
20. HCD, 13 October 1932.
21. Glenbow-Alberta Institute, Agnes Macphail, "The Economic Crisis and the C.C.F." (1933).
22. *Border Cities Star*, 15 November 1932. SFP, Grace MacInnis to Doris French, 23 March 1957. HCD, 14 April and 24 May 1932.
23. AMP, vol. 6, weekly newsletter, 22 April 1933. Contrast the views on universities in Agnes Macphail, "Advantages of

Higher Education," *Family Herald and Weekly Star*, 22 July 1931, with "Out of My Experiences."

24. Woodsworth Collection, vol. 10a, Macphail to Bert Robinson, secretary of the Socialist Party of Canada, n.d. [August, 1932]. Niagara Falls *Gazette*, 30 March 1932.

25. *Border Cities Star*, 15 November 1932.

26. Ottawa *Citizen*, 18 July 1932; London *Free Press*, 21 July 1932. SFP, Macphail interview notebook. The relevant background can be found in NAC, R. B. Bennett Papers, M-592: 52776, Bennett to Macphail, 28 May 1932; 52784, Bennett to Morrison, 21 June 1932; and other papers in this section.

27. Ottawa *Citizen*, 2 August 1932.

28. The Calgary program and the Regina Manifesto are reprinted in Walter D. Young, *The Anatomy of a Party: The National CCF, 1932-61* (Toronto, 1969), pp. 303-13.

29. SFP, interview with D. M. LeBourdais, 11 April 1958. Toronto *Star*, 1 December 1932. Concerning these events, see Gerald Caplan,*The Dilemma of Canadian Socialism: The CCF in Ontario* (Toronto, 1973).

30. Hanover *Post*, 8 December 1932. *Farmers' Sun*, 1 December 1932.

31. Terry Crowley, "The New Canada Movement: Agrarian Youth Protest in the 1930s," *Ontario History* 80(1988): 311-25.

32. Toronto *Star Weekly*, 11 February 1933. AMP, vol. 6, weekly newsletter, 4 March 1933.

33. London *Free Press*, 20 March 1933. Kitchener-Waterloo *Record*, 30 January 1933. AMP, vol. 6, weekly newsletter, 3 March 1933. HCD, 1 February 1933.

34. Ottawa *Journal*, 22 December 1932. Agnes Macphail, "If I Were Prime Minister," *Chatelaine*, January 1933, pp. 19, 46. Robert Caygeon, "Agnes Macphail, A Romantic Evangelist," *Saturday Night*, 29 July 1933, p. 4. R.T.L., "Miss Macphail," *Maclean's*, 15 June 1933, pp. 12-13.

35. A. M. Mowat, "The Dollar and the Pound," *Saturday Night*, 18 February 1933.

36. Macphail, "The Economic Crisis and the C.C.F.," 1933.

37. Woodsworth Memorial Collection, vol. 8, A. H. Downs, Jr., to D. Williams, 2 March 1934.

38. Ibid., Ernest Winch to Bert Robinson, 17 October 1932; [Robinson] to Winch, 12 February 1933; Bernard Loeb to Robinson, 1 April 1933.

39. Woodsworth Collection, vol. 1, minutes, 5 February and 7 May 1933. AMP, vol. 3, Provincial Council minutes, 5 June 1933.

40. SFP, interview with Elmore Philpott—4, 1957; interview with D. M. LeBourdais.

41. SFP, interview with Eugene Forsey, 1957.
42. *Weekly Sun*, 27 July 1933. *Western Producer*, 27 July 1933. NAC, CCF Papers, vol. 1, National Council minutes, 18 July 1933.
43. *Western Producer*, 27 July 1933.
44. SFP, Grace MacInnis to Doris French, n.d. [1957]. UCO, file 510, Frank Underhill to Leonard Harmon, 16 May 1957.
45. See the detailed account provided by Caplan, *Dilemma*, pp. 41-58.
46. Woodsworth Collection, vol. 8, Elizabeth Morton to CCF Clubs, 17 November 1933; Bert Robinson to Socialist Party, 7 November 1933. NAC, CCF Papers, vol. 41, Elmore Philpott to J. S. Woodsworth, 7 October 1933.
47. Toronto *Globe*, 18 November 1933.
48. Woodsworth Collection, Bert Robinson to A. H. Downs, Jr., 26 September 1933. NAC, CCF Papers, vol. 5, J. S. Woodsworth to Norman Priestley, 11 December 1933.
49. AMP, vol. 1, Elmore Philpott to Macphail, 19 February 1934. Woodsworth Collection, vol. 1, Provincial Council minutes, 17 February 1934.
50. Toronto *Star*, 19 February 1934. Smith later criticized the way in which his statement was reported.
51. CCF Papers, vol. 41, [J. S. Woodsworth] to Arthur Mould, 19 February 1934.
52. AMP, vol. 1, file 3, H. H. Hannam to Macphail, 22 February 1934, and other correspondence in this file.
53. Woodsworth Collection, vol. 8, A. H. Downs, Jr., to D. Williams, 7 March 1934. Contrast Woodsworth's position with that of the Labour Conference in CCF Papers, vol. 41, "Statement to the CCF Provincial Council" and "Statement to the Labour Conference Executive."
54. AMP, vol. 6, weekly newsletter, 23 June 1934.

Chapter 7

1. SFP, interview with W. B. Megloughlin, 13 September [1957].
2. AMP, vol. 9, file 19, "The Three Great Things in Life."
3. HCD, 12 June 1929, p. 3629.
4. See ibid., 28 March 1928, pp. 1794-97.
5. See the speech by Hugh Guthrie, HCD, 25 June 1934, p. 4293, and Macphail, 14 February 1934, p. 565. Toronto *Globe*, 21 March 1935. *Report of the Superintendent of Penitentiaries Re Kingston Disturbances 1932* (Ottawa, 1933). SFP, Agnes Macphail, "Canada's Prison Problem," 1935, and "A Report on Prison Reform," *Canadian Forum*, December 1946, pp. 206-8.
6. HCD, 14 February 1934, p. 8569.
7. SFP, file 16, Lilla Bell.

8. HCD, 14 February 1934, p. 565,
9. Ibid., 14 February 1934, p. 568.
10. Ibid., 4 February 1933, p. 2101. See J. Petryshyn, "'Class Conflict and Civil Liberties': The Origins and Activities of the Canadian Labour Defense League," *Labour/Le Travail* 10 (1982): 39-64.
11. AMP, vol. 1, file 3, Macphail to Edward Baynes, 28 March 1934.
12. Ibid.
13. Toronto *Globe*, 4 April 1935.
14. HCD, 30 June 1934, p. 458. On Fry, see Michael Ignatieff, *A Just Measure of Pain: The Penitentiary in the Industrial Revolution, 1750-1850* (London, 1989), p. 179.
15. HCD, 4 April 1935, p. 2413.
16. Ibid., 25 June 1934, p. 4292.
17. Toronto *Globe*, editorial, 16 February 1934.
18. Ibid., 12 June 1935.
19. Ottawa *Journal*, 20 March 1935.
20. Ottawa *Citizen*, 18 February 1935; Toronto *Globe*, 19 February 1935. HCD, 4 April 1935.
21. Ottawa *Journal*, 20 March 1935; Toronto *Globe*, 19, 20, and 21 March, 4 and 5 April 1935.
22. AMP, vol. 1, Hugh Guthrie to Macphail, 30 April 1935; Macphail to J. C. McRuer, 27 May 1935.
23. HCD, 28 June 1938, p. 4346.
24. AMP, vol. 6, weekly newsletter, 8 June 1935.
25. Toronto *Globe*, 23 May 1935.
26. SFP, interview with W.B. Megloughlin, 13 September [1957].
27. SFP, interview with Gerard Beaudoin, 6 September 1957.
28. Toronto *Star*, 12 June 1935. On Kingsley, see Tim Buck, *Yours in the Struggle: The Reminiscences of Tim Buck* (Toronto, 1977), p. 201.
29. AMP, vol. 1, Nellie McClung to Macphail, [1935].
30. Toronto *Mail and Empire*, 13 June 1935.
31. AMP, vol. 7, file 7, 1935.
32. AMP, vol. 6, weekly newsletter, 20 March 1936.
33. HCD, 28 January 1938, p. 4345.
34. *Ask No Quarter*, p. 212.
35. See Agnes Macphail, *Convict or Citizen? The Urgent Need for Prison Reform* (Toronto: CCF Literature Department, n.d.), and "A Report on Penal Reform." A summary of the recommendations of the Archambault report can be found in C. P. Stacey, *Historical Documents of Canada*, vol. 5, *The Arts of War and Peace, 1914-1945* (New York, 1972), pp. 130-34.

Chapter 8

1. AMP, vol. 6, weekly newsletter, 8 February 1936.

2. Doris French Shackleton, *Tommy Douglas* (Toronto, 1975), p. 94.
3. AMP, vol. 5, file on Russia. UCO, file 510, Brandon *Sun*, n.d. Macphail, "Mother and Child Clinics," Owen Sound *Sun-Times*, 8 October 1936.
4. AMP, vol. 9, file 18, Macphail, "Lessons from Scandinavia"; "The Sweden That I Saw."
5. *Globe and Mail*, 12 July 1941.
6. MTPL, Macphail biographical file, ca. 1940.
7. Woodsworth Collection, vol. 47, Macphail to S. B. McCready, 16 May 1941. Windsor *Star*, 21 May 1936.
8. See Ron Faris, *The Passionate Educators* (Toronto, 1974), p. 98.
9. Toronto *Star*, 29 November 1932.
10. See UFO Cooperative Company minutebook, 15 February 1936 and 27 November 1941. W. C. Good, *Farmer Citizen* (Toronto, 1958), pp. 238-43. Ian MacPherson, *Each For All: A History of the Cooperative Movement in English Canada, 1900-1945* (Toronto, 1979),pp. 141-45.
11. AMP, vol. 2, Clara Johnston to Agnes Macphail, 21 March 1938.
12. HCD, 3 March 1930, p. 225.
13. Owen Sound *Sun-Times*, 23 May 1936.
14. Toronto *Star*, 23 September 1937.
15. Walkerton *Herald*, 8 July 1937.
16. Quoted in H. Blair Neatby, *William Lyon Mackenzie King*, vol. 2, *The Prism of Unity* (Toronto, 1976), p. 156.
17. HCD, 9 March 1937, pp. 910-11; 21 February 1935, p. 1070.
18. Agnes Macphail, "Go Home Young Woman? Ha! Ha!" *Chatelaine*, October 1933, pp. 13-14.
19. AMP, vol. 10, file 23, 26 February 1937.
20. These personal letters are in AMP, vols., 1, 2.
21. AMP, vol. 1, Macphail to Arlene Smith, 9 April 1936. There are other instances involving university women in this volume and farm women in NAC, Louise Lucas Papers, Neva Myrick to Louise Lucas, 22 March 1931. The larger context is admirably established in Strong-Boag, *The New Day Recalled*.
22. HCD, 19 March 1937, pp. 1965-67. *New Commonwealth*, 27 March 1937.
23. AMP, vol. 6, weekly newsletter, 13 May 1939.
24. See Susan Ware, *Beyond Suffrage: Women in the New Deal* (Cambridge, Mass., 1981).
25. This assessment is based on Jean Graham, "Among Those Present," *Saturday Night*, 18 June 1932; Cairine Wilson, "Women and Education" and "Women's Opportunities," *Family Herald and Weekly Star*, 22 July 1931, 20 July 1932; "Speech to the Women's Canadian Club," 22 January 1931,

NAC, Cairine Wilson Papers, vol. 5; NAC, Charles Clay Papers, vol. 3, article, July 1943. See also Valerie Knowles, *First Person: A Biography of Cairine Wilson* (Toronto, 1988).

26. See Franca Iacovetta, "'A Respectable Feminist': The Political Career of Senator Cairine Wilson, 1921-1962," in Kealey and Sangster, *Beyond the Vote*, pp. 63-88.

27. Thérèse Casgrain, *Woman in a Man's World*, trans. Joyce Marshall (Toronto, 1972), p. 117.

28. AMP, vol. 6, weekly newsletter, 18 May 1939.

29. AMP, vol. 5, file 28. On Whitton, see P. T. Rooke and R. L. Schnell, *No Bleeding Heart: Charlotte Whitton, A Feminist on the Right* (Vancouver, 1987), p. 213.

30. London *Free Press*, 7 November 1936. AMP, vol. 5, file 28, Nora Frances Henderson, "Canadian Women Socially Conscious, Not Politically," [1939]. Winifred Strangeways, "She's a City Father," *Saturday Night*, 25 May 1935.

31. AMP, vol. 10, "Women in the Present World," [1936].

32. Ibid., vol. 10, file 23, Macphail, "Women in Government," [n.d.].

33. AMP, vol. 2, L. M. Phillips to Macphail, 10 March 1937.

34. Ibid., Macphail to Harold Peat, 11 March 1937.

35. University of Guelph Special Collections, Farm Movement Papers, interview, R. Alex Sim, Arthur Haas, Elizabeth Haas, 12 May 1987.

36. Violet McNaughton Papers, Macphail, "Peace—How Do We Get It?" 19 May 1935. Railroad Workers of America, *Labour*, 28 May 1935.

37. SFP, Marion Hunter to Doris French, 25 March 1958.

38. United Cooperatives of Ontario archives, file 510, "Touch of Humour."

39. HCD, 4 April 1935, p. 2434.

40. Montreal *Star*, 7 March 1936.

41. AMP, vol. 7, file 7, 1935.

42. Buffalo *Evening News*, 24 May 1937; Buffalo *Courier-Express*, 24 May 1937. Swarthmore College Peace Collection, U.S.–Canadian Peace Committee, press release [1937].

43. Oshawa *Times*, 29 March 1938.

44. Toronto *Mail and Empire*, 6 December 1935; Toronto *Telegram*, 5 December 1935. AMP, Norman MacKenzie to Macphail, 8 December 1935. For other occasions when Reid incurred similar displeasure, see *Radical Mandarin: The Memoirs of Escott Reid* (Toronto, 1989), pp. 82-106.

45. Montreal *Gazette*, 30 March 1939.

46. AMP, vol. 3, Macphail, "National Organization for Agriculture," 21 November 1939. A similar spirit animates the account of the Depression in Robert Bothwell, Ian

Drummond, and John English, *Canada, 1900-1945* (Toronto, 1987), pp. 245-58.

On developments in agricultural organization, see Ian MacPherson, "An Authoritative Voice: The Re-orientation of the Canadian Farmers' Movement, 1935-1945," *Historical Papers/Communications historiques 1979*, pp. 164-81.

47. AMP, vol. 3, press clipping, 21 November 1939.
48. SFP, Macphail interview notebooks.
49. AMP, vol. 7, file 10, 1938. HCD, 13 May 1939, p. 4039.
50. HCD, 13 May 1939, p. 4040.
51. Ibid., 27 January 1939, p. 390.
52. Owen Sound *Sun-Times*, 20 February 1937.
53. NAC, Edith Holtom Papers, vol. 1, Macphail to Holton, 2 May 1940; ibid., 16 October 1939
54. E. B. Joliffe, "Agnes," Ontario Woodsworth Foundation, *Newsletter*, 1, no. 6 (March 1954): 3.
55. David Lewis, *The Good Fight: Political Memoirs, 1909-1958* (Toronto, 1981), p. 183.
56. Dundalk *Herald*, 15 February 1940.
57. AMP, vol. 4, election flyer, 1940.
58. See the interview with Oliver in Karen Knight, "Agnes Macphail paved road for women in Canadian politics," Durham *Chronicle*, 24 March 1982.
59. AMP, vol. 2, Mrs. Hugh MacDonald to Macphail, 27 March 1940.
60. Dundalk *Herald*, 28 March 1940.
61. AMP, vol. 7, press clipping, 1940.
62. Toronto *Star*, 3 April 1940. Ottawa *Citizen*, 28 March 1940.
63. AMP, vol. 2, Cairine Wilson to Macphail, 27 March 1940; Margaret Hyndman to Macphail, 28 March 1940.
64. Ibid., Adelaide Plumptre to Macphail, 28 March 1940.
65. Toronto *Globe and Mail*, 23 February 1940. NAC, Cairine Wilson Papers, vol. 6, file 9, "Women in the Parliament of Canada," 28 September 1942.
66. This written after Caleazzo Ciano, 1946.

Chapter 9

1. Woodsworth Collection, vol. 47, Macphail to S. B. McCready, 1940.
2. AMP, vol. 10, file 22, Agnes Macphail, "Defence of Canada Regulations," 13 May 1940. Toronto *Star*, 14 May 1940. Montreal *Gazette*, 20 May 1940.
3. Thomas Berger, Fragile Freedoms: Human Rights and Dissent in Canada (Toronto, 1981), provides an introduction to this problem.

4. Violet McNaughton Papers, Macphail to McNaughton and McNaughton to Macphail, 31 May and 3 June 1940.

5. Saskatoon *Star-Phoenix*, 18 and 30 July, 20 August 1940.

6. SAB, Agnes Macphail, *Unity Means Victory*, 1940.

7. AMP, vol. 8, file 4.

8. AMP, vol. 1, McClung to Macphail, n.d.

9. King Papers, C4866:26214-21, Macphail to Mackenzie King, 16 May 1941; King to Macphail, 12 April 1941, and other letters on 7 and 30 March. SFP, H. H. Hannam interview, 1957.

10. King Papers, C6809: 280448-49, Macphail to King, 11 January 1942. *Globe and Mail*, 12 January 1942. J. L. Granatstein, *The Politics of Survival: The Conservative Party of Canada, 1939-1945* (Toronto, 1967), pp. 103-4, establishes the larger context for this event.

11. King Papers, C6809: 289450. Macphail to King, 26 March 1942.

12. Owen Sound *Daily Sun-Times*, 25 April and 4 May 1942. Interview with E. B. Joliffe, 4 April 1990.

13. AMP, vol. 9, file 12, "Elements of Greatness in Persons I Have Known."

14. Andrew Brewin in CCF, *25th Anniversary Souvenir* (Toronto, 1957).

15. Woodsworth Collection, vol. 1, CCF Provincial Council minutes, 7 August and 27 September 1942. Toronto *Globe*, 13 May 1942.

16. AMP, vol. 3, file 5, radio transcript; vol. 8, file 1, Macphail, "Should the CCF Gain Power in 1943—What of Agriculture?"

17. CCF Papers, vol. 198, Ruth Joliffe to David Lewis, 2 December 1942; Macphail to Lewis, 1 February 1943.

18. Toronto *Globe and Mail*, 24 June 1943.

19. AMP, vol. 9, file 16, Macphail, "Rural Citizenship."

20. AMP, vol. 10, file 23, "The Power of Women Is Unlimited," 5 December 1942.

21. See Patricia Shultz, *The East York Workers' Association: A Response to the Great Depression* (Toronto, 1975).

22. Toronto *Star*, 22 February 1944. McKenty, *Hepburn*, p. 272.

23. *Globe and Mail*, 24 February 1945. Toronto *Star*, 14 February 1945. Montreal *Gazette*, 15 February 1945. Chatham *Daily News*, 8 June 1949.

24. Montreal *Gazette*, 15 February 1945.

25. Quoted in Caplan, *Dilemma*, p. 155.

26. Lewis, *Good Fight*, p. 318.

27. Interview with E. B. Joliffe 2 April 1990. Lewis, *Good Fight*, pp. 215, 263-71, 304-19, carefully documents these and

other events surrounding the 1945 defeat of the CCF in Ontario and the federal election that year.

28. NAC, R. B. Bennett Papers, M3147: 554765, Macphail to Bennett, 4 October 1946.
29. Anne A. Perry, "Is Woman Suffrage a Fizzle?" *Maclean's*, 1 February 1928. Charlotte Whitton, "Is Woman a Flop in Politics?" *Saturday Night*, 26 January 1946. Dorothy Livesay,"Women in Public Life—Do We Want Them," *Saturday Night*, 19 July 1949, p. 17.
30. NAC, Catherine Cleverdon Papers, Macphail to Cleverdon, 22 November 1946. Charlotte Whitton Papers, vol. 4, Macphail to Whitton, 24 February 1945.
31. NAC, CCF Papers, 60 (Ontario Women's Committee), Marjorie Mann to David Lewis, 16 February 1948. This issue is discussed in Louise Watson, *She Never Was Afraid: The Biography of Annie Buller* (Toronto, 1976), pp. 87-91, and Joan Sangster, *Dreams of Equality: Women on the Canadian Left, 1920-1950* (Toronto, 1989).
32. CCF Papers, vol. 55, David Lewis to Macphail, 16 January 1948.
33. *Canadian Parliamentary Guide*, 1951, p. 626. Ontario, Debates of the Legislative Assembly (ODLA), 24 March 1949.
34. "Women and Politics," and G. M. Grube, "The Ontario Election," *Canadian Forum*, July 1948, pp. 77, 83. The course of the CCF during this decade can be followed in Caplan, *Dilemma*; Lewis, *Good Fight*; and the structural analysis provided in Leo Zakuta, *A Protest Movement Becalmed* (Toronto, 1964).
35. Dean Beeby, "Women in the Ontario C.C.F., 1940-1950," *Ontario History* 74(1982): 275. See also Joan Sangster, *Dreams of Equality*.

Chapter 10

1. Quoted in Helen Beattie, "Old Warrior," *Canadian Home Journal*, February 1949.
2. Ibid.
3. ODLA, 24 February 1949.
4. MTPL, biographical files, vols. 15-16.
5. Chatham *Daily News*, 8 June 1949. On these events, see Bothwell, Drummond, and English, *Canada Since 1945*.
6. ODLA, 24 February 1949.
7. SFP, obituary, 1954.
8. ODLA, 24 February 1949.
9. Eileen Sufrin, *The Eaton Drive: The Campaign to Organize Canada's Largest Department Store, 1948 to 1952* (Toronto, 1982), p. 99. SFP, Grace MacInnis to Doris French, 23 March 1957.

While Grace MacInnis associated this description of capitalism with Macphail, it had also been used by Tommy Douglas in years previous.

10. Beattie, "Old Warrior," and for what follows, AMP, vol. 10, "Our Responsibilities," (n.d.), Macphail, "Men—Hogs," and Toronto *Star*, 26 October 1951.

11. CCF Papers, vol. 198, "Draft Suggestions for a CCF Policy on the Employment of Women," 1948. Beeby, "Women in the C.C.F.," pp. 258-83, and Sangster, *Dreams of Equality*, pp. 215-22. British and American developments can be found in Vicky Randall, *Women and Politics* (New York, 1982), pp. 183-91.

12. Beattie, "Old Warrior."

13. ODLA, 7 April 1949.

14. Macphail, "Men Want to Hog Everything."

15. Toronto *Star*, 19 October 1951. See also Beeby, "Women in the CCF," and Elizabeth Forbes, *With Enthusiasm and Faith, History of the Canadian Federation of Business and Professional Women's Clubs* (Toronto, 1974), pp. 75-78, 136.

16. SFP, C.B.C., "Portrait in Memory."

17. Ibid.

18. SFP, Agnes Macphail, "My Ain Folk," and Clara Wilmot to Margaret Stewart, 19 February 1958.

19. *Saturday Night*, 25 April 1950.

10. SFP, interview with Muriel Kerr, 1957.

21. SFP, Macphail interview notebooks.

22. AMP, vol. 10.

23. Toronto *Globe and Mail*, 17 June 1954.

24. SFP, "Agnes Macphail: In Memoriam," *K.P. Telescope*, March 1954. NAC, Louis St. Laurent Papers, 208, opposition parties, 1953-55.

25. Toronto *Globe and Mail*, 15 February 1954; Toronto *Telegram*, 15 February 1954.

26. *Le Devoir*, 20 February 1954.

27. CCF Papers, vol. 309, Macphail file. Toronto *Globe*, 10 March 1941. A replica of this bust was presented to the Ontario legislature in 1961. The Elizabeth Fry Society created a scholarship in her honour at the school of social work in the University of Toronto.

28. See Strong-Boag, *The New Day Recalled*, Sangster, *Dreams of Equality*, and Kealey and Sangster, *Beyond the Vote*.

29. Burt, "Legislators, Women and Public Policy," p. 145. Yolande Cohen, ed., *Women and Counterpower* (Montreal, 1989), provides a differing perspective.

30. Political scientists have framed their inquiries within an integration model. See M. Janine Brodie and Jill M. Vickers,

Canadian Women in Politics: An Overview, CRIAW paper no. 2 (Ottawa, 1982); Janine Brodie, *Women and Politics in Canada* (Toronto, 1985); Bashevkin, *Toeing the Lines*. Journalist Penny Kome's book, *Women of Influence: Canadian Women and Politics* (Toronto, 1985) is more discursive.

Comparative perspectives within the West include Sandra Baxter and Marjorie Lansing, *Women and Politics: The Invisible Majority* (Ann Arbor, 1980); Pippa Norris, *Politics and Sexual Equality: The Comparative Position of Women in Western Democracies* (Boulder, Colo., 1987); Jane Lewis, ed., *Women's Welfare, Women's Rights* (London, 1983); Louise Tilly and Patricia Gurin, eds., *Women, Politics and Change* (New York, 1990).

31. Jill Vickers, "Feminist Approaches to Women in Politics," in Kealey and Sangster, eds., *Beyond the Vote*, p. 27.
32. Seymour Martin Lipsett, *Continental Divide: The Values and Institutions of Canada and the United States* (New York, 1990), p. 129.
33. Lloyd Axworthy, "Buying Power," *Canadian Forum* 69 (June 1990): 5-6.

Select Bibliography

Primary Sources

National Archives of Canada
    CCF Papers and Records
    Catherine Cleverdon Papers
    R. B. Bennett Papers
    Good Family Papers
    Edith Holtom Papers
    William Lyon Mackenzie King Papers and Diaries
    Agnes Macphail Papers (AMP)
    J. J. Morrison Papers
    Louis St. Laurent Papers
    Louise Lucas Papers
    Charlotte Whitton Papers
    Cairine Wilson Papers

Archives of Ontario (Toronto)
    Stewart-French Papers (SFP)

Saskatchewan Archives Board (Saskatoon)
    Violet McNaughton Papers
    United Farmers of Canada (Saskatchewan Section) Papers

British Columbia Archives and Records Service (Victoria)
    Nellie McClung Papers

Swarthmore College Peace Collection

Thomas Fisher Library (Toronto)
    Woodsworth Collection

Metropolitan Toronto Library. Bibliographical Scrapbooks, Volumes 15 and 16

University of Guelph Library Archival and Special Collections
    Frank Harding Collection
    Farm Movements Papers

United Cooperatives of Ontario (Mississauga)
    Minutebooks of the United Farmers and United Farm Women of Ontario and related Papers (UCO, UFO, and UFWO)

Canada, Parliament, House of Commons, *Debates* (HCD)

Ontario, Legislative Assembly, *Debates* (ODLA)

Newspapers and magazines: Boston *Herald*; *Canadian Magazine*; Dundalk *Herald*; *Farmers' Sun* (later, *Weekly Sun*); *Farmer's Ad-*

vocate (eastern edition); Flesherton *Advance*; *Grain Grower's Guide*; Hanover *Post*; *Maclean's*; Montreal *Gazette*; New York *Times*; Owen Sound *Sun-Times*; Saskatoon *Star-Phoenix*; *Saturday Night*; Toronto *Telegram, Star, Globe,* and *Mail*; and *Western Producer*.

Secondary Sources

Bacchi, Carol Lee. *Liberation Deferred? The Ideas of the English Canadian Suffragists, 1877-1918.* Toronto, 1983.

Bashevkin, Sylvia B. *Toeing the Lines: Women and Party Politics in English Canada.* Toronto, 1985.

Beeby, Dean. "Women in the CCF, 1940-1950." *Ontario History* 74(1982): 258-83

Brodie, Janine. *Women and Politics in Canada.* Toronto, 1985.

Burt, Sandra, Lorraine Code, and Lindsay Dorney, eds. *Changing Patterns: Women in Canada.* Toronto, 1988.

Bussey, Gertrude, and Margaret Tims, *The Women's International League for Peace and Freedom, 1915-1965.* London, 1965.

Caplan, Gerald. *The Dilemma of Canadian Socialism: The CCF in Ontario.* Toronto, 1973.

Casgrain, Thérèse. *Woman in a Man's World.* Translated by Joyce Marshall. Toronto, 1972.

Cook, Ramsay. "Tillers and Toilers: The Rise and Fall of Populism in Canada in the 1890s." *Historical Papers/Communications Historiques 1984.*

Crowley, Terry. "The Origins of Continuing Education for Women: The Ontario Women's Institutes," *Canadian Woman Studies 7,* no. 3 (Fall 1986): 78-81.

—, "The New Canada Movement: Agrarian Youth Protest in the 1930s." *Ontario History* 80(1988): 311-325.

Flanagan, Thomas. "Equal Pay for Work of Equal Value: An Historical Note." *Journal of Canadian Studies* 22(1987): 5-19.

Good, William Charles. *Farmer Citizen: My Fifty Years in the Canadian Farmers' Movement.* Toronto, 1955.

Hall, Roger, William Westfall, and Laurel Sefton MacDowell, eds. *Patterns of the Past: Interpreting Ontario's History.* Toronto, 1988.

Johnston, Charles M. *E. C. Drury: Agrarian Idealist.* Toronto, 1986.

Kealey, Linda, ed. *A Not Unreasonable Claim: Women and Reform in Canada, 1880s-1920s*. Toronto, 1979.

Kealey, Linda, and Joan Sangster, eds. *Beyond the Vote: Canadian Women and Politics*. Toronto, 1989.

Kechnie, Margaret. "The United Farm Women of Ontario: Developing a Political Consciousness." *Ontario History* 77(1985): 267-80.

Kleinberg, S. Jay, ed. *Retrieving Women's History*. Oxford, 1988.

Knowles, Valerie. *First Person: A Biography of Cairine Wilson*. Toronto, 1988.

Laycock, David. *Populism and Democratic Thought on the Prairies, 1910-1945*. Toronto, 1990.

Lewis, David. *The Good Fight: Political Memoirs, 1909-1958*. Toronto, 1981.

McClung, Nellie. *In Times Like These*. Toronto, 1915 (reprint, Toronto, 1972).

MacGillivray, Don. "Military Aid to the Civil Power: The Cape Breton Experience in the 1920s." In Don Macgillivray and Brian Tennyson, eds., *Cape Breton Historical Essays*. Sydney, N.S., 1980.

McNaught, Kenneth. *A Prophet in Politics: A Biography of J. S. Woodsworth*. Toronto, 1959.

Macpherson, C. B. *Democracy in Alberta*. Toronto, 1953.

MacPherson, Ian. *Each for All: A History of the Cooperative Movement in English Canada, 1900-1945*. Toronto, 1979.

—, "An Authoritative Voice: The Re-orientation of the Canadian Farmers' Movement, 1935-1945." *Historical Papers/Communications Historiques 1979*.

Mardiros, Anthony. *William Irvine: The Life of a Prairie Radical*. Toronto, 1979.

Morton, Desmond, and Terry Copp. *Working People: An Illustrated History of Canadian Labour*. Ottawa, 1980.

Morton, W. L. *The Progressive Party in Canada*. Toronto, 1950.

Neatby, H. Blair. *William Lyon Mackenzie King*. Vol. 2. *The Lonely Heights, 1924-1932*; Vol. 3. *The Prism of Unity*. Toronto, 1963, 1976.

Owram, Doug. *The Government Generation: Canadian Intellectuals and the State, 1900-1945*. Toronto, 1986.

Palmer, Bryan D. *Working-Class Experience: The Rise and Reconstitution of Canadian Labour, 1800-1980.* Toronto, 1983.

Pierson, Ruth Roach. *'They're Still Women After All': The Second World War and Canadian Womanhood.* Toronto, 1986.

—, ed. *Women and Peace: Theoretical, Practical and Historical Perspectives.* London, 1987.

Prentice, Alison, and Susan M. Trofimenkoff, eds. *The Neglected Majority.* Vol. 2. Toronto, 1985.

Randall, Vicky. *Women and Politics.* New York, 1982.

Rolph, W. R. *Henry Wise Wood of Alberta.* Toronto, 1950.

Rooke, P.T., and R.L. Schnell. *No Bleeding Heart: Charlotte Whitton, A Feminist on the Right.* Vancouver, 1987.

Sangster, Joan. *Dreams of Equality: Women on the Canadian Left, 1920-1950.* Toronto, 1989.

Socknat, Thomas. *Witness against War: Pacifism in Canada, 1900-1945.* Toronto, 1987.

Stewart, Margaret, and Doris French. *Ask No Quarter: A Biography of Agnes Macphail.* Toronto, 1959.

Strong-Boag, Veronica. *The Parliament of Women: The National Council of Women of Canada, 1893-1929.* Ottawa, 1976.

—, *The New Day Recalled: Lives of Girls and Women in English Canada, 1919-1939.* Toronto, 1988.

Thompson, John, and Allen Seager. *Canada, 1922-1939.* Toronto, 1985.

Ware, Susan. *Beyond Suffrage: Women in the New Deal.* Cambridge, Mass., 1981.

Young, Walter. *The Anatomy of a Party: The National CCF, 1932-61.* Toronto, 1969.

Young, W. R. "Conscription, Rural Depopulation and the Farmers of Ontario." *Canadian Historical Review* 53 (1972): 289-320.

Index

Addams, Jane, 66, 99, 101
Agrarian issues, 16-19, 23, 27, 35, 46-47, 71-72, 106, 166, 183, 187
Anderson, Harry, 135, 143, 145
Antigonish movement, 150
Archambault, Joseph, 145
Astor, Nancy, 59, 63-64, 154
Atholl, Duchess of, 163

Bailey, Hugh (brother-in-law), 35, 149
Bailey, Lilly MacPhail (sister), 7, 35, 200
Ball, R.J., 40-41
Bank Act, 74
Bank of Canada, 113
Baynes, Charles, 128-29, 135, 136, 137, 139-41
Beaudoin, Gerald, 142, 143
Beauharnois scandal, 105
Beder, E.A., 121
Bland, Henri, 61
Bell, Lilla, 178
Bence, Alfred, 177-78
Bennett, R.B., 92, 104, 107, 114, 115, 145, 148, 154, 189
Bernier, Germaine, 204
Birth control, 185
Black, George, 155
Black, Louise, 155-56
Blake, Katherine, 101
Bland, Salem, 117
Borden, Robert, 22, 24, 29, 33
Bourassa, Henri, 89
Bracken, John, 165
Braden, Sam, 18
Brewin, Andrew, 180, 181, 182, 186, 197
Brewin, Margaret, 186, 198
British Women's Party, 25
British Empire Steel Corporation, 63
Bruce County, 16, 17
Brown, Walter G., 177
Buck, Tim, 107, 125
Burnaby, R.W.E., 28, 29
Byng, Lord Julian, 89

Campbell, Jean Black (grandmother), 5, 6, 10-11, 34, 47
Campbell, John (grandfather), 5
Campbell, L.G., 82, 104, 144
Campbell, Margaret Haxton (aunt), 180, 199
Campbell, Robert (uncle), 180-81
Campbell, Ruby (niece), 181-82, 199
Canadian Association of Consumers, 190
Canadian Chamber of Agriculture, 165
Canadian Congress of Labour, 193, 196
Canadian Co-operative Federation (CCF), 116-27, 149, 164, 167, 168, 180, 182-91, 187, 188, 189, 190, 191, 200, 203, 204, 205
Canadian Council of Agriculture, 31, 37, 50, 5
Canadian Labour Defence League, 107, 124, 125, 136
Canadian Labour Party, 23
Canadian Manufacturers' Association, 25, 38-39
Canadian Radio League, 116
Canadian Reconstruction Association, 25
Canadian Women's Party, 25
Cape Breton, 63, 80-82
Carefoot, R.L., 202
Casgrain, Pierre, 158
Casgrain, Thrse, 11, 89, 158, 206
Cass-Beggs, Barbara, 197
Catt, Carrie Chapman, 101
Chatauqua, 98
China, 95, 96
Civil liberties, 97, 176, 181-82
Cody, Maurice, 150
Coldwell, M.J., 203
Communism, 43, 97, 107, 119, 148, 178, 188
Communist party of Canada, 107, 125
Congress of Industrial Organizations, 152
Conner, J.M., 121
Conscription, 22-23, 44

Conservative Party, 17, 27, 45, 46, 69, 83, 92, 104, 108, 156, 188, 198, 199, 207
Cooperative Union of Canada, 150, 151
Cooperatives, 149-51
Coote, George, 62, 72
Crerar, Thomas, 49, 51, 69
Cuden, Thomas, 122
Customs scandal, 85

Daly Inquiry, 143, 145
Dawson, J.D., 139-40, 142, 143, 145
Denison, Flora MacDonald, 90
Denmark, 148-49
Depression, 102, 106-10, 113
Dominion Elections Act, 62
Dorchester Penitentiary, 133
Douglas, T.C., 154, 156, 190
Drayton, Henry, 30
Drew, George, 185-86, 187, 188, 193
Drury, E.C., 37, 40, 45, 49, 51, 60-61
Dundalk Farmers' Cooperative, 149
Duplessis, Maurice, 167
Durham Farmers' Cooperative, 150
Durham Review, 33-34
Dyke, Eunice, 79

East York Neighbourhood Workers' Association, 185, 204
Edward VIII, 163
Edwards, Bob, 48
Edwards, Stewart, 29
Elections Act, 62, 176
Elizabeth Fry Society, 193, 202, 204
Elliot, Preston, 72
Ethiopia, 162, 163
Equal Rights Association, 31
Equality for women. *See* Women's equality

Fair Employment Practices Act, 198, 199
Fairclough, Ellen, 204
Fallis, Iva, 157
Farmers' movements. *See* Patrons of Husbandry; United Farmers of Alberta; United Farmers of Ontario
Farmer's Sun, 23, 26, 28, 41
Fascism, 159, 163, 188
Federal elections, 19, 27. *See also* Macphail, Agnes, elections by year
Feminism, 65, 90, 91, 195-96, 206
Ferguson, Howard, 69, 96, 97, 201

First Cooperative Packers, 150
Flavelle, Joseph, 27
Forke, Robert, 69, 75, 82
Forsey, Eugene, 193
Fowke, Edith, 197
French, Doris, 202
Frost, Leslie, 194, 199

Gardiner, James, 179
Gardiner, Robert, 72, 110-11, 116, 123, 178, 189
Garland, Ted, 55, 72, 126
Gender discrimination, 11-12, 93-94, 184-85, 196, 197. *See also* Women's equity
General Motors, 84, 152
Ginger Group, 75-76, 85, 93, 116
Globe, 18, 95-96
Good, W.C., 34, 69-70, 71, 72, 75, 76, 86, 118, 122, 123, 150, 151, 183
Gowanlock, Wattie, 15
Graham, George P., 131, 156
Graham, Howard, 72
Grange, the. *See* Patrons of Husbandry
Graydon, Gertrude, 24
Greer, Richard, 142
Grey County, 16, 17, 32-34
Griesbach, Emma, 26
Guthrie, Hugh, 62, 87, 135-37, 138-39, 141-42

Haas, Arthur, 161, 183
Hall, Dr., 144
Hall, Alfred G., 140, 141
Hamilton, William C., 192
Hannam, H.H., 116, 126, 151, 166, 176

Harman, Leonard, 151
Harris, Grace, 170
Harris, Walter, 170
Healey, Mr., 114
Heaps, A.A., 84
Henderson, Nora Frances, 158-59
Henderson, Rose, 121
Hepburn, Mitchell, 89, 124, 127, 145, 152, 170, 185, 188
Holdfast Club, 79
Houde, Camillien, 154
Housewives Consumers' Association, 190
Howe, C.D., 180
Hughes, Ada Marean, 24
Hughes, James, 24

Hughes, Laura, 24
Humphrey, John, 196
Hyndman, Margaret, 172, 196, 198

Immigration Act, 107
Imperial Economic Conference, 1932, 114, 115
Independent Labour party, 23, 24, 25, 33, 45
International League, 66, 99
Irvine, William, 34, 55, 71, 72, 74, 94, 116-17, 126

obs, Sam, 72
Jamieson, David, 34, 35
Jamieson, Laura, 65, 99, 102, 105
Japanese, and World War II, 176, 181
Johnson, S.C., 122-23
Joliffe, Edward Bigelow, 180, 183, 186, 188, 200, 203
Joliffe, Ruth, 183, 204
Junior Farmers, 79

Keenleyside, Hugh, 100-101, 175, 189
Kerr, Muriel, 72
King, J.H., 83
King, William Lyon Mackenzie, 49, 50, 51, 63, 75, 82, 83, 84, 85, 86, 93, 99, 101, 113, 118, 123, 144, 148, 153, 169, 175, 178, 179, 180
Kingsley, W.T., 143
Kingston Penitentiary, 107, 130, 131, 133, 139-40, 204

Labour Conference, 120, 124, 125
Labour Progressive party, 188, 190, 194
Lambert, Norman, 183-84
Lapointe, Ernest, 94, 141, 144
Latter Day Saints, 13
Laurier, Wilfrid, 18, 22, 44
League for Social Reconstruction, 113, 120, 122
League of Nations, 65, 66, 99-102, 162, 163, 165
League of Nations Society, 102, 157
League of Women Voters, 189
Leavens, B.E., 183
LeBourdais, D.M., 124
Lewis, David, 169, 183, 191
Lewis, Sophie, 191
Liberal party, 27, 45, 46, 49, 69, 83, 108-9, 127, 156, 177, 207
Livesay, Dorothy, 17, 189

Lloyd, Mr., 129
Loeb, Alice, 123
Loeb, Bernard, 123
Long, Huey, 160
Luckock, Rae Morrison, 185, 189, 190

McClung, Nellie, 21, 37, 88-89, 143, 158, 171, 178, 189
McCullagh, George, 179-80
Macdonald, John A., 17
MacDonald, Donald C., 203
MacDonald, J. Ramsay, 100
McGill, Helen Gregory, 92
McGregor, Daniel (uncle), 13
McGregor, Margaret (aunt), 13
MacInnis, Angus, 123, 126, 167
MacInnis, Grace Woodsworth, 185, 200, 206
MacKenzie, Norman, 165
McLachlan, J.B., 80
McMaster, A.R., 72
MacMurchy, Marjorie, 25
McNaughton, Violet, 25, 34, 99, 105, 202
Macphail, Agnes
  birth, 3
  education, 8, 11, 12-13
  teaching, 14-16, 19-21, 28, 30
  physical appearance, 14
  and voting rights for women, 18-19
    health, 20, 28, 101, 102, 111, 135, 161-62, 187-88, 192, 200
  1911 election, 19
  and the UFO, 26-30
  1920 by-election, 29
  1921 election, 33, 34-52
  and the press, 42, 46-49, 57-60, 100
  peace activism, 65-68
  1925 election, 82-84
  1926 election, 86-87
    speaking tours, 98, 101, 102, 160-61
  1930 election, 104-5
  and prison reform, 13, 126, 128-46, 192-93
  1935 election, 143-44
    visit to USSR and Scandinavia, 148-49
    and cooperatives, 73-74, 149-51
    and labour unions, 152, 195
    and World War II, 164, 167-68, 169

  1940 election, 169-71
  1940 by-election, 175, 177-78

as *Globe* columnist, 179-80
1943 provincial election, 185-86
1945 provincial election, 188-89
1948 provincial election, 191
1951 provincial election, 200
travel to Scotland, 201
death, 203
MacPhail, Alexander (grandfather), 4-5
MacPhail, Dougald (father), 4, 6, 8-9, 103
MacPhail, Gertha (sister). *See* Reany, Gertha
MacPhail, Henrietta (Etta) (mother), 4, 6-7, 8, 9, 10, 14, 79, 103, 161
MacPhail, Jean Jack (grandmother), 5, 10, 14, 47
MacPhail, Lilly (sister). *See* Bailey, Lilly
McRuer, J.C., 142, 143, 145, 181

Mail and Empire, 18
Marks, Joseph, 45
Marsh, Leonard, 148
Martin, Paul, 114, 158
Megloughlin, William B., 133-34, 140-41, 142-43
Meighen, Arthur, 33, 35, 83, 86, 87
Miller, Mr., 203
Moore, Tom, 88
Morris, William, 44
Morrison, J.J., 25, 28, 39, 41, 45, 46, 51, 86, 116, 151
Morrow, Fred, 179
Morton, Elizabeth, 185
Multiculturalism, 95, 96
Murdock, James, 179
Murphy, Emily, 157
Murray, Mr., 12-13

National Committee on Refugees, 157
National Council of Women, 143
National Equal Franchise Union, 25
National Federation of Liberal Women of Canada, 89, 172
National Labour party, 120
National Policy, 17
National Progressive party. *See* Progressive party
New Deal, 108, 156
Nickle, W.F., 134, 179
Nielsen, Dorise, 172, 176, 177, 178
Non-Partisan League, 71

North Battleford, 178

O'Day, Caroline, 154
Old Age Pensions, 84, 105
Oliver, Farquhar, 80, 87, 170, 186
Oliver, John, 80
Ontario Federation of Agriculture, 176
Ontario Hydro, 44
Ontario provincial elections, 69, 80, 87, 127, 170, 185-85, 188-89, 191, 200
Ormond, D.M., 134, 141, 145

Padlock Law, 167
Pankhurst, Emmeline, 25, 106
Parkinson, Joseph, 122
Parlby, Irene, 25, 37
Patrons of Husbandry, 16, 37
Patrons of Industry, 16-17, 25
Pay equity, 196-98
Pearson, Lester, 194
Peat, Harold, 160
Philpott, Elmore, 122, 124-25, 126, 127, 170, 178
Pidgeon, George, 66
Plaunt, Alan, 116
Plumptre, Adelaide, 172
Populism, 26
Pouliot, Jean-Franois, 72, 102, 163
Power, C.G., 73, 204-5
Powers, A.A., 41
Prison reform, 128-46, 186, 192-93
Prison riots, 133
Progressive party, 38, 45, 46, 47, 49-50, 64, 68-69, 70-71, 75, 83-84, 85, 86

Reagan, Frank, 134
Reany, Gertha MacPhail (sister), 7, 16
Reany, W. Meredith (brother-in-law), 16
Reciprocity, 17, 18
Reconstruction party, 144, 159
Regina Conference, 121, 122-23
Reid, Escott, 165
Robinson, Bert, 121, 125
Roosevelt, F.D., 108
Ross, Alexander, 139
Ross, John C., 26, 41, 46
Royal Canadian Mounted Police, 107-8
Ryan, "Red," 144-45

St. Laurent, Louis, 184, 204
St. Vincent de Paul Penitentiary, 133
Salsberg, Joseph, 194
Scott, R.J., 126, 176
Selassie, Haile, 163
Senate, 102-3, 175, 176, 202
Shaw, J.T., 76
Sifton, Clifford, 29, 43
Sim, R. Alex, 76, 149, 161
Simpson, James, 66
Sissons, C.B., 183
Smith, A.E., 107, 125, 126
Smith, Goldwin, 17
Smith, Mary Ellen, 37, 99
Social Credit, 110
Social legislation, 38, 73, 74, 91, 105, 151, 152, 193, 194
Socialism, 73, 109, 113, 114, 118, 188
Socialist party of Canada, 120-21, 125, 126-27
Soviet Union, 81, 148
Spanish Civil War, 162-63
Spencer, Henry, 55, 72
Spry, Graham, 116
Staples, Ralph, 151
Stevens, H.H., 102, 144
Stewart, Margaret, 202, 203
Stony Mountain Penitentiary, 129, 132, 133, 139
Sweden, 148-49

Tariffs, 17-18, 28, 29, 30, 46, 84-85, 102, 112, 115
Taschereau, Louis Alexandre, 89
Telegram, 59, 84
Tinker, Lila, 189, 198
Toronto Labour party, 120
Towers, Graham, 166
Trades and Labour Congress, 23, 23, 88, 131
Tucker, Robert, 16, 21, 22

Unemployment, 109-110
Unionist government, 22, 24
United Church of Canada, 73, 201
United Cooperatives of Ontario, 15
United Farm Women of Ontario, 26, 30, 31, 33, 52, 65, 69, 79
United Farm Young People of Ontario, 79-80, 118
United Farmers of Alberta, 21, 38, 50, 76, 87, 110

United Farmers Cooperative Company, 150-51
United Farmers of Manitoba, 50
United Farmers of Ontario, 23, 24, 25, 27-30, 34, 37-40, 50, 51, 60, 75, 76, 78-80, 82, 83, 104, 114-15, 116, 117-18, 122, 126, 150, 165-67, 176, 182, 205
United Grain Growers, women's section, 25
United Nations, 194, 196
United Reform Movement, 177
Universal Declaration of Human Rights, 196

Waldron, Gordon, 150
Wheat Board, 50
Whitton, Charlotte, 158, 189, 190
Whitmore, J.G., 150
Wilmot, Clara, 200-201
Wilmot, William, 201
Wilson, Cairine, 89, 156-57, 171, 172, 204
Women voters, 24-25, 35, 36, 40, 89, 105-6, 172, 188-89
Women's equality, 88-94, 152-54, 196-99
Women's Institutes, 25, 79
Women's International League for Peace and Freedom, 65, 99, 101, 102, 105,204
Women's Peace Union, 65
Women's suffrage, 11, 18, 22, 25, 45
Women's Trade Union League, 189
Wood, Henry Wise, 38, 39, 110
Woodsworth, James Shaver, 66, 71, 73-74, 76, 80, 81, 84, 87, 89, 94, 96, 118-19, 123, 126, 127, 153, 156, 167, 168, 182, 183
Woodsworth, Grace. See MacInnis, Grace
Woodsworth, Lucy Staples, 66
Workers' Unity League, 107
World Disarmament Conference, 102

World War II, 164, 167-68, 169, 176

Young, Alexander, 86

Zonta Club, 72